Handbook of Woodworking Plans, Patterns and Projects

Other Books by Bert Holtje:

*Handbook of Exterior Home Repairs:
A Practical Illustrated Guide—1979*

*How to Double and Triple the Useful
Life of Everything You Own—1977*

*The New Homeowner's Illustrated
Handbook: A Do-It-Yourself Repair Guide
to Problems That Are Sure to Occur—1977*

*100 Ways to Make Money in your Spare Time,
Starting with Less Than $100—1972*

*How to Borrow Everything You Need
to Build a Great Personal Fortune—1974*

Handbook of Woodworking Plans, Patterns and Projects

Abe Finkelstein
and
Bert Holtje

Illustrated by Roger Engelke

Parker Publishing Company, Inc.
West Nyack, New York

© 1980 by

PARKER PUBLISHING COMPANY, INC.
West Nyack, N.Y.

All rights reserved. No part of this
book may be reproduced in any form or
by any means, without permission in
writing from the publisher.

Library of Congress Cataloging in Publication Data

Finkelstein, Abe
  Handbook of woodworking.

  Includes index.
  1. Woodwork. I. Holtje, Herbert, joint author.
II. Title.
TT180.F57   684'08   79-26025
ISBN 0-13-382853-0

Printed in the United States of America

50 Ways You Can Profit from the Pleasure of Woodworking

Woodworking has a way of repaying those who take the time to work with tools. In addition to being fun, the projects in this book can be practical and profitable as well as decorative. Moreover, it's possible for you to make each of these useful items for a fraction of what you might pay in a store. Whatever your interest in woodworking, here is all the information you need to create 50 projects that are helpful, practical, entertaining, money-saving and money-making.

How this Book Will Help You

Whether you're an experienced woodworker, or simply planning your first project, this book provides fresh ideas and projects to give you the reputation of "master craftsperson" in a hurry. Here are just a few of the ways this book will be of benefit to you:

- It is organized to help you select practical projects with a purpose. For example—
    - Projects which help you . . . and others
    - Projects for your hobby
    - Projects for wildlife
    - Projects for indoors
    - Projects for sports

- The right project—and you. There is no better way to be successful in woodworking than to pick the right projects. Look over all of the projects before you decide on the first one, and then go on to success.
- You can even use many of these projects as a springboard for your own ideas. The laminated jewelry projects, for example, will give you excellent ideas for other projects of this type.
- You can easily progress from the simple projects to those which require a reasonable amount of skill. Not only will you be able to gauge your progress, you will be able to tell when you are ready to go on to more elaborate woodworking.
- Clear, step-by-step instructions ensure that you have very little chance to make a mistake. If you check yourself each step of the way, the finished project is bound to be perfect. Whether or not you already have woodworking skills, the easy-to-use drawings will help to further simplify each project.
- And what if you have only a few tools? Do not worry! All of these projects can be made with only the most basic, inexpensive woodworking tools.
- There is no need for an elaborate workshop. About the only thing you need is a strong table and a good vise. Whether it's in the basement, the garage, or any spare room, you can make these projects anywhere.
- Many of the projects can be mass-produced, and are easy to sell. Handmade craft projects are very popular, and if you follow our instructions, you can make them for very little money and sell them at a handsome profit.

- We have also given you instructions for buying wood which will enable you to do the best job at the best price—never specifying anything that would cost more and add nothing to the finished project.

One man who made the tugboat and barge for a relative's son was immediately besieged by friends for sets for their children. After he made them, he decided that he would mass-produce them for sale in local toy and craft stores. His venture has since expanded from the simple tug and barge to many other projects and a full-time business.

Another person, with a flair for design, began making the laminated jewelry described in Chapter 3. When a set of earrings caught the eye of an arts and crafts teacher in school, he found himself not only teaching part-time, but in the business of creating custom laminated jewelry for patrons of a local craft gallery.

A number of photography enthusiasts have saved a lot of money by making the simple darkroom paper safe and light box we describe. Bought commercially, these items could cost over a hundred dollars. But, for less than $25, you can make *both*.

Some of the projects can make your life a lot easier and more productive. For example, the little compost collector can make fertilizer for your garden and help get rid of garden and kitchen scraps. And who hasn't wanted to help an ambitious kid build a downhill racer, but not known where to begin? We think we've got one of the best—and fastest—right in Chapter 6. If you want to save money with interior remodeling, just look at our plans for a wall-mounted desk, key rack and a most unusual and practical wine glass rack.

There you have it—a woodworking book for everyone. Now pick a project. If it's a holiday time, you might want to make one of the wooden jewelry items for a friend. Or a local scout troop might appreciate the bike rack. Perhaps it's that time of year when migrating birds would make a home in your yard if you built a house for them. It's not difficult to see how these projects can make your life brighter and easier, and help you do something for a friend that will be remembered for a long, long time.

Abe Finkelstein
Bert Holtje

Table of Contents

Introduction: Fifty Ways You Can Profit from the Pleasure of Woodworking 5

Chapter 1. Money and Time-Saving Tips on Wood and Woodworking 13

Chapter 2. Seven Profitable Projects You Can Sell or Give as Gifts 27

Newspaper gatherer, sandwich tray, child's step stool, tugboat and barge, Colonial spoon rack, party cheese board, portable planter

Chapter 3. Eight Hobby Projects That Will Save You Time and Money 55

Double-sided easel chalkboard, laminated wood jewelry, photo blind, photo darkroom paper safe, do-all kit box, sewing basket, photographers' and artists' light box, bicycle rack

Chapter 4. Six Nature and Wildlife Projects You Can Use or Sell 87

Cage for small animals, contemporary doghouse, birdhouse, rabbit castle, bird feeding box, birdbath watering hole

Chapter 5.	**Ten Projects for Indoors That Everyone Wants** **115**
	Colonial sugar scoop, set of serving boards, folk toys, wall-mounted desk, memo pad/pencil holder, farmer's hat rack, key rack, wine glass rack, set of puzzles, kitchen slate reminder
Chapter 6.	**Nine Easily Made Projects That Make the Outdoors More Fun** **153**
	Combination picnic box/tabletop, compost collector, jet boat, pathway lamp, lawn chair, picnic salad set, old-fashioned wagon racer, house number signboard, garden caddy
Chapter 7.	**Ten Sports Projects for You or for Profit** **189**
	Beach clogs, two kites and a kite reel, storable ping-pong table, indoor tether ball, bowl-a-ball, basketball backboard, checker shuffleboard, live fish box, sandbox play center, bounce-ball game.
Index	.... **227**

Handbook of Woodworking Plans, Patterns and Projects

1

Money and Time-Saving Tips on Wood and Woodworking

Woodworking has been and will continue to be one of the most popular crafts people choose to express themselves—not only is it personally rewarding, but it is possible to save money on what you would ordinarily have to buy, and to make money by selling the things you make. Whether you have set your sights on creating artistic forms of wood sculpture or simply building practical projects such as cabinets and furniture, woodworking is indeed a most rewarding way to develop personal skills and self-expression.

You will find this an extraordinarily helpful book because each intriguing project is described in careful step-by-step fashion, including all the dimensions you need for the finished product. By reading the instructions carefully and following the illustrations closely, you will be able to save a great deal of time and effort.

A wide range of rewarding, practical and helpful projects are included, and most can be assembled with either hand or power tools. In the latter case, only the most basic, inexpensive power tools need be used. Whatever your interest and level of skills, here are a few practical suggestions to consider before undertaking any of the projects:

- Before you start any actual shop work, read the instructions through carefully and be sure you understand the drawings. As soon as you are able to envision the steps that are to be taken, as well as the finished project, you are ready to begin.

- If any of the steps or tools are unfamiliar to you, practice first on the materials you have bought for the project. Try making the cuts with the tools suggested in scrap wood, drive a few nails and screws in the wood that will be used, and see how the finishing will go with the tools suggested.
- Be sure that you have completed each step before you go on to the next. If it's not quite right, make it right before you go on.
- Accept nothing but the highest standards of workmanship from yourself. It may take a little longer in the beginning, but when you set high standards, it will be worth it.
- Observe all safety precautions. Later in this chapter we will discuss basic safety for the home workshop.
- Learn to use wood sparingly. Not only does this make good economic sense, but it will help reduce the drain of one of our most important natural resources.

How to Measure Lumber Accurately

Before you tackle any of the projects, consider these points:

1. Materials are given in nominal sizes for thickness and width. For example, 1 × 2 × 60 really is ¾ × 1½ × 60.
2. Measurements on the drawings are the correct, actual sizes.
3. In many cases, types of wood are not specified.

Money and Time-saving Tips on Woodworking 17

Only where strength, color, weathering and other considerations are important are actual woods specified.
4. Measurements are given in English units—inches and feet. Metric equivalents are given in parenthesis immediately following the English units.

How to Buy Wood

There was a time when you could take a ten-dollar bill to the lumber yard and load up the trunk of your car. And you might even have had some change left over to buy hardware and finishes. But today, the price of all wood is very high and likely to go higher. So it pays to plan your projects carefully and buy only enough wood for the project you are going to make.

Because of the many sizes and shapes of lumber required for all types of woodwork, the board foot is the basic measure by which quantities of wood are sold. Because some comparison shopping will definitely help your woodworking dollar go further, all you need to know is the price per running foot of each size.

But remember that if a piece of wood ½ × 8 costs a certain price per foot, a piece of ¾ × 8 will probably cost the same price, because pieces were probably surface milled from a piece of 1 × 8 rough, unfinished lumber.

The board foot is equivalent to 144 cubic inches of lumber. It is a base standard by which mills and yards can price their wood, and the system makes it very easy to estimate a job. Since you almost never think of wood in terms of its cubic volume, the term may be confusing, but let's see just what one board foot looks like.

A piece of wood 1″ thick and 12″ on each side is exactly a board foot. However, this is the raw measure of unfinished lumber, not the wood you would buy at a local lumber yard. The finished board foot would look more like this: ¾″ to $^{13}/_{16}$″ thick, 11½″ to 11⅝″ wide, and 12″ long.

A board with the nominal dimensions of 2″ thick by 6″ wide by 12″ long is also one board foot. Boards less than an inch thick are usually figured as being an inch thick.

You may wonder why the board foot measure is important, when all you will use are the dimensions given on the drawings. As we mentioned, economy is important. When you know the number of board feet and multiply it by the cost per board foot for the lumber you have chosen, you will have the cost of the wood. If the yard is to do some of the cutting for you, there may be a charge, but the price will vary with suppliers.

Let's just see how you can use the board foot formula. Use this formula to obtain the number of board feet:

$$\frac{\text{No. of pieces} \times \text{thickness} \times \text{width} \times \text{length}}{12} = \text{board ft.}$$

Try this to see if you understand the formula:
3 pieces
1″ thick
8″ width
10 feet long

$$\frac{3 \times 1 \times 8 \times 10}{12} = 20 \text{ board feet}$$

If the wood you have selected is selling for 80¢ a board foot, the wood you need will cost $16.

What Kind of Wood Should You Use?

With few exceptions, the wood used in the projects in this book is softwood. In general, hardwoods are used for such projects as furniture, cabinetry and architectural work. Softwoods, while they can be used for these applications, are most often used in building construction.

Softwood has a natural resin; hardwood lacks this component. Both hardwood and softwood are cut to standard thickness and width, but only softwood is cut to standard lengths. Hardwood is more scarce than softwood, so it is cut in whatever lengths that are possible from the log. Softwoods are generally sawed in even number widths ranging from 2 to 12 inches. The lengths are also cut in even measures such as 8, 10, 12 and 14 feet. If there is a sufficiently large order, mills can cut wood in just about any size that is required. The standard sizes simplify production and keep costs down.

Because hardwood is most often used where its surface will show, it is graded so that one side of the board is clear, or completely free of knots or rot. The other side must be considered structurally "sound," or free from any problems that could cause weakness.

The highest grade of hardwood is called Firsts. The second grade, obviously, is called Seconds. However, Firsts and Seconds are often combined and graded as F.A.S. (Firsts and Seconds). The third grade is called Selects, and the other grades follow in this order: Number one common, number two common, sound wormy, number 3A common and number 3B common.

The best advice we can give you is not to buy by designation alone. The higher the grade, the more expensive the wood will be. But if you select from lesser grades carefully, you should be able to have the kind of wood you want at a lower price.

The system of grading hardwood is relatively simple, but softwood grading is another story. The problem with softwood grading stems from the fact that there are a number of different softwood associations in the United States, all with their own system of grading. However, there are some general parameters you can use when you plan to buy softwood.

In general, softwood is graded by its method of preparation, intended use and whether it is dried or green. Dry lumber has a moisture content of less than 19% and is much less likely to warp than wood with a greater content of moisture.

When softwood is called yard lumber, it is intended for use in building construction. Structural lumber has a thickness of over 2". Factory or shop lumber is used for craft and cabinetry. Shop lumber is the wood we advise you to use for many of the projects described in this book.

This, however, is only the beginning of the maze of softwood classifications. Select wood is the top grade, but within this category, there are a number of rank-ordered grades. Wood designated as A in the select category is perfect and blemish free. B is just blemish free. C might have some small defects, such as small knots and variations in coloring. Grade D has more pronounced defects.

Factory and shop lumber has a "common" grade which is useable for construction. Common is further graded from 1 to 4, the last grade being coarse, knotty wood.

As you can see, selecting the proper softwood is a problem. Since it is unlikely that you are a professional woodworker, we suggest that you don't try to become an expert on wood grading. Just pick the least expensive grade that will meet your needs, regardless of what it is called. You may be surprised at the savings. With a little experience, you will be able to select the best wood for the job—and save quite a bit over what you might pay if you simply ask for select.

It's difficult to comprehend just what the differences are between hard and softwoods. Not all wood is of the same hardness or softness. Until you have worked with woods at the extremes, it is difficult to know just what kind of effort is required. For example, you can drive a nail through basswood, with almost no effort, but any attempt to nail walnut will probably result in a bent nail.

Here, to help you get a feel for the relative hardness and softness of wood, is a simple table:

- *THE SOFTEST WOODS*

    Basswood, butternut, cedar, cottonwood, fir, pine, yellow poplar and spruce.

- *THE WOODS OF INTERMEDIATE HARDNESS*

    Chestnut, cyprus, Douglas fir, red gum, hemlock and redwood.

- *THE HARDEST WOODS*

    Ash, beech, yellow birch, eastern red cedar, cherry, elm, hickory, locust, maple, oak, sycamore, tupelo, walnut.

Softwoods tend to deteriorate faster than hardwoods. Hardwoods have a closer grain than softwoods and can last for centuries. It's easier to nail softwoods, and most hardwoods require other methods of joinery. When a nail must be driven through a piece of hardwood, it's best to drill a pilot hole first.

Basic Workshop Safety

Even though you may be using only hand tools, you should read and observe these basic safety tips. A cut from a fast moving hand saw can be as bad as that from a power tool. We urge you to observe these safety rules:

1. Some of the projects in this book will require you to do some lifting of heavy wood. Lift with your arm and leg muscles; never use your back.
2. Never test the sharpness of a tool on your finger; always use the material it will cut.
3. Your thumb is a very handy part of your hand. But you can damage it badly if you use it as a sawing guide.
4. Whenever you use a knife or other cutting tool, be sure to use it in such a way that you push the edge of the blade away from you as you work.
5. Keep your hands and fingers away from the edge of any cutting tools.
6. Always use safety goggles or a plastic face shield when you work.
7. Wear clothes that are unlikely to contribute to an accident. Loose belts, long sleeves and floppy collars are all prime targets for trouble with tools. Never wear a tie near power tools.
8. When your tools are not in use, store them so that the cutting edges face away from you. Never let tools rest extended over the edge of a bench.
9. Make sure that your hammer handles fit their heads tightly. A handle that has dried out and loosened can often be fixed by soaking it in water until it expands to fit the head snugly again, and hammering the wedge deeper into the handle.
10. Never use a file without a handle. The point of a file is a dangerous weapon.

Money and Time-saving Tips on Woodworking

11. Be sure that all your cutting tools are well-sharpened. Dull tools force you to strain, and the added effort can make you loose a grip and cause serious damage to yourself or someone standing nearby. If the edges are dull, the tool may slip.
12. Never use tools for work other than that for which they are intended. Don't pry with a screwdriver or chisel; don't use a ball-peen hammer to drive nails and be sure that you have a cross-head screwdriver when you encounter a Philips head screw.
13. Never carry any tools in your pocket, except a closed pocket knife.
14. Don't let sawdust build up in your shop. It's quite flammable under the right conditions.
15. Don't keep oily rags around. Oil and air can cause spontaneous combustion. If you must store oily rags, keep them in a sealed metal container.

Where to Work

A workshop is a very handy place to have, but if you don't have a space that you can set aside just for your woodworking, almost any other place will do for the projects we have outlined in this book. Naturally, you'll want to choose a place that won't be damaged by sawdust, paints, stains and general abuse. A cellar, garage or even an outside porch (in good weather) will do.

You should consider your tools as well as yourself when you select a spot for your shop. A damp basement may not be too uncomfortable for you when you plan to spend only a few hours a week at your work. But dampness will rust tools, warp wood and prevent paint and stains from drying.

We have heard of some pretty fine workshops that have been built in home attics. Of course, the attic must have sufficient headroom in which to work, and large enough access through which you can bring in power tools and big pieces of wood. And don't forget to make sure that you can remove your finished project once it has been built. You know the old story of the guy who built the boat in the cellar, but was never able to launch it because he couldn't get it out of the house. An attic can be hot in the summer and cold in the winter. But with good insulation, a heater and an air conditioner, it can be a great place to work.

Many fine workshops have been set up in garages. It's not a big problem to bring power to a garage, and to insulate it well enough so that it can serve as a year-round workshop. In fact, because of the large doors, the garage makes an ideal workshop.

What About a Workbench?

There is nothing handier than a sturdy workbench. If you are fortunate enough to have a commercial unit, it will have a built-in vise and a lot of other handy features.

But there really is no need to spend a lot of money on a cabinet maker's bench when you can make one for a lot less that will serve your purposes well. This bench is easy to make and a pleasure to use. A vise can be attached easily, and, if you like, you can add a shelf or two under the top to store your tools.

What About Tools?

A nail hammer, crosscut saw, coping saw, screwdriver, chisel, hand drill, pocket knife, a few files, a ruler,

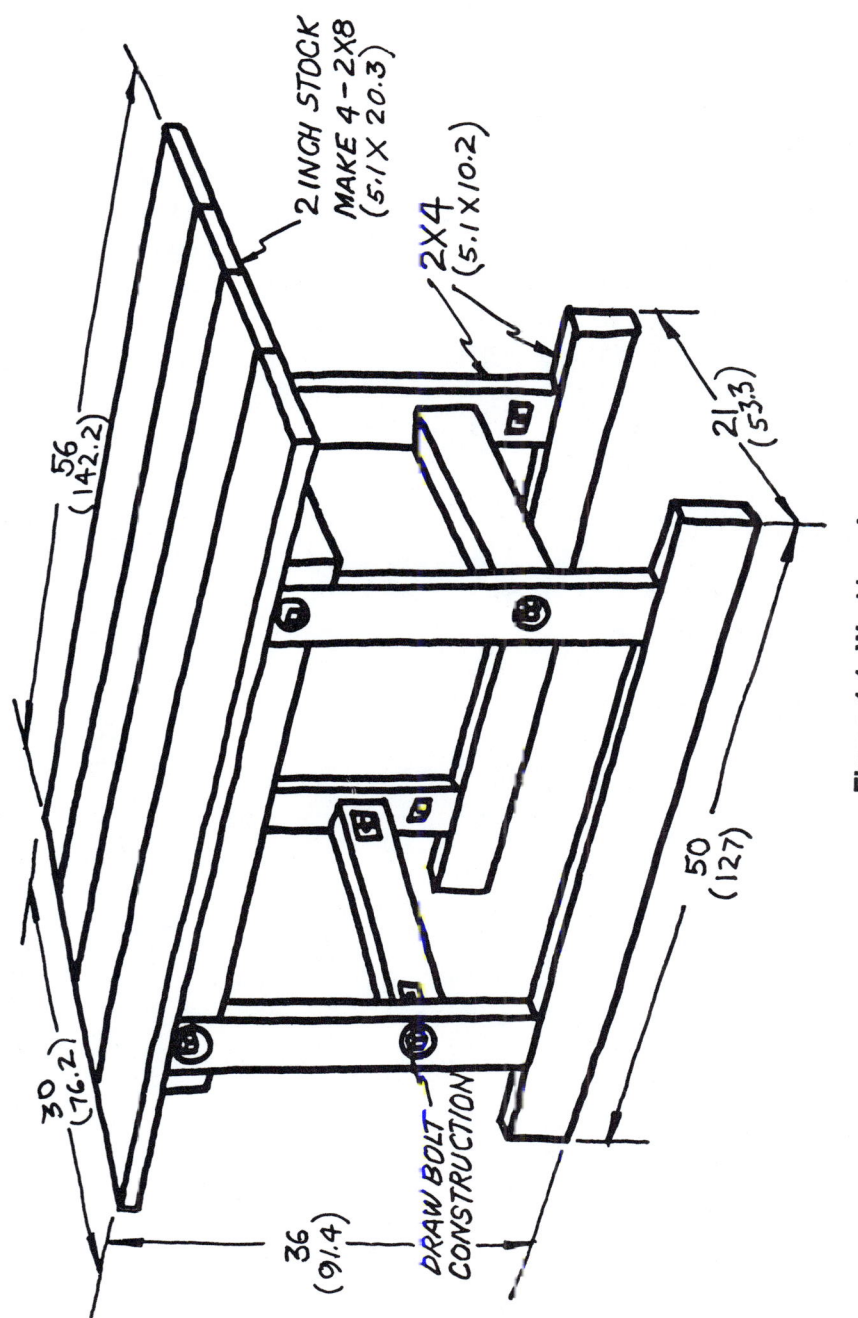

Figure 1-1. Workbench

plane and some sandpaper are all you need to make many of the projects we have described.

These are all hand tools, and there is little you can't do with them. If we were to suggest one power tool that would be most helpful in a wood shop, it would be the six-inch circular hand saw. You won't be able to do any better work with it, but you certainly will be able to do it faster.

Now, on to the projects.

2

Seven Profitable Projects You Can Sell or Give as Gifts

NEWSPAPER GATHERER

Sunday just isn't Sunday unless the living room is strewn with newspapers. The funnies are usually in one corner, the sport section is in another, and everything else is left where it was read. But come Monday, that pile and the other papers that arrive daily can be a bother unless you plan a way to keep them in one place. This newspaper gatherer is a device that will solve your problems forever. It just sits quietly in a corner gathering papers until you are ready to get rid of them. And if you put a set of casters under the gatherer, you can push it to the curb for pick-up or anywhere else you want.

Here's What You'll Need:

- Base—2 pcs 1 × 4 × 12 (2.5 × 10.2 × 30.5)
- Base—2 pcs 1 × 4 × 15½ (2.5 × 10.2 × 39.4)
- Uprights—2 pcs 1 × 2 × 12 (2.5 × 5.1 × 30.5)
- Cross pieces—2 pcs 1 × 2 × 15½ (2.5 × 5.1 × 39.4)
- Diagonal braces—2 pcs 1 × 2 × 24 (2.5 × 5.1 × 61)
- Diagonal braces—2 pcs 1 × 2 × 6 (2.5 × 5.1 × 15.2)

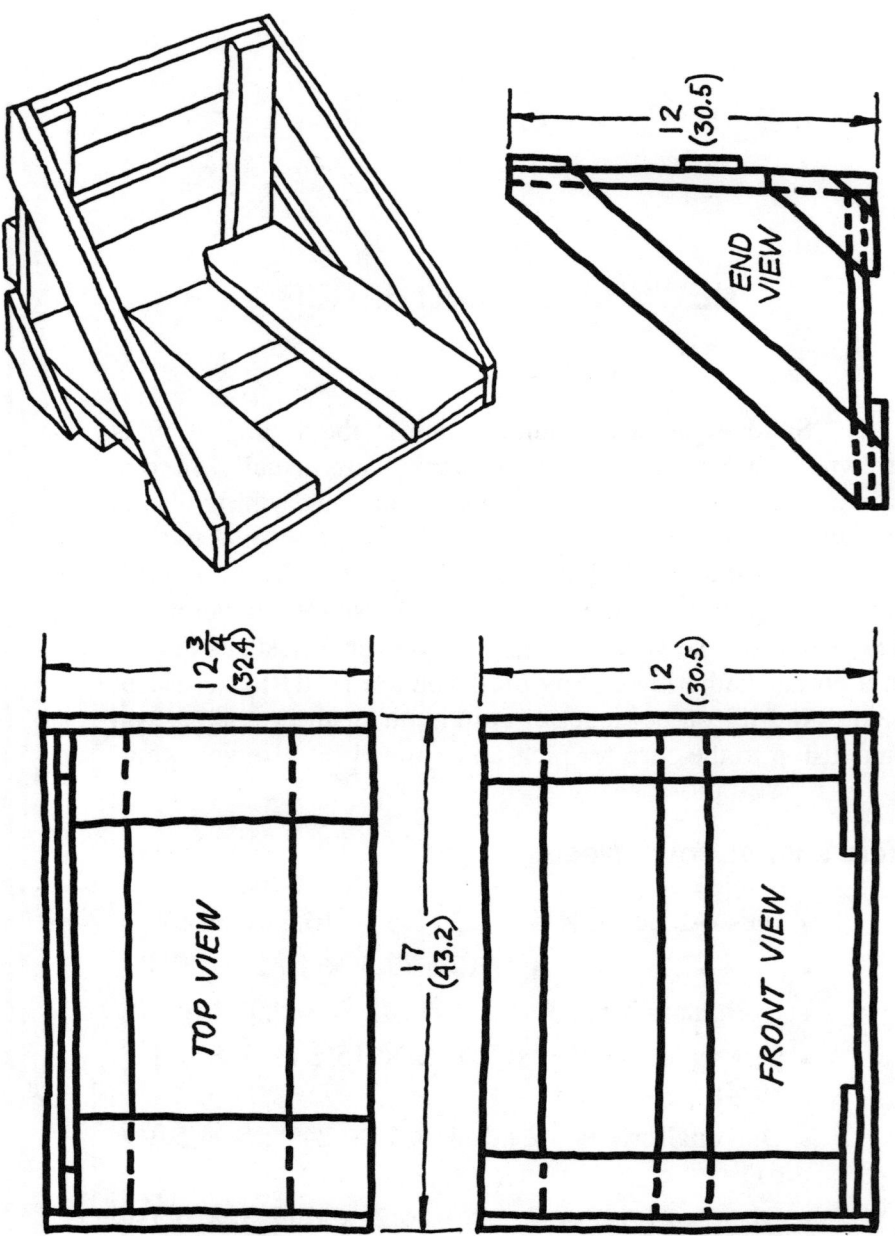

Figure 2-1. Newspaper Gatherer.

Projects You Can Sell or Give as Gifts 31

- Assorted nails and screws, paint, varnish or shellac, as required

Here's How to Make It:

Begin by cutting the two larger and two small base pieces to size. Assemble these four boards by nailing the short boards on top of the longer base sections, as shown in Figure 2-1. This provides an opening on the bottom of the gatherer through which you can pass a string when you tie the bundles.

Next, assemble the crosspieces to the uprights, as shown in Figure 2-1. The upper crosspiece is fastened at the top of the uprights, and the lower piece to the midpoint of the uprights. Now, fasten this subassembly along the long edge of the base, and position the crosspieces outside the gatherer.

Stand the assembly on its side, and use a try square or a triangle to make sure you have a 90° angle. Position and fasten the diagonals from corner to corner; the wood should straddle the corners. Use a cross-cut saw to trim the corners of the diagonal branches to conform to the shape of the structure.

Finish the surface and edges with sandpaper, even if you don't plan to paint it. This is a working tool, and you might pick up some splinters as you tie and remove paper bundles if you don't do some sanding.

As we mentioned earlier, you can mount casters in each corner to make the gatherer mobile.

SANDWICH TRAY

Here's a project, although easy to make, that will give you an opportunity to be quite creative. Your chance lies in the choice of materials, and with very little imagination you can have a tray that is much more than practical. Some of the most beautiful woodwork we have seen is of simple design, but stands out because of the craftsperson's choice of grain and wood colors.

If you feel like working with hardwood, think of using combinations such as walnut, mahogany or birch. You can even use veneered lumber, such as furniture core woods. Even veneered chipboard can be used.

If you decide to work with woods of varying color and grain, why not try to coordinate the projects with colors and textures in the room in which the tray will be used.

Here's What You'll Need:

- Base—1 pc ¾ × 5½ × 18 (1.9 × 14 × 45.7) (Exact size)
- Rails—2 pcs ¼ × 1¼ × 18 (.6 × 3.2 × 45.7)
- Handles—2 pcs ¼ × 1 × 7½ (.6 × 2.5 × 19) (Do not cut apart.)
- Waterproof glue, brads or screws, stain, varnish

Here's How to Make It:

These instructions are based on the use of solid wood. If you plan to use veneered wood, first see the notes at the end of these instructions.

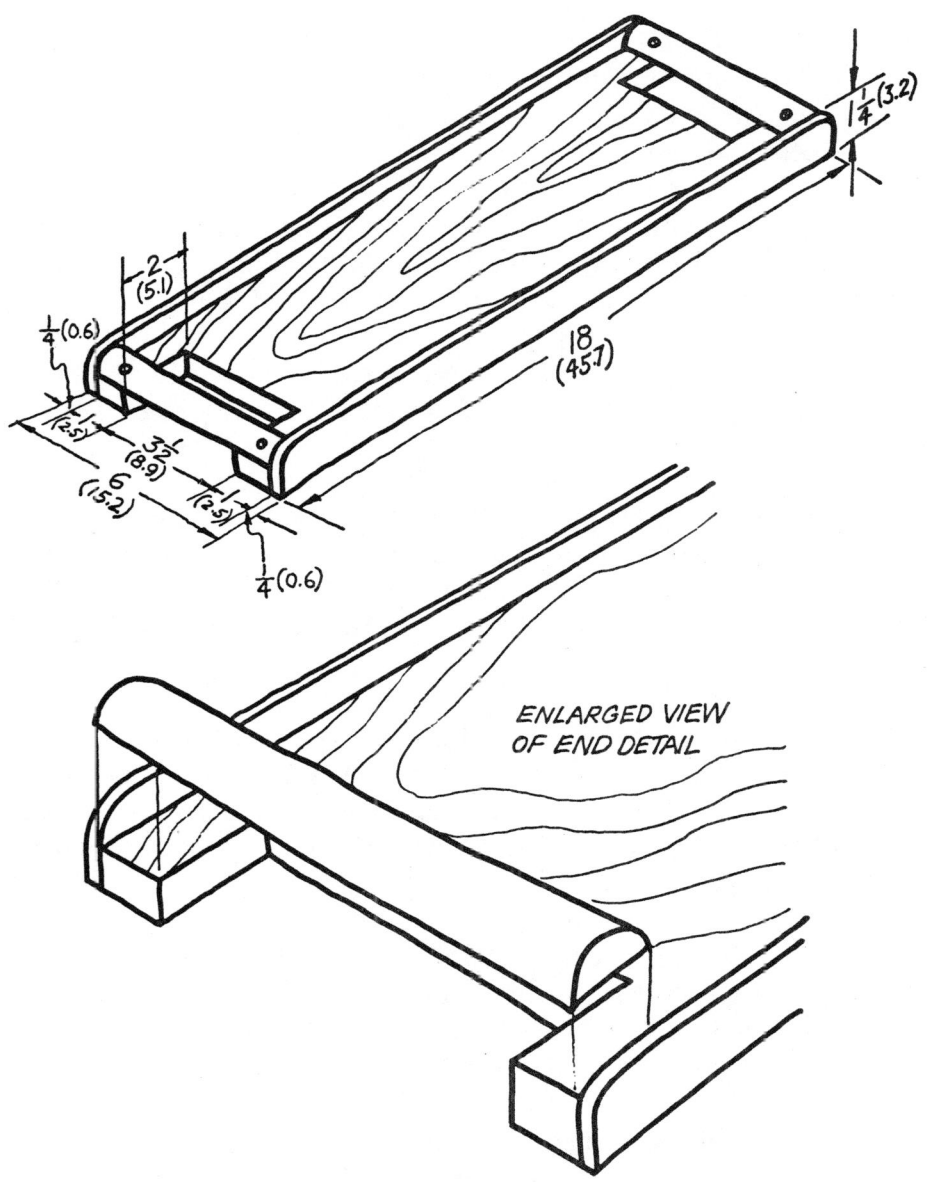

Figure 2-2. Sandwich Tray.

Begin by cutting the base to shape. Make sure it is square and straight. Lay out the hand openings and cut them out with a coping or jig saw. Smooth all the inside edges before you go on to the next step.

Cut the side rails to size, but leave the upper corners square for now. Next, fasten the side rails in place with a good waterproof glue. Use clamps to hold the rails in place as the glue dries. Smooth all the edges and surfaces, using a medium and then a fine sandpaper.

Shape the handle stock to a smooth convex form. You can use a power tool, such as a belt sander, or you can do the job with hand tools. A surface-forming tool is effective, as is a rasp, or the careful use of a well-sharpened knife. Do not cut the handles apart until all of the shaping and sanding has been done. This will insure that both handles have the same shape.

Cut the handles to size, and make sure they fit easily, but not loosely, between the rails. See Figure 2-2. When you are sure you have a good fit, smooth the handles with fine sandpaper.

The handles can be fastened with brads or decorative screws. If you decide to use screws, be sure to drill pilot holes before driving the screws. Whether you use screws or brads, it's a good idea to add some strength to the handles by using waterproof glue as well.

Now you can shape the rails to follow the contours you created for the handles. This shaping can be done by hand or power tools. Perhaps the best tool for the job is the surface-forming tool. Finish the shaped ends with sandpaper and then apply a coat of shellac to the entire tray.

When the shellac dries, use a fine grade of steel wool to smooth the surface. Two or three coats of spar varnish, either gloss or matte, will finish the job. Be sure to rub each dried coat with fine steel wool before applying the next.

After the last coat of varnish, apply a good grade of furniture wax and buff the surface well.

Projects You Can Sell or Give as Gifts

NOTES: If you plan to stain the wood before applying any varnish, first wipe all pieces of wood end grain with boiled linseed oil. This will prevent the stain from deepening the color too much.

If you plan to use veneered wood, carefully peel small pieces of veneer from scrap pieces and glue them in place along the end grain of the base. Use the linseed oil if the rails are to be made of veneered plywood.

You may want to glue a piece of felt to the bottom of the tray. With this protection you will be less likely to damage surfaces on which the tray is placed.

CHILD'S STEP STOOL

Have you ever noticed how many kid's toys are based on things owned by their parents? Toy cars, boats and houses are among the most popular. Well, why not make something practical for a small person, who can't reach to the cookie jar, that looks just like the steps in his parent's house? An ordinary step stool would do the job, but this set of miniature stairs will look like part of the house and extend a growing reach very nicely.

We have given suggested sizes that work well, but you can make these steps any size you want. And, if you want to add to the number of steps, just extend the set by another step unit.

Here's What You'll Need:

- Sides—2 pcs 1 × 8¼ × 10½ (2.5 × 21 × 26.7)
- Treads—2 pcs 1 × 6½ × 15 (2.5 × 16.5 × 38.1)
- Risers—2 pcs ½ × 3¾ × 15 (1.3 × 9.5 × 38.1)
- Rear reinforcer—1 pc 1 × 2 × 13½ (2.5 × 5.1 × 34.3)
- Nails—1½" or 2" brads

Here's How to Make It:

Begin by cutting all the pieces to size. Be sure that your cuts are straight and edges are square. Even a slight irregularity will result in a stool that rocks when a child tries to

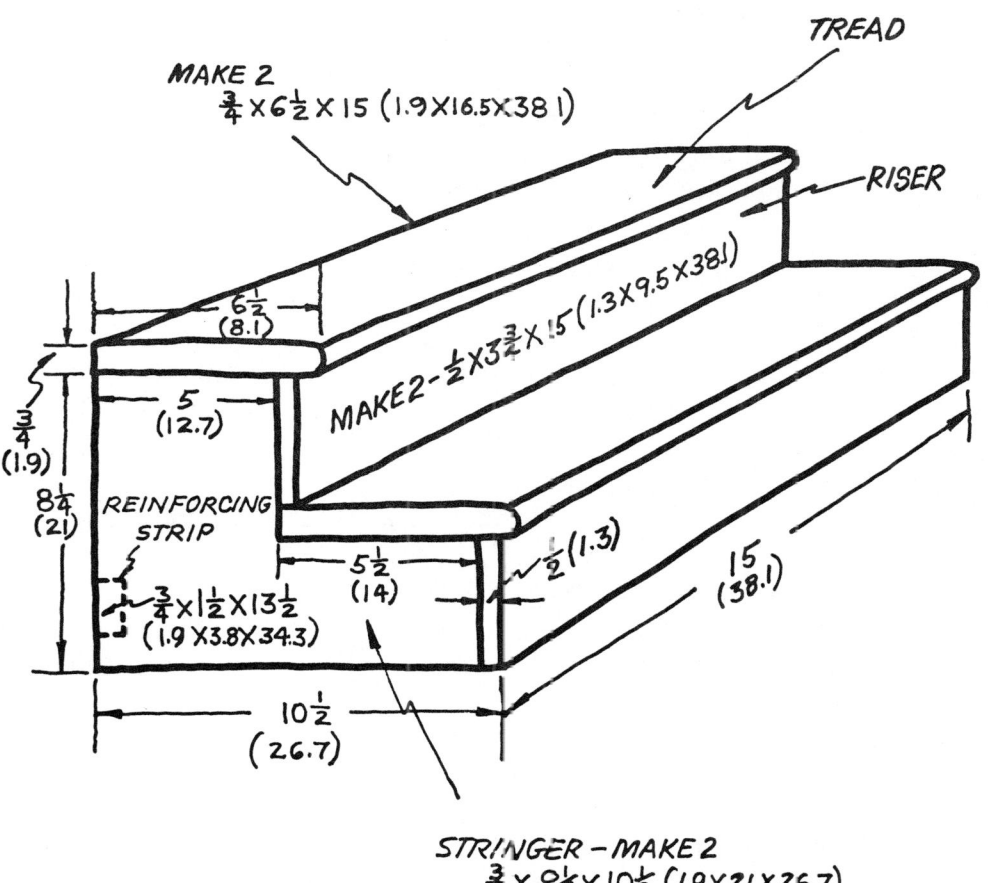

Figure 2-3. Child's Step Stool.

stand on it. If you were making a full size set of stairs and had an angle or two slightly off, you would have a set of squeaky stairs. Normally, stairs are made of hardwood, such as oak, but little feet and little use mean that you can make this project of a lighter wood, such as pine or plywood.

Before you begin any assembly, use a plane, rasp or surface-forming tool, such as the Stanley Surform, to round off the nosing of the treads. Finish the nosing with sandpaper, beginning with a coarse grade and putting on the final touches with a fine paper or steel wool.

Lightly mark the nailing lines on the treads and risers. These lines should be measured off as ½ the thickness of the stringer. If you use the 1" nominal size we suggested for the stringer, it will be ¾" thick. Half of this is ⅜", and this is the distance you should measure off for your nailing line. But first, make sure of the thickness of the wood you use.

You can add strength to these, and any stairs, by driving the nails at alternating angles, rather than straight into the wood. This increased holding power will help keep your steps together if they get rough treatment.

Begin the assembly by setting and nailing the two risers to the two stringers. After the risers are positioned, add the two treads. Be sure to sink the nail heads and fill the holes with putty.

Position the reinforcing strip in the back and nail it in place. Even though this is a small piece of lumber, it completes the box structure and greatly stabilizes the stairs.

After the assembly has been completed, go over the stairs with sandpaper to remove splinters and to smooth all surfaces and edges.

You can finish the surface any way you want, but these three ways will give you good wearing qualities. Think about matching a color scheme in the home, and the steps will look as though they were custom-made for the child.

Projects You Can Sell or Give as Gifts

- *Style 1*. For a wood finish, other than the color of the wood you used, try a stain followed by shellac or spar varnish.
- *Style 2*. To show the color and grain of the wood you used, just apply shellac or spar varnish. If you go this route, make sure that you fill the nail holes with a material the same color as the wood, or all the little dots of filler will stand out.
- *Style 3*. You can use a primer and oil paint. If the steps are to be used outside, a waterproof paint should be used.

If you have any carpet remnants, why not apply pieces to the treads to soften the steps for little feet. If you have enough material, try your hand at a "wall-to-wall" installation. Simply tack the carpeting down tightly over the treads and risers, and trim the sides flush with the wood.

TUGBOAT AND BARGE FOR MASS PRODUCTION

This tub-toy was so popular with the first kid who got it that we decided to include instructions to multiply the fun. With some simple jigs you can mass-produce the tug and barge for every budding sea captain you know. Make it for your own little friends, or think of it the next time you're asked to make toys for a fair or fund-raising project. With a few imaginative strokes of the paint brush, you can make a fascinating fleet of boats and barges that will turn any child's bath into a sea adventure.

Even if you want to make only one set, read on. We have included instructions for making one or many.

Here's What You'll Need:

- *Tugboat*

    Hull—1 pc ¾ × 3½ × 9 (1.9 × 8.9 × 22.9)
    Deck—1 pc ¾ × 2 × 5½ (1.9 × 5.1 × 14)
    Pilot house—1 pc ¾ × 1½ × 2 (1.9 × 3.8 × 5.1)
    Mast—1 pc ¼ dowel × 4 (.6 × 10.2)
    Stack—1 pc ¾ dowel × 2 (1.9 × 5.1)

- *Barge*

    Hull—1 pc ¾ × 3½ × 8 (1.9 × 8.9 × 20.3)
    Cabin—2 pcs ¾ × 1½ × 2, or 1 pc 1½ × 1½ × 2 (3.8 × 3.8 × 5.1)
    Glue, nails, screw eyes, string and paint

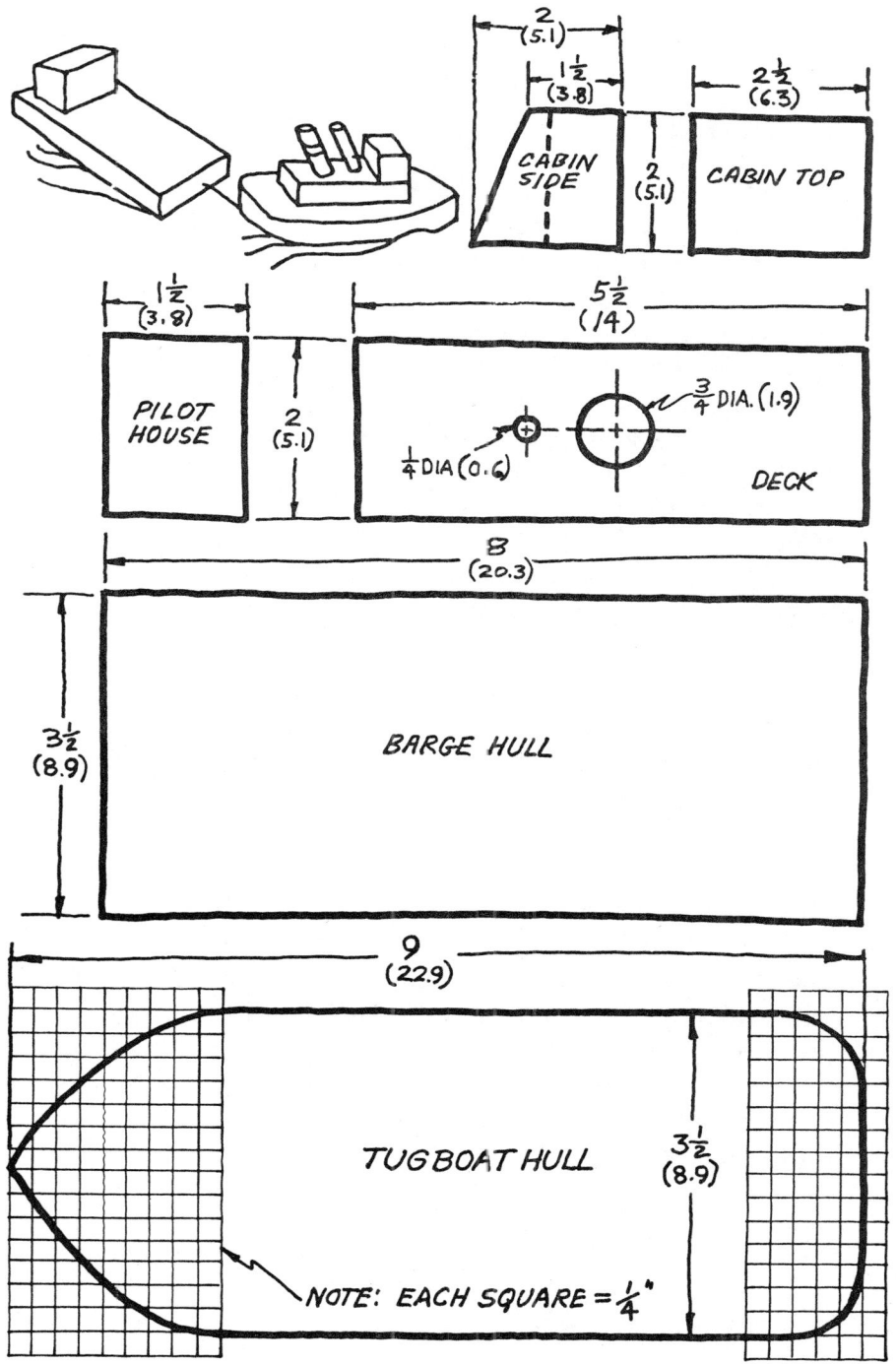

Figure 2-4. Tugboat and Barge for Mass Production.

Here's How to Make One:

Begin by cutting all wood blanks to size. After this, mark off all curves and angles, and make the appropriate cuts. Using the drawings, lay out the positions for the holes and then drill each ½" deep (1.3 cm).

See Figure 2-4 for the positions of all the parts. Mark the positions lightly with a pencil, and then complete the assembly with a waterproof glue and finishing nails. Only two finishing nails will be required for each assembly; the glue does the job and the nails merely hold everything in place until the glue sets. Be sure to sink the nails with a nail set and fill the holes with putty or caulking compound before you paint. Smooth all the edges, and lightly sandpaper the surfaces.

We have placed the parts in the general position they would appear on a real tug and barge. If you like, you can vary the position to add some variety and interest to your fleet. For example, if you slide the tug pilot house slightly forward so it overhangs the deck section, you will give the impression of a flying bridge. The barge cabin can be placed anywhere, as long as it centers on the narrow measure. Try a few of your own ideas before you glue and nail everything together.

If the boat is to be used in the water, it might be a good idea to give it a coat of shellac before you apply the paint. This will seal the wood and make the paint less susceptible to peeling.

Don't forget the screw eyes aft on the tug and forward on the barge. Connect both with a short piece of string and the set is ready for launching.

Here's How to Make a Fleet of Boats and Barges:

Mass production of this set is best handled with a few power tools. Use cutting stops on a table saw to make it easy to

Projects You Can Sell or Give as Gifts

cut a number of blanks quickly. Be sure to set the table saw to rip the angle of the barge cabin tops before they are cut to length.

Drilling the deck holes can be speeded up by making a drilling jig from either metal or a piece of hardboard. You can use this pattern by itself, or you can make an open-ended box to hold the work during drilling operations. The latter is helpful only if you are really going into the shipbuilding business.

You can add your own touches when you drill and mount the mast and the stack. For a very rakish look, mount both parts at a slight angle. Or you can position the mast vertically and mount the stack at a slight angle. When both the stack and mast are mounted vertically, you will have a boat with an older look. Take your choice, but try various positions before you set the drill angle and make the holes.

The final step in your mass production efforts will be a pattern for the tug prow. This can be made of heavy cardboard or even a piece of light scrap wood.

COLONIAL SPOON RACK

This project is as practical as it is decorative. If you want to display a collection of old spoons, the colonial spoon rack will show them to their best advantage. And, if you like the practicality of having your everyday spoons ready for use, this is the perfect project for you. Any kind of wood can be used, but pine is easiest to work with and it can be stained to match just about any decorating scheme. It's easy enough to make one, but consider buying enough wood for several; they make fine gifts. The construction lends itself to simple productions, and you can make several people happy with colonial spoon racks.

Here's What You'll Need:

- Sides—2 pcs ½ × 2 × 14 (1.3 × 5.1 × 35.5)
- Back—1 pc ¼ × 10 × 15 (.6 × 25.4 × 38.1)
- Holders—2 pcs ⅜ × 1¼ × 11 (1 × 3.2 × 27.9)

Here's How to Make It:

Begin by cutting all the blanks to size. Trace the outlines of the shapes and transfer them to the appropriate wood blanks. You can use carbon paper to do this, or just bear down lightly on the pencil and retrace the shape on the tracing paper to make a light indentation of the outline on the wood. Temporarily, nail the two blanks together for cutting.

You can use a coping saw or a power jig saw to cut the

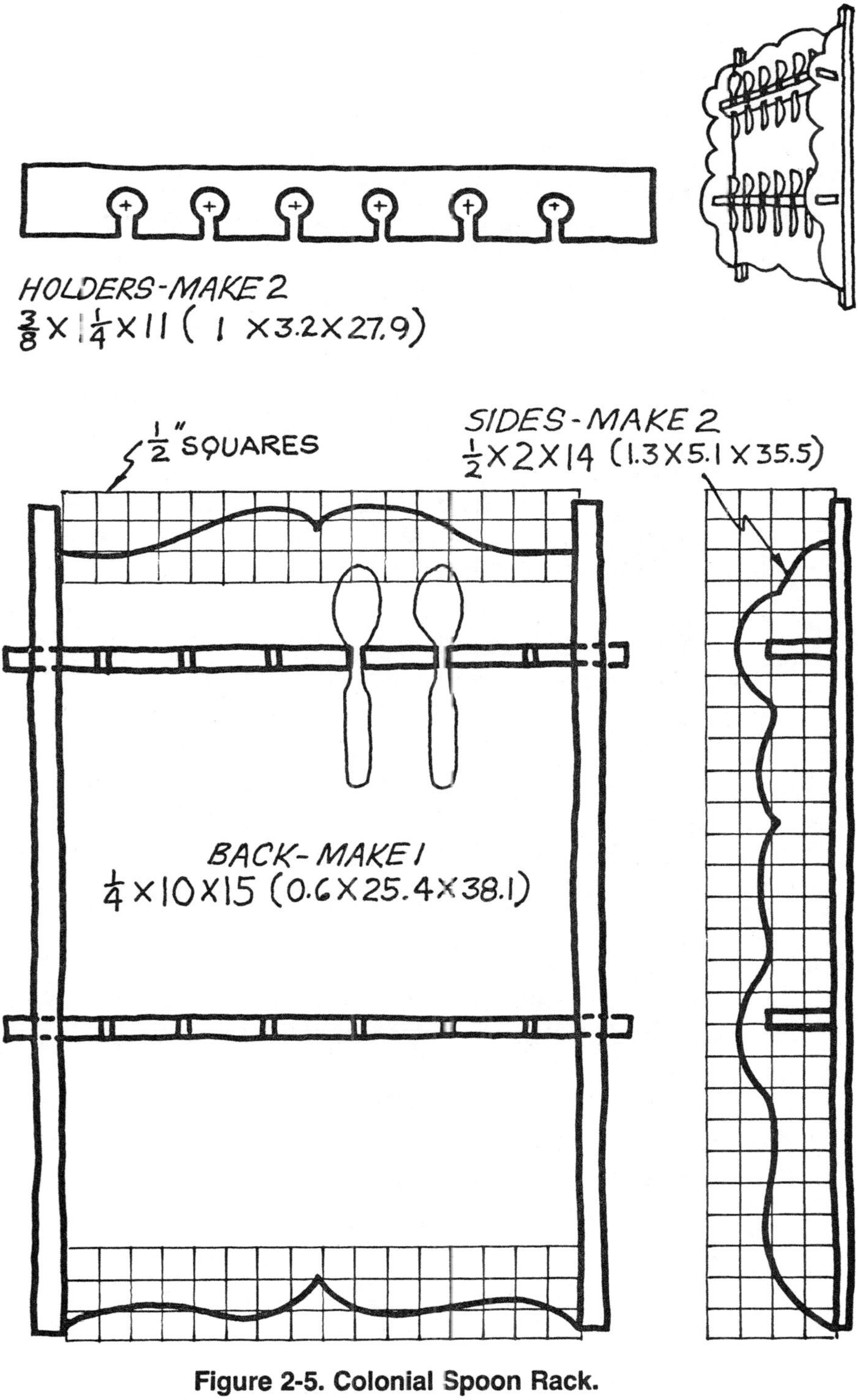

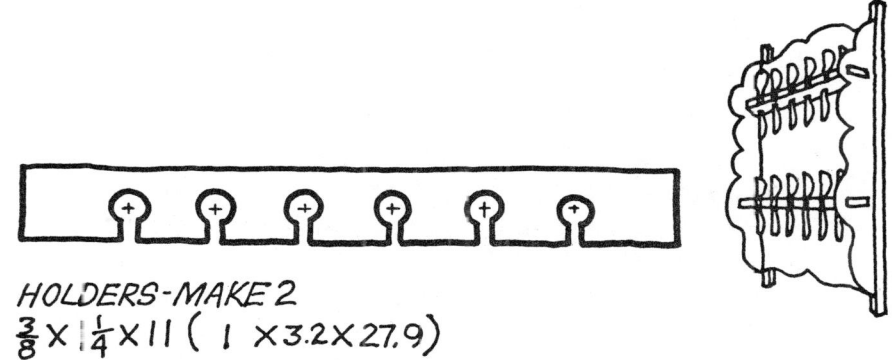

HOLDERS-MAKE 2
$\frac{3}{8} \times 1\frac{1}{4} \times 11$ ($1 \times 3.2 \times 27.9$)

$\frac{1}{2}$" SQUARES

SIDES-MAKE 2
$\frac{1}{2} \times 2 \times 14$ ($1.3 \times 5.1 \times 35.5$)

BACK-MAKE 1
$\frac{1}{4} \times 10 \times 15$ ($0.6 \times 25.4 \times 38.1$)

Figure 2-5. Colonial Spoon Rack.

shapes. The slots should be cut very carefully with a back saw. Smooth all sides and edges with fine sandpaper.

To make the spoon holders, first follow the same instructions given above to transfer the pattern. Drill the spoon holes ¼" in diameter along the center line of the holders. See Figure 2-5 for the measurements. Cut the ⅛" spoon slots with a back saw.

Make a trial fit into the side slots, and trim to insure a snug fit. Round off the front edges, except for the part which fits into the slots. Test and adjust the slots to fit the spoons you plan to display.

To make the back, first cut the wood to shape. Lay out the patterns for the top and bottom by tracing, as described in the last two sections. Cut out the shape and round all curved edges.

Before final assembly, make a trial fit of all the pieces. When you are sure that everything fits snugly and is squared up, fasten the sides to the back with brads and glue. After the glue has dried, sand and smooth all of the surfaces and edges.

This piece is a replica of a colonial spoon rack, and will look good stained and finished with matte varnish. Apply several coats of varnish, sanding each coat lightly before putting on the next. A good coat of paste wax will finish the job nicely.

If the spoon rack is to be mounted on a wall, you will not want to see mounting screws or nails. An effective way to mount the rack so that it can be taken down easily is to drill two ⅜" holes halfway through the back of the upper left- and right-hand corners. Heavy brads driven in the wall at a slight angle, so that each will catch a hole and support the rack, is all that is needed. The brads will be unseen, insuring that nothing will detract from the appearance of your work.

PARTY CHEESE BLOCK

Gift-shop cheese boards may accent your decor and look as though they just came from a photo spread in *Gourmet* magazine, but when you try to use them, you usually find that they are woefully small and impractical. We've tried to solve this problem without making a concession to style. This cheese board is a replica of the old butcher block. It's attractive as well as practical. We've even included a pocket for your favorite cheese knife.

Here's What You'll Need:

- A & K ⅜ (or ½) × 5 × 10 (1 (or 1.3) × 12.7 × 25.4)
- B & J ¾ × 5 × 10 ea. (1.9 × 12.7 × 25.4)
- C-I ¾ × 4 × 10 ea. (1.9 × 10.2 × 25.4)

To heighten the appearance of this butcher-block cheese board, we have designed it using light and dark wood lamination. The woods you choose should be of the same relative hardness or softness, open grain woods should be avoided. We suggest that pieces A and K be made of walnut. Pieces B and J can be made of lighter birch. To continue the alternate pattern in the block itself, make three of the C through I pieces of birch, and four of walnut.

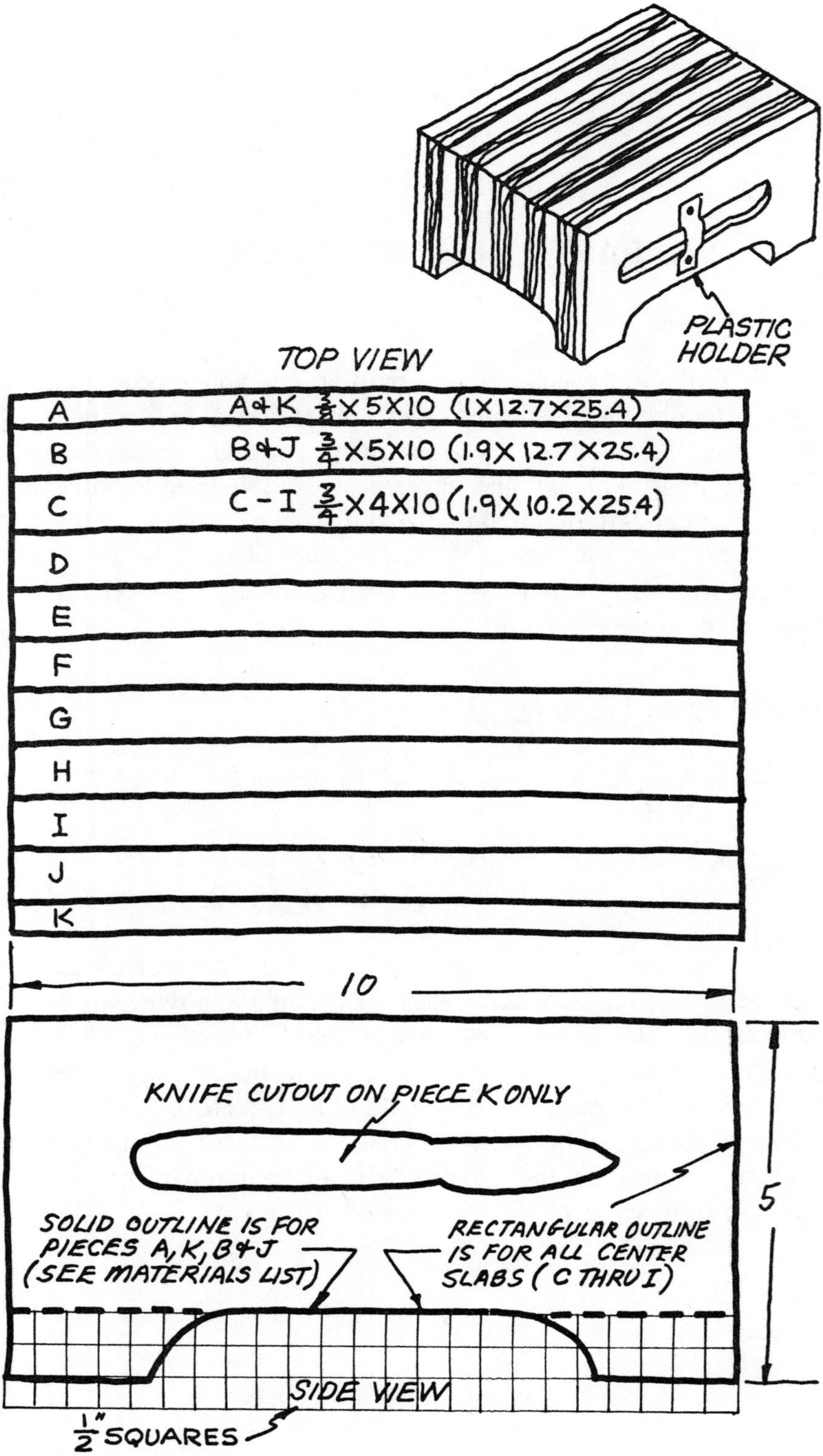

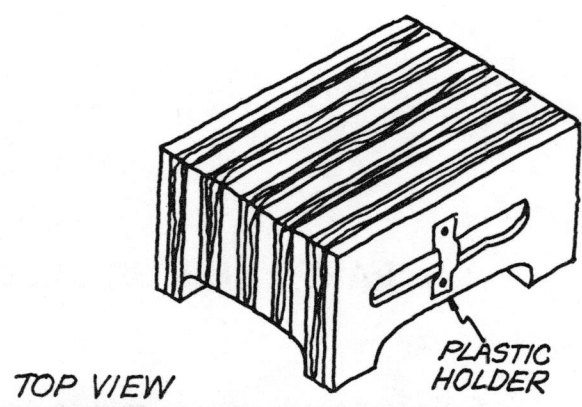

PLASTIC HOLDER
TOP VIEW
A
A&K 3/8 X5X10 (1X12.7X25.4)
B
B&J 3/4 X5X10 (1.9X12.7X25.4)
C
C-I 3/4 X4X10 (1.9X10.2X25.4)
D
E
F
G
H
I
J
K
10
KNIFE CUTOUT ON PIECE K ONLY
5
SOLID OUTLINE IS FOR PIECES A, K, B&J (SEE MATERIALS LIST)
RECTANGULAR OUTLINE IS FOR ALL CENTER SLABS (C THRU I)
SIDE VIEW
1/2" SQUARES

Figure 2-6. Party Cheese Block.

Projects You Can Sell or Give as Gifts

Here's How to Make It:

Begin by tracing the pattern and transferring the shapes to the wood that will be used. The end sections are made up of one thick and one thin piece to form a heavy foot to support the block. Pay particular attention to the placement of the dark and light woods. See Figure 2-6 for wood positioning, and note that the two end pieces are made of the darker walnut.

Next, cut all pieces to size and shape. If you are planning to include a cutout for your favorite cheese knife, trace it lightly with soft pencil on one of the end pieces. Position the knife so that it centers in both directions on the block. Drill a hole large enough to accomodate the end of a coping saw blade in the part of the wood that will be removed. Fit a blade to the saw and cut out the outline. Try the knife for a fit. If it's too snug, use a file and sandpaper to loosen the fit. If your knife is too thick to be held in the single cutout, it may be necessary to gouge or drill the next layer of wood to make more room. This can be done with a bottom-beveled gouge or an ordinary wood chisel. Be sure to sand the finished cutout before you assemble the block.

The next step is to glue all of the pieces together. Be sure to assemble the pieces in the pattern shown in Figure 2-6. Different species of woods expand and contract at different rates, and because you will be using birch and walnut for this project, it is important to use a strong plastic resin thermo-setting glue. Once a thermo-setting glue has cured, it will always maintain its consistency and will not be affected by heat.

Be sure that all pieces are smooth and dust free. Line them up in the proper order and coat each surface to be joined with glue. A small paint brush is an excellent tool for applying glue. Apply enough glue to cover the surface completely, but not so much that the clamping pressure will force a lot of it to run out.

Once the glued pieces have been positioned and assembled, they should be clamped until the glue dries. Clamping time varies with the glue you have chosen; check the label on the can or bottle. You can use C-clamps or cabinet-makers handscrew clamps, but be sure to place scrap wood between the face of the clamps and the wood being laminated. The pressure should be even; four clamps, one at each corner will do the job. If you do not have a set of clamps, you can place the glued assembly under a weight, such as a cinder block. Be sure to protect the piece under the block with a piece of scrap wood. To insure that excess glue doesn't cause problems, you can cover the surface of your bench with wax paper. Be sure to remove any excess glue before it hardens. Use a scraper blade, wood chisel or just a damp rag.

After the glue has dried, cut a chamfer at each corner and then lightly plane all the surfaces. A file can be used to smooth the inside curves of the legs before the entire block is finished with a fine grade of sandpaper.

This cheese block will look best with only a few applications of any odor-free cooking oil. Apply several coats, and allow a day or two in between. It's not necessary to apply any other kind of finish.

To protect the surface of the table on which you will use the cheese block, glue squares of felt to each of the legs.

If your cheese knife tends to fall out, you can mount an elastic strap across the opening. You can hold the strap in place with decorative upholstery nails.

Now all you need is the cheese!

PORTABLE PLANTER

Anyone who lives in a house with limited garden space, or in an apartment with no garden at all will appreciate this portable planter. The chances are that no one window will allow enough sun into a room to keep plants really healthy, so it is often necessary to shift plants from window to window during the day. This planter not only gives you a good planting capacity, it's also easy to move to follow the sun. It's an ideal gift for a shut-in who would like to raise plants inside. It's easy to make and leaves plenty of room for your creative energies if you would like to enhance it with your own design. Simple floral designs on the sides will make this planter look as though it were the product of a professional craftsperson.

Here's What You'll Need:

- Sides—2 pcs ½ × 7 × 16 (1.3 × 17.8 × 40.6)
- End—#1 1 pc ½ × 7 × 9 (1.3 × 17.8 × 22.9)
- End—#2 1 pc ½ × 7½ × 9 (1.3 × 19.1 × 22.9)
- Handles—2 pcs ½ × 1¼ × 24 (1.3 × 3.2 × 61)
- Wheels—2 pcs ½ × 7D (1.3 × 17.8D)
- Leg—1 pc ½ × 2½ × 8 (1.3 × 6.3 × 20.3)
- Bottom—1 pc 1 × 8 × 12 (2.5 × 20.3 × 30.5)
- Axles—2 pcs ¼ dowel, 1 to 2" long (.6 × 2.5 to 5.1)

Note that the bottom is made of 1" stock (¾" actual thickness). This was done to provide a heavier base for the dirt and plants. A lighter piece of wood might warp and split.

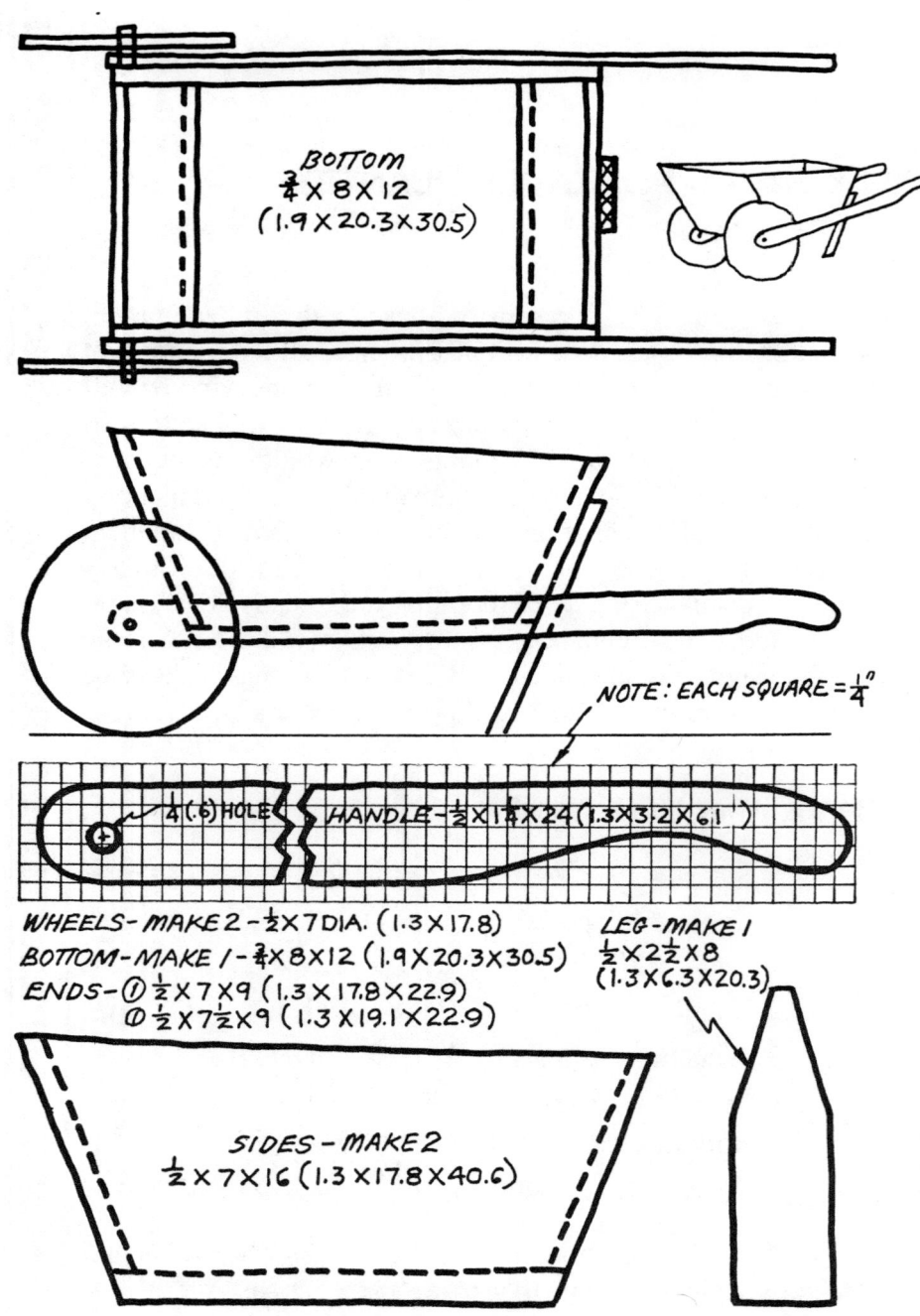

Figure 2-7. Portable Planter.

Projects You Can Sell or Give as Gifts 53

Here's How to Make It:

Begin by cutting all the wood to size. The pieces are shown part-scale, so you will have to enlarge the patterns before transferring them to the wood blanks. Once you have transferred the patterns to the wood, cut all pieces to shape. Round off the handles to provide a comfortable grip. Drill ¼" holes in the wheel centers and, as indicated in the drawings, at the ends of the handles. Using the side pattern as a template, mark off and cut all the angles.

See that all parts of the planter box fit neatly and then use a waterproof glue and nails or screws to put it together. Be sure to use nails or screws made of noncorroding metals, such as copper, brass or aluminum. The dampness from the dirt in the planter can cause problems with other metals.

Fasten the handles to the box at the same level as the bottom, and extend them 2" (5.1) from the front. Measure from the hole to the bottom front of the box.

Round off the ends of the ¼" dowels and glue the wheels in place. Allow about ¼" space between the outside of the handle and the inside of the wheel for a pleasant appearance. Even though the wheels do not turn, the planter can be slid easily from one sunny location to another by lifting and pulling on the handles.

Fasten the leg to the planter box in the center of the rear panel. Position the leg so that the handle is level.

The inside of the planter should be finished with several coats of waterproof paint or a good spar varnish. If there are any openings at the joints of the box, seal them with caulking compound or putty before painting.

The outside of the planter can be painted or finished with just about anything from stain and varnish to any paint you have handy. As we mentioned, the sides of the planter can be hand decorated. If such artwork is not your forte, you can apply any of the many decals that are now sold in craft stores.

3

Eight Hobby Projects That Will Save You Time and Money

DOUBLE-SIDED EASEL CHALKBOARD

Why do kids draw on the walls? Maybe because their parents didn't give them this nifty chalkboard. Not only is it a sound idea to have some equipment at home that is like that found in school, but it's also a good idea just to provide a place where budding artists can make their marks—not on the wall. And, it's convertible. Wipe the chalk marks and position a few clips, and you have an easel. Because it's two-sided, you can leave one side as a chalkboard and the other as an easel.

No matter how you look at it, this project will make a lot of people happy.

Here's What You'll Need:

- Rails—4 pcs 1 × 3 × 60 (2.5 × 7.6 × 152.4)
- Stretchers—4 pcs 1 × 3 × 30 (2.5 × 7.6 × 76.2)
- Panels—2 pcs ¼ × 20 × 30 hardboard (.6 × 50.8 × 76.2)
- Lockstrips—2 pcs ⅛ × ½ × 15 soft steel (.3 × 1.3 × 38.1)
- Tray bottoms—2 pcs ¼ × 4 × 30 hardboard (.6 × 10.2 × 76.2)
- Tray backs—2 pcs ½ × 3 × 30 (1.3 × 7.6 × 76.2)

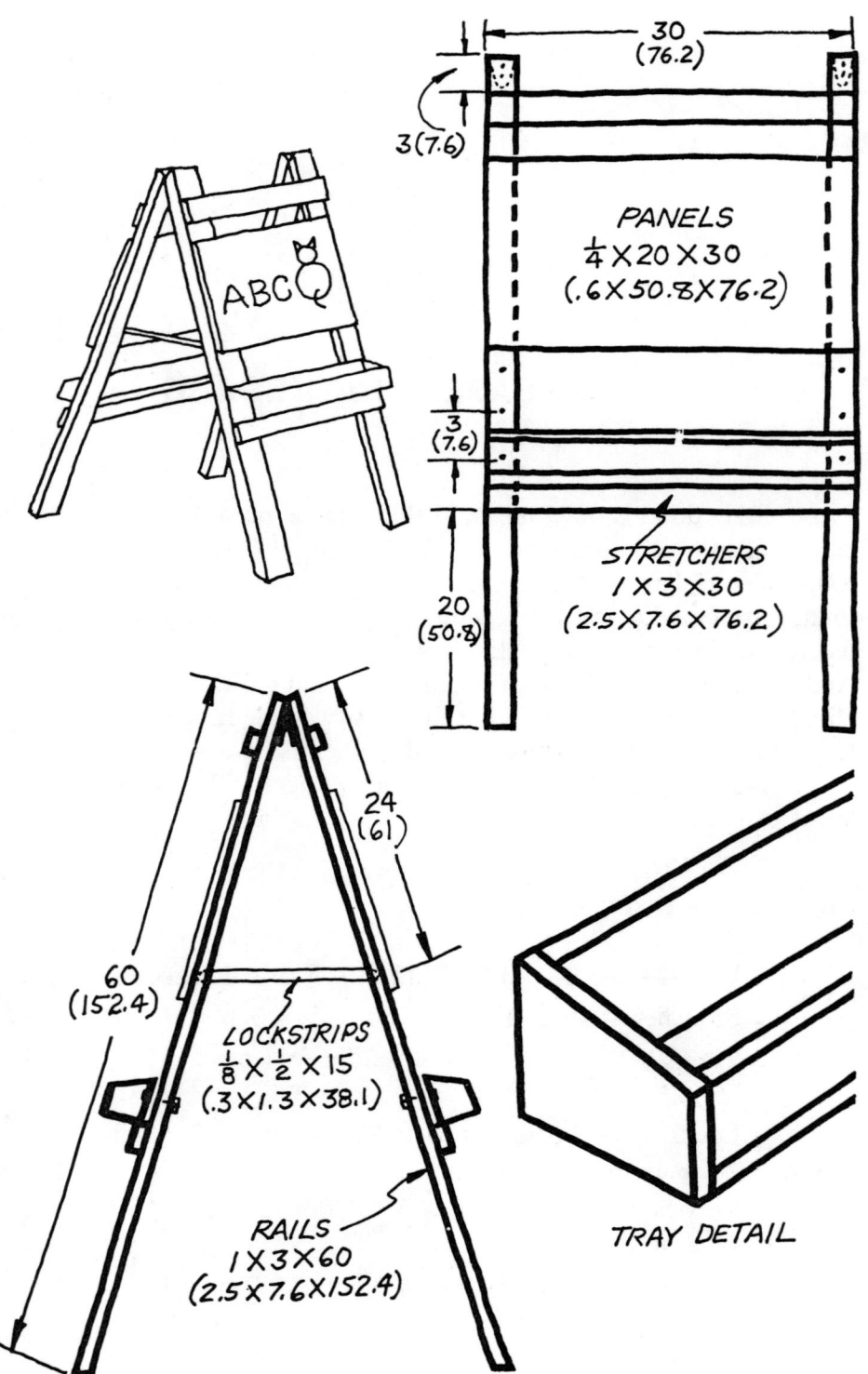

Figure 3-1. Double-Sided Easel Chalkboard.

- Tray fronts—2 pcs ½ × 2 × 30 (1.3 × 5.1 × 76.2)
- Tray ends—4 pcs ½ × 3¼ × 4 (1.3 × 8.2 × 10.2)
- Glue, finishing nails
- 2 pcs—3" strap hinges
- 4 wingnuts and bolts $^3/_{16}$ × 2 (.5 × 5.1)
- Paint for panels (green chalkboard paint)

Here's How to Make It:

Panels

Cut the panels to size and smooth all edges. Apply two coats of chalkboard paint. Follow the paint manufacturer's instructions for time between coats.

Easel

Cut the rails to size and touch up all rough edges. Lay out and fasten the stretchers with nails and glue. Be sure that each subassembly, front and back, is square or it will be a rocky affair when it is finished. See Figure 3-1 for proper placement. Place the rail assembly upside-down on the floor, with the tops touching. Hold them down with either clamps or weights. Position the strap hinges so that each hinge pin straddles the touching point of the rails, and then fasten the hinges with wood screws.

Tray

Cut all the tray parts to size and shape. Assemble the parts with nails and glue. See Figure 3-1 for assembly details. Drill holes at the back of the trays to facilitate fastening to the rails. See Figure 3-1 for the location of the holes.

The trays can be made adjustable by drilling several evenly spaced holes above and below the original hole. You can use ¼-20 nuts and bolts, or use "T" nuts to prevent the bolts from protruding.

Lock Strips

Round off all the ends. At each end, in the center of the strip, drill a $^3/_{16}''$ (.5) hole ½" (1.3) from the end. Lay out and cut a "V" shape into *one* of the holes in each strip.

Smooth all sharp edges.

Measure down from the hinge a distance of 24" (61) on the inside of each rail and make a mark with a brad. Fasten the closed lock strip end into each of these spots with a round head screw and washer on each side of the strip. Fasten a screw into the other part of the rail, allowing enough of the screw to project and act as a latch when the lock strip is swung down.

Assembly and Finishing

You can fasten the panels several ways, depending on your needs and available hardware. Here are some options:

1. Bolt in place.
2. You can make them adjustable with equally spaced holes, as was done with the trays.
3. Resting on dowel supports.

You can finish the frame to match your room. Paint, stain and varnish, or just a waxed surface will be fine.

LAMINATED WOOD JEWELRY

This is a craft that has been raised to a fine art by a number of talented people. With a little imagination, you can take the basic instructions we give you and turn out original jewelry designs that will impress anyone.

Basically, the technique depends on the lamination process. With today's epoxy glues and a few simple tools, you can make laminations that once required considerable effort and special equipment. The appeal of jewelry made this way is the variation of color that is possible by laminating different types of wood. The color, layers of lamination and the shape of the finished pieces all combine to create pieces that can be subtle or startling.

Here are some of the more popular woods that can be used for lamination:

Wood	*Color*
Walnut	Brown
Rosewood	Red black
Padouk	Vermillion
Amaranth	Purple
Prima vera	Light yellow
Coco bolo	Dark orange
Teak	Light brown

Many of these colorful woods can be bought in small pieces in craft shops or specialty lumber yards. The wood is also available by mail from Albert Constantine & Sons, Bronx, New York.

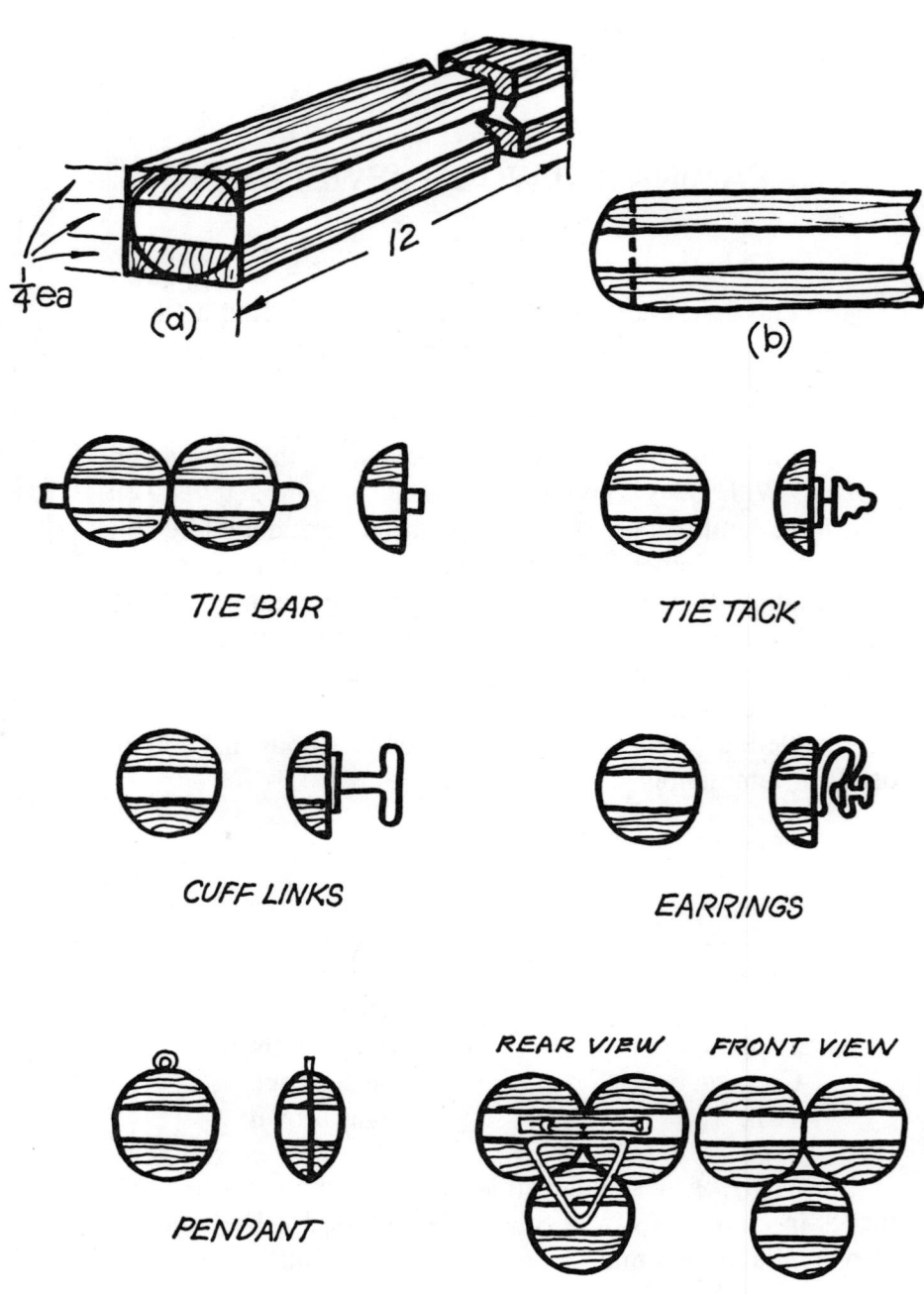

Figure 3-2. Laminated Wood Jewlery.

Hobby Projects That Save Time and Money

Here's What You'll Need:

- 3 pieces of wood in different colors ¼ × ¾ × 12 (.6 × 1.9 × 30.5)
- Assorted jewelry findings, such as earring clips, tie clip, tie tack, cuff links, etc.
- Epoxy glue
- 1 pc clothes hanger wire 3' long (91.4)

Here's How to Make It:

This is the kind of project you will want to plan carefully before you start. Think in terms of the shape of the piece you are going to make, as well as the relationship of the colors of the pieces of wood you will laminate. You might want to sandwich a dark wood between two lighter pieces of the same wood. Or you can reverse this or arrange the wood in sequence from dark to light. Whichever arrangement you choose, plan it to be harmonious with the shape you will make. For example, if you are planning a teardrop shape, you can accentuate the form by laminating wood in steps of progressive color, from light at the top thin section, to dark at the lower heavier part.

How to Make the Master Block:

The sizes and measurements are not critical; make the block to suit the ideas you have for original jewelry or the designs we have included.

Before you do the laminating, smooth all adjoining surfaces with fine sandpaper. Use an epoxy glue to join the pieces in the pattern you want, clamp the assembly tightly and allow it to harden. When the epoxy has cured, shape the block into a cylinder by using either a lathe, or a rasp and sandpaper.

Each of the elements used to make the jewelry is rounded in front and flat on the back. The easiest and safest way to make the elements is to round the end of the cylinder, and then cut off the shaped piece. After you cut off each element, round the end of the cylinder again and cut off the next piece.

When you have shaped and cut all of the buttons you plan to use, smooth the surfaces and edges with fine 3/0 sandpaper.

To make the cuff links, earrings, tie bar or tie tack, simply fasten the appropriate jewelry finding to the back with the same epoxy you used to make the lamination.

The brooch is made by joining the three buttons on the back with a wire triangle, held in place with epoxy. Attach a pinback as shown in the drawing, and the assembly is completed.

To make the pendant, two buttons are attached to each other, back to back. Before you attach the buttons, prepare a wire loop with a twisted pigtail. Gouge out an area on the back of one of the buttons just enough to accomodate the wire pigtail. Fasten the two buttons and the pigtail with epoxy.

Laminated jewelry can be finished to suit the costume with which it will be worn. It can be left natural, but if this is contemplated, it is best to apply several coats of a good wax. An oil finish adds depth, and shellac or varnish will produce a lustrous shine.

PHOTO BLIND

Anyone who has tried to take nature pictures without some kind of a blind knows the real meaning of the word frustration. You simply must have something that blends with the surroundings and is large enough to hide behind. This description also implies something that would take two men and a boy to carry into the field.

But, when you get two photographers who write about woodworking projects and who don't like to carry heavy things, the answer turned out to be light, simple and concealing.

Here's What You'll Need:

- Supports—8 pcs 1 × 2 × 48 (2.5 × 5.1 × 121.9)
- Filler blocks—4 pcs 1 × 2 × 3 (2.5 × 5.1 × 7.6)
- Bolts—12 pcs ¼—20 × 3 carriage bolts with washers and wing nuts (6 mm—1.0 mm × 7.6)
- Pivot—1 pc ⅜—16 × 36 threaded rod with nuts and four washers (9 mm—1.0 × 91.4)
- Cover—6 yards of mosquito netting 36" wide (6m × 1m wide)
- Grommets—1 dozen large grommets

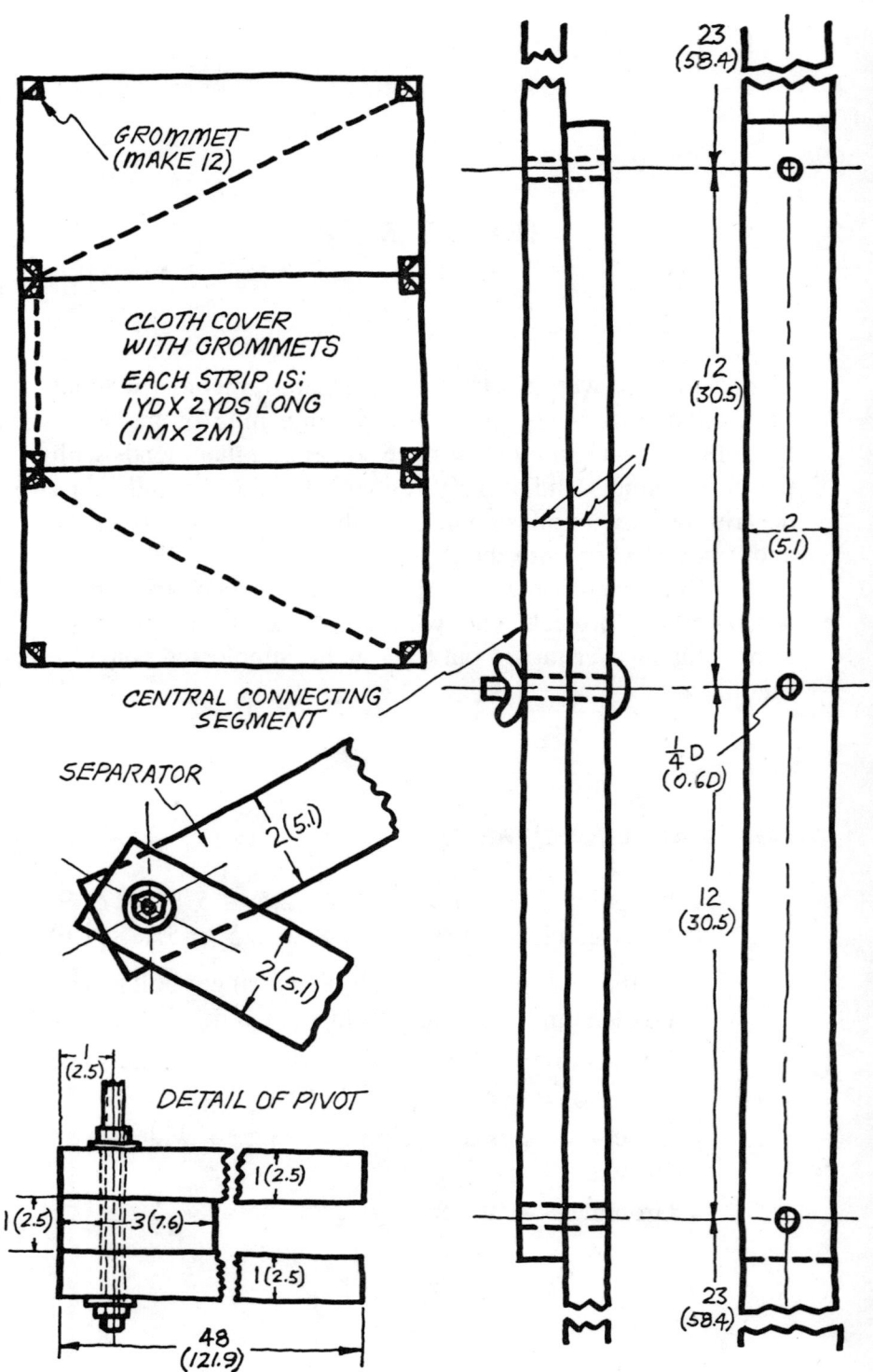

Figure 3-3. Photo Blind.

Hobby Projects That Save Time and Money

Here's How to Make It:

Cut all the supports to size; make sure they are evenly trimmed and square. Lay out the supports and clamp them together in pairs.

Drill each pair and label them to insure that when one of the pair is reversed, the holes will match. When drilling the end holes, do both pieces so that in a pinch you can use the pairs right side up or upside down. This will permit quicker field assembly.

Lay out, cut and drill the separators. They are only used to insure even stacking in the traveling position. Do not glue them to either leg.

Stain the legs a medium tone to blend with ground and surroundings. If you plan to varnish, use only a matte finish; gloss will produce reflections that could warn of your presence.

Make the cover of any lightweight, open-weave material which is semiopaque. Mosquito netting is ideal, but you can also use voile, batiste or even an open-weave burlap.

Seam the material inside so you end up with a piece that is 2 by 3 yards. Before stitching together, turn each corner and fasten a grommet. The grommets slip over the bolt ends when the blind is erected.

In traveling position, each leg swings into half its length by removing the outer wing nuts and bolts.

When in open position the blind is 6' high.

PHOTO DARKROOM PAPER SAFE

It's a big pain to keep opening and closing packages of photographic paper when you're making prints in the darkroom. You can buy a commercial paper safe, or for one-tenth the cost you can make this one. It's easy to make, and makes darkroom work go much more smoothly.

Here's What You'll Need:

- Top—1 pc ¾ × 12 × 20 plywood or particle board (1.9 × 30.5 × 50.8)
- Bottom—1 pc ¾ × 12 × 20 plywood or particle board (1.9 × 30.5 × 50.8)
- Ends—2 pcs ¾ × 10 × 12 plywood or particle board (1.9 × 25.4 × 30.5)
- Door—1 pc ¾ × 11½ × 20 plywood or particle board (1.9 × 29.1 × 50.8)
- Back—1 pc ¼ × 11½ × 20 hardboard (.6 × 29.1 × 50.8)
- Inserts—4 pcs ¼ × 12 × 19 (.6 × 30.5 × 48.2)
- Door ledge—1 pc ¼ × 2 × 20½ hardboard (.6 × 5.1 × 52)
  2 pcs ¼ × 2 × 11½ hardboard (.6 × 5.1 × 29.1)
- Bottom strip—1 pc 1 × 1 × 20 (2.5 × 2.5 × 50.8)
- Seal—⅛ × 60 soft leather or rubber (.3 × 152.4)
- Heavy-duty triple magnet with keeper
- Nails, glue, hinges, handle
- Flat black paint

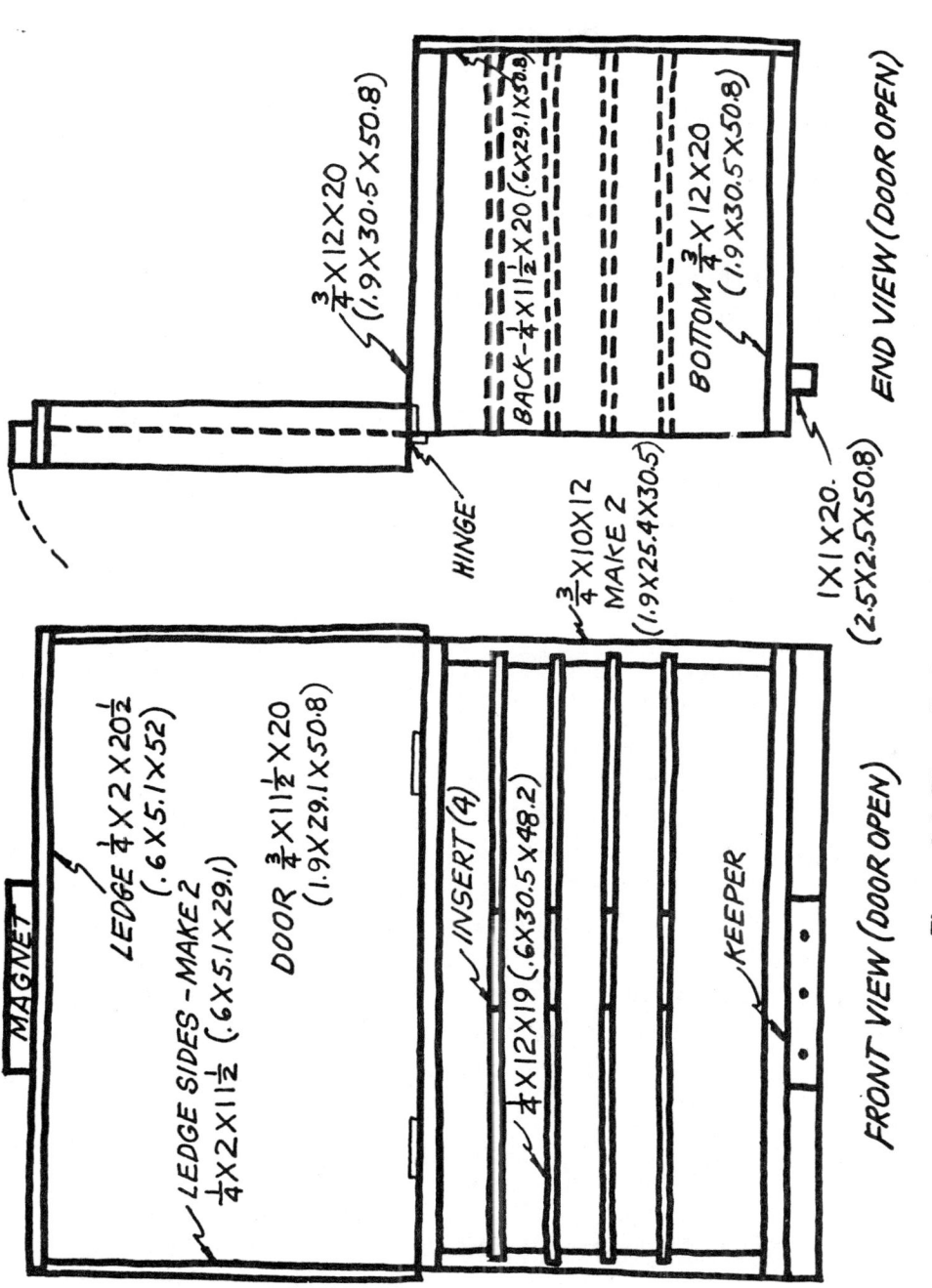

Figure 3-4. Photo Darkroom Paper Safe.

Here's How to Make It:

Begin by cutting all pieces to size.

The grooves on the sides of the box that support the shelves should be laid out as shown in Figure 3-4. If you have a table saw, make cuts in the sides to hold the shelves when the box is assembled. Make the cuts a little wider than ¼" to allow for the thickness of paint that will be applied later. If you don't have a table saw, you can make supports of wood strips that are 1½" wide and ⅜" thick. Cut them each 12" long, and nail and glue them to the sides where the grooves would have been. Leave a little more than a ¼" space between them. The strip grooves should be in the same position as the cut grooves shown in the drawing. If you do it this way, remember that the shelves should be shorter by ¾".

After you have made the grooves, assemble the box by using glue and nails. Be sure that the box is perfectly square, and then glue and nail the back in place.

Next, cut a 3" (7.6) semicircle in the center front edge of each shelf insert. This will provide a finger grip for the paper when the safe is in use.

Turn the box on its back, position the door in place and tack it lightly with several nails. Now attach the hinges to the top. Doing this, you will eliminate the usual space taken up by the hinges. Before you remove the nails, attach the side ledge strips and the bottom strips to the door.

Now remove the nails and try the door. It should swing freely, yet fit snugly. Line the inside of the door with some shielding material, such as sponge rubber or leather, to make the door absolutely light-tight.

Mount the magnetic catch to the bottom of the door, and mount its keeper to the bottom strip. When the keeper has been mounted on the bottom strip, mount the strip on the

Hobby Projects That Save Time and Money 71

bottom of the box. Position the strip so that when the door is closed, the force of the magnet pulls the door snugly against the lining material inside.

You should paint the inside and outside with several coats of flat black paint. Paint the shelves and allow them to dry before you slide them in place within the box.

The bottom of the box has only one "foot," the strip under the front which supports the magnet keeper. There is a reason for this unevenness. In such a tilted position the door will not catch on the table or shelf when closing, and the photo paper will always slide to the back of the cabinet, helping to prevent you from spilling paper when working in the dark.

Before you put the box into use, it's a good idea to test it first. Put a piece of photographic paper on each shelf. Do this in a darkroom. Close the door, and then let the box stand either in a lighted room or outside in the sun. Make sure that enough time passes so that all surfaces of the box are exposed to light. Then bring the box back to the darkroom, remove the paper and process each sheet. If there are any leaks, you will see dark areas on the paper. You can seal leaks with black electricians' tape, or by filling cracks with a black silicone sealing compound.

DO-ALL KIT BOX

If you have no place to store tools, this is the project for you. Even if you have a well-equipped shop, this kit box will do a lot of organizing for you. Keep whatever tools or hobby parts you want in it, and if they are heavy enough, you can mount a set of casters on the box so it can be rolled away. It's especially handy for a router with accessories and a drill with accessories.

The box should be divided into compartments to accomodate whatever you plan to store. We have given no dimensions for the dividers because it is impossible to tell what you will store in the box. However, when you plan your dividers, it's best to make heavy cardboard mock-ups of dividers and tools that will be stored before you cut and assemble the plywood dividers.

Here's What You'll Need:

- Front—1 pc ½ × 16 × 20 plywood (1.3 × 40.6 × 50.8)
- Back—1 pc ½ × 16 × 20 plywood (1.3 × 40.6 × 50.8)
- Ends—2 pcs ¾ × 12 × 15¼ (1.9 × 30.5 × 38.6)
- Top—1 pc ¾ × 12 × 20 (1.9 × 30.5 × 50.8)
- Bottom—1 pc ¾ × 12 × 18½ (1.9 × 30.5 × 47)
- Dividers—Assorted lengths of ¼ × 6" plywood
- Drawer dividers—¼ "U" channel with mounting points

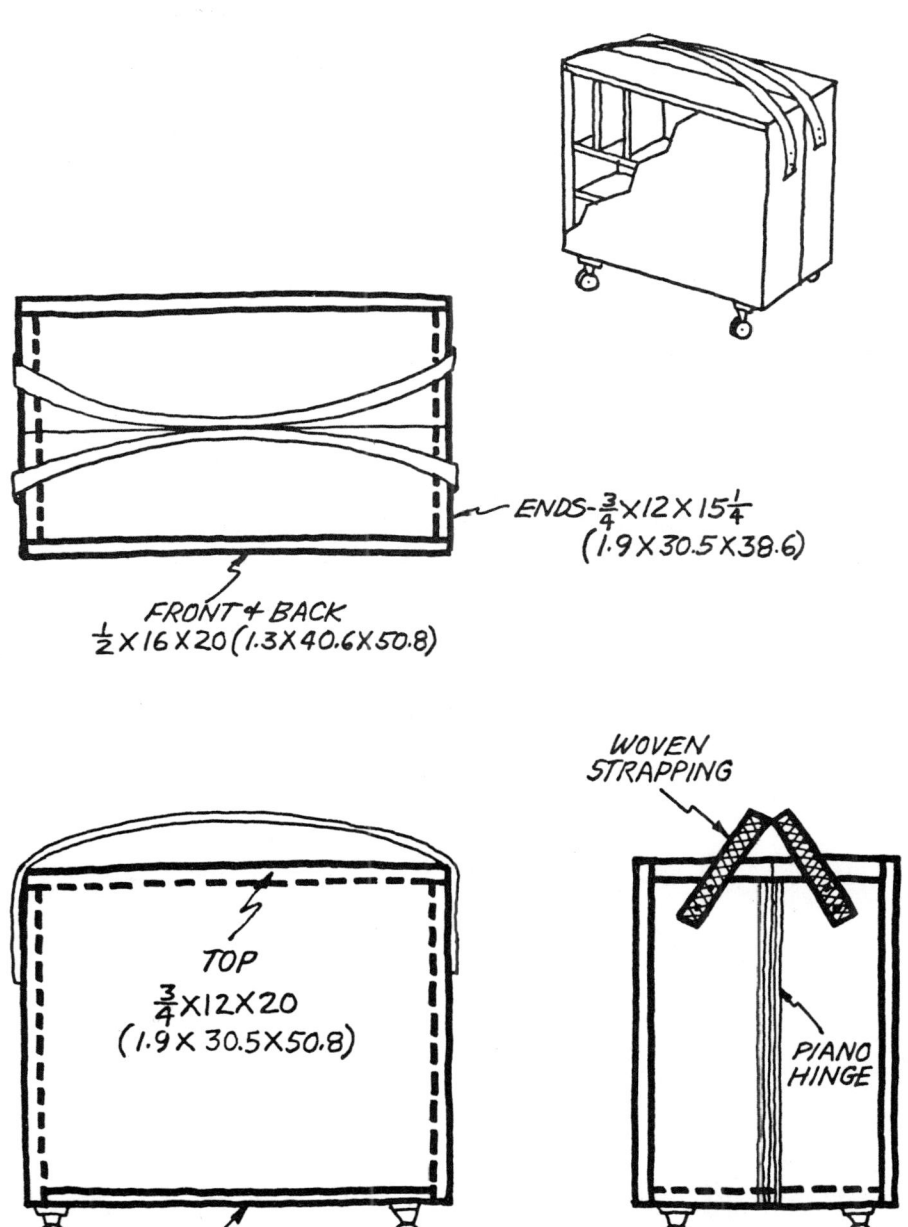

Figure 3-5. Do-All Kit Box.

- Piano hinge—16" (40.6) long
- Trunk latches (4)
- Woven strapping for handles—2 pcs, each 30" long
- Screws with washers

Here's How to Make It:

First, cut all pieces to size. Make sure they butt properly and can be assembled into a neat box.

Using the front, back, end, top and side pieces, make a box. Use nails and glue, but be careful not to use nails that will interfere with the saw when the box is cut in half. Before you clamp the nailed and glued pieces, check the assembly to make sure it squares up.

When the glue has dried, cut the box in half on a table saw. If possible, use a blade with cross-cut or plywood teeth to insure a smooth finish. After the box has been halved, smooth the edges to make sure you have a close fit.

Next, you will join the two halves with the piano hinge. The hinge mounts on the outside. Before you mount the hinge, use either clamps or rope to insure that the two sides are tight and perfectly matched.

After you have mounted the hinge, open the box and begin to arrange the tools or supplies that will be stored. Don't rush into installing the dividers; plan the placement carefully. The fewer the dividers you have, the lighter the box. The box will be heavy enough if you store power tools, so why add more weight? It's wise to make a trial cardboard arrangement before you start cutting wood and fastening the dividers.

You can use small plastic drawer organizers that are available in most hardware stores. Some are 6 to 6½" deep, and will fit when stacked in one side of the kit.

Hobby Projects That Save Time and Money 75

Lightly mark off the tentative location of the dividers, after you are sure that your cardboard templates are in the right position. Cut the dividers to the proper length from the plywood and fasten them in place. For storage of lightweight tools, brads and glue will do, but if you have heavy tools, it's best to reinforce the dividers with small angle irons or brackets.

Gliders, rollers or casters fastened to the bottom will add to the usefulness of the box. We have suggested webbed strapping as a material for the carrying handles, but some very nice handles that are sold in home centers will also do the job.

You might want to reinforce all inside angles with angle braces or mending plates if you plan to store and carry heavy tools.

NOTES: The front view of the sketch is shown without the front piece in order to illustrate the method used to fasten the ends, top and bottom.

Dividers may be installed by using ¼" metal divider strips used in department store displays, or from pieces of ¼" "U" channel aluminum. You can even combine these two systems.

The main use for the box is to hold such tools as a router with accessories, a drill with accessories, a model maker's vise, hand tools and a plastic or metal drawer organizer. But, you are only limited by your own needs and imagination.

SEWING BASKET

Nothing can be messier than a disorganized sewing basket. This was as true in colonial times as it is today. In fact, this basket is based on designs used during that period to try to solve the same problem. There is a drawer for such things as scissors and other sewing tools. A set of spool racks will help keep thread organized, and a pincushion keeps pointy things where they belong.

Here's What You'll Need:

- For the drawer:
  Front—1 pc ¼ × 3 × 10 (.6 × 7.6 × 25.4)
  Front back-up—1 pc ¼ × 2⅛ × 8⅞ (.6 × 5.4 × 22.5)
  Back—1 pc ¼ × 2⅜ × 8⅞ (.6 × 6.1 × 22.5)
  Sides—2 pcs ¼ × 2⅜ × 9⅛ (.6 × 6.1 × 23.2)
  Bottom—1 pc ¼ × 8⅞ × 8⅞ (.6 × 22.5 × 22.5)
- Spool rack—1 pc ½ × ¾ × 8 feet (.6 × 1.9 × 243.8)
- Spool holders—12 pcs ¼ dowel × 5 (.6 × 12.7)
- Drawer pull
- Glue, small brads or headless nails
- Pincushion—muslin, sawdust, patterned cloth, cardboard

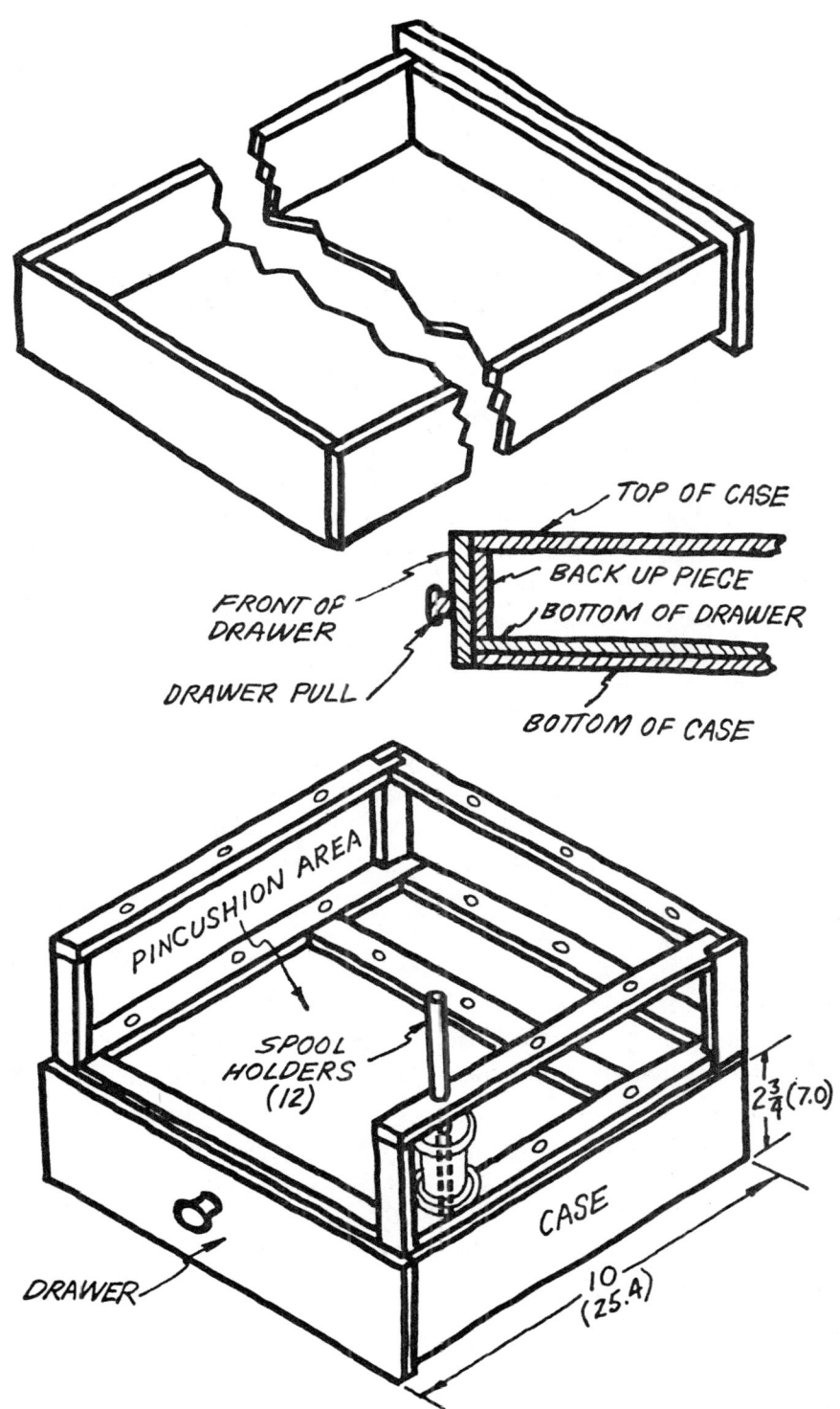

Figure 3-6. Sewing Basket.

Here's How to Make It:

Begin this project by making the case first. Follow the sketch carefully and you will hide many of the raw edges. Cut all wood to the proper size. Glue and nail the sides and back to the bottom section. Before the glue hardens, make sure that all the pieces are square with each other. Glue and nail the top to complete the open case.

Next, make the drawer. Cut all pieces to size, but test each piece for fit in the case before you begin any assembly. The design allows for $1/16"$ clearance on all sides. Fasten the back piece to the bottom, from the back, as shown in Figure 3-6. Fasten the sides in the same way, coming flush with the back to allow for nailing and gluing. Fasten the drawer-front back-up piece to the back of the drawer facing. See Figure 3-6 for positioning details. Clamp and glue these pieces; allow plenty of time for the glue to dry. Position the drawer-front and back-up piece; glue and nail in place.

The spool racks are next. Assign a number or letter to each piece before you cut it to size. Pairs should be identified with the same number or letter, for example a-a, 2-2. Cut each piece to size and shape.

Temporarily, fasten the upper and lower pairs together for drilling. Mark the strips for drilling, 3 holes in each section, evenly spaced. Drill ¼" holes and then enlarge them slightly with a round file. If you use a hand drill, make sure that the upper holes are perfectly aligned with the lower. File and smooth the edges of the holes. Now you can assemble the rack on the top of the case. Use glue and small brads.

Cut the dowels to length and round off all ends. Cut three dowels, each 3" long for the center spool rack. There is no upper rack for this section, and these are the only dowels that will be glued. Glue them in place and make sure they are

Hobby Projects That Save Time and Money

perfectly vertical. You might want to make a simple jig of corrugated cardboard to hold the dowels while the glue dries. All the other dowels should be left loose.

Sand and finish all edges and surfaces, and apply a finish that will complement the room in which the basket is to be used. Because this basket is based on a colonial design, a maple stain followed by several coats of shellac and or varnish is appropriate.

Next, you can mount the drawer pull. A small white porcelain knob will complete the colonial look.

To complete the project, make the pincushion. Start by cutting a piece of stiff cardboard to fit loosely in the larger section in the spool rack. Make a bag of muslin that is about 1½" wider and longer than the cardboard. Sew the muslin with a ½" seam all around, except for a ¾" opening. Turn the bag inside out. Now, fill the bag with sawdust; sew up the hole.

Cut a piece of the patterned cloth to the same shape as the cardboard, but leave 2" of extra cloth on all sides. Place the sawdust-loaded muslin bag on the cardboard. Cover the bag with the patterned cloth, pulling it over on all sides and under the cardboard. Use a needle and heavy thread to pull the cloth and secure it over the cardboard. Do this by taking several stitches on each of the opposite sides until the cloth is tight over the cardboard and the sawdust bag. A little white glue at each of the corners will help hold the cardboard and cloth securely together.

Position the pincushion on the basket and the job is done.

PHOTOGRAPHERS' AND ARTISTS' LIGHT BOX

It's a lot easier to judge a photographic negative when you have a well-diffused light behind it. And there are many times when an artist would like to trace a design on a piece of opaque paper. The solution to both of these problems is our easy-to-make light box. It can even be used to bottom-light glassware for photography.

Here's What You'll Need:

- Long sides—2 pcs ½ × 6 × 20 (1.3 × 15.2 × 50.8)
- Short sides—2 pcs ½ × 6 × 15 (1.3 × 15.2 × 38.1)
- Base—1 pc ¾ × 15 × 19 plywood (1.9 × 38.1 × 48.2)
  or 2 pcs ¾ × 8 (20.3) × 19 stock shelving
- Edging—2 pcs ¾ × ¾ × 20 corner guard molding (1.9 × 1.9 × 50.8)
- Edging—2 pcs ¾ × ¾ × 16 corner guard molding (1.9 × 1.9 × 40.6)
- Top—1 pc ⅛ × 16 × 20 (.3 × 40.6 × 50.8) white transluscent plastic, such as Rohm & Haas Plexiglas #W-2447
- Switch—One single pole, single throw, toggle switch
- Lamp and lamp fixtures—3 cool white type fluorescent tubes (15 watts, 18" long) with fixtures to match

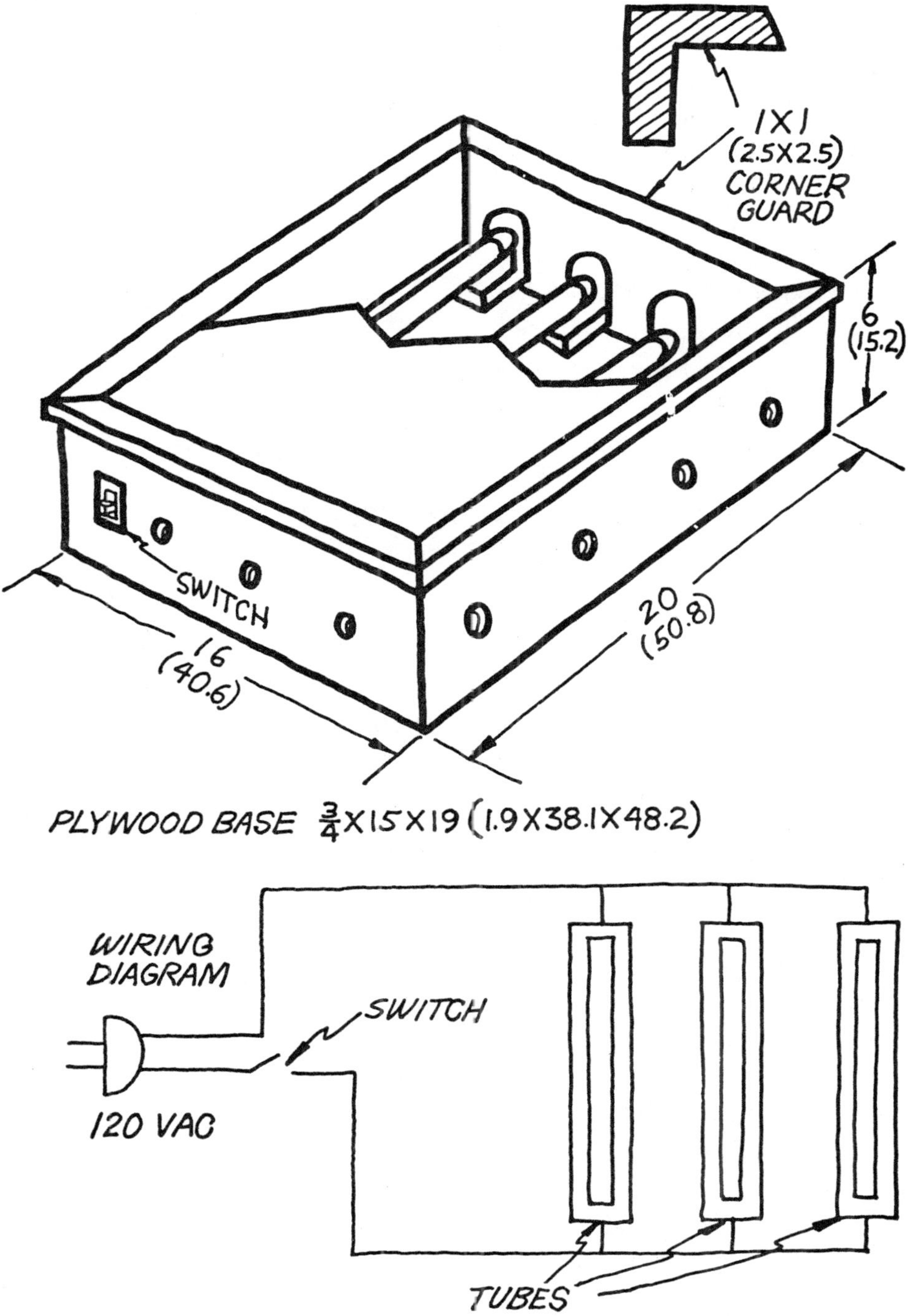

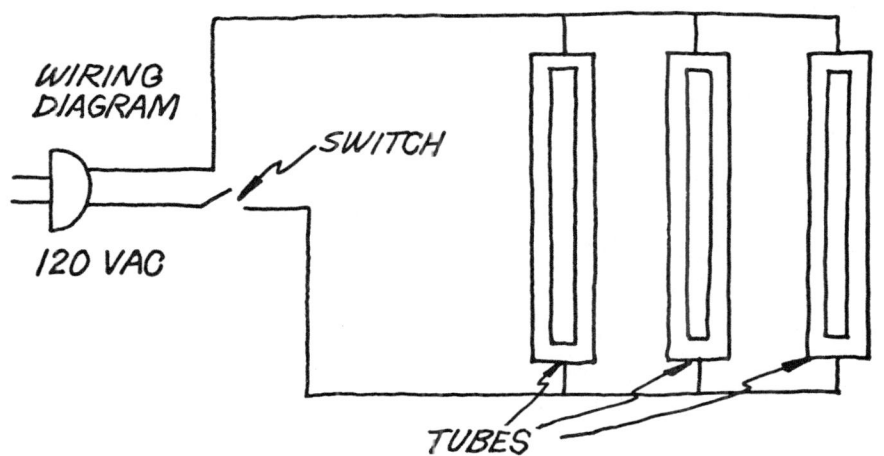

Figure 3-7. Photographers' and Artists' Light Box.

- Wire—approximately 15′ (70 cm) of standard zip cord
- Glue and nails

Here's How to Make It:

Cut the base and all side pieces to the correct size.

The wiring diagram we have shown (Figure 3-7) is simplified. Although most fluorescent tubes used today are instant-start, the diagram for wiring will vary if you use rapid-start or other pre-heat tubes. When you buy the tubes, be sure that they match the accessories and fixtures. The electrical supply dealer can help you to understand the appropriate wiring.

Next, assemble the fluorescent fixtures to the base. Be sure they are evenly spaced to insure well-distributed light. You can wire the fixtures at this point, but leave enough wire to make the connection to the switch and to the line cord. These lamps should be wired-in parallel—*not series*—and it makes a safer job if you can solder and tape all connections. If you don't have soldering tools, use electrician's speed nuts to make tight, safe connections.

Drill evenly spaced holes in the side pieces for ventilation. Drill or cut a hole in one side for the switch you purchased. A round shank toggle switch merely requires a hole drilled to the proper size. But, if you are using another type of switch, you can use a keyhole saw to make the appropriate mounting hole.

Now you can assemble the sides to the base, but be sure that the fluorescent tubes are *not* mounted in their sockets. And be sure that you keep them stored well away from your work area; they can be dangerous if broken. Use brads and glue to fasten the sides.

Hobby Projects That Save Time and Money

If you are going to paint, stain or varnish the box, now is the time to do it.

Next, finish the wiring. Solder the connections or use speed nuts. You can let the power cord run from the box by way of one of the ventilation holes, but it's better to drill a special hole just for the wire. The wire should be snug, but not tight. Be sure to tie a stress relief knot in the wire inside the box. This will prevent electrical problems if the cord gets yanked accidentally.

Now you can test the fit of the plastic. If it is larger than the sides, trim it carefully with a file until it is about ⅛" smaller all around to allow for expansion.

Miter the corners of the molding at 45°, and check the fit of all the pieces on the assembled box. When they all fit properly, position the plastic sheet and fasten the molding in place.

The chances are that limited use of the light will preclude the need for a tube replacement for a long time. But, to save yourself the trouble of having to remove one of the pieces of corner molding to get at the tubes, you can use two small wood screws on one of the pieces of molding. Simply remove the screws, slip off the edging and you will be able to slide the plastic free to get at the tubes.

BICYCLE RACK

Bikes are usually left just where the ride ended—in the driveway, on a lawn or even in the garage where a car can back over it. There is seldom one place to put a bike—unless you make this rack. It'll hold all the family bikes, plus those of visitors.

Lean it against a house or garage, or even prop it against a tree, and your bike problems will be solved. A 45° angle is just enough, but you can set it up any way you want, as long as it keeps your bikes where they belong.

Here's What You'll Need:

- Separators—5 pcs 1" dowels × 30" (2.5 × 76.2)
- Rails—4 pcs 2 " × 4 × 24 (5.1 × 10.2 × 61)
- Side rails—2 pcs 1 × 4 × 33 (2.5 × 10.2 × 83.8)
- Carriage bolts ¼ × 4 with nuts and washers, galvanized iron, copper or stainless
- 1 can of penta-chlorophenol wood preservative

Here's How to Make It:

Cut the dowels and side rails to size. Cut the 2 × 4's to size. Measure dowel holes in two of the 2 × 4's four inches apart. Drill 1" holes at each of the points you just marked. The holes should be centered on the width of the 2 × 4's.

Fasten one of the drilled and one of the undrilled 2 × 4's face to face. Use carriage bolts as well as a good water-

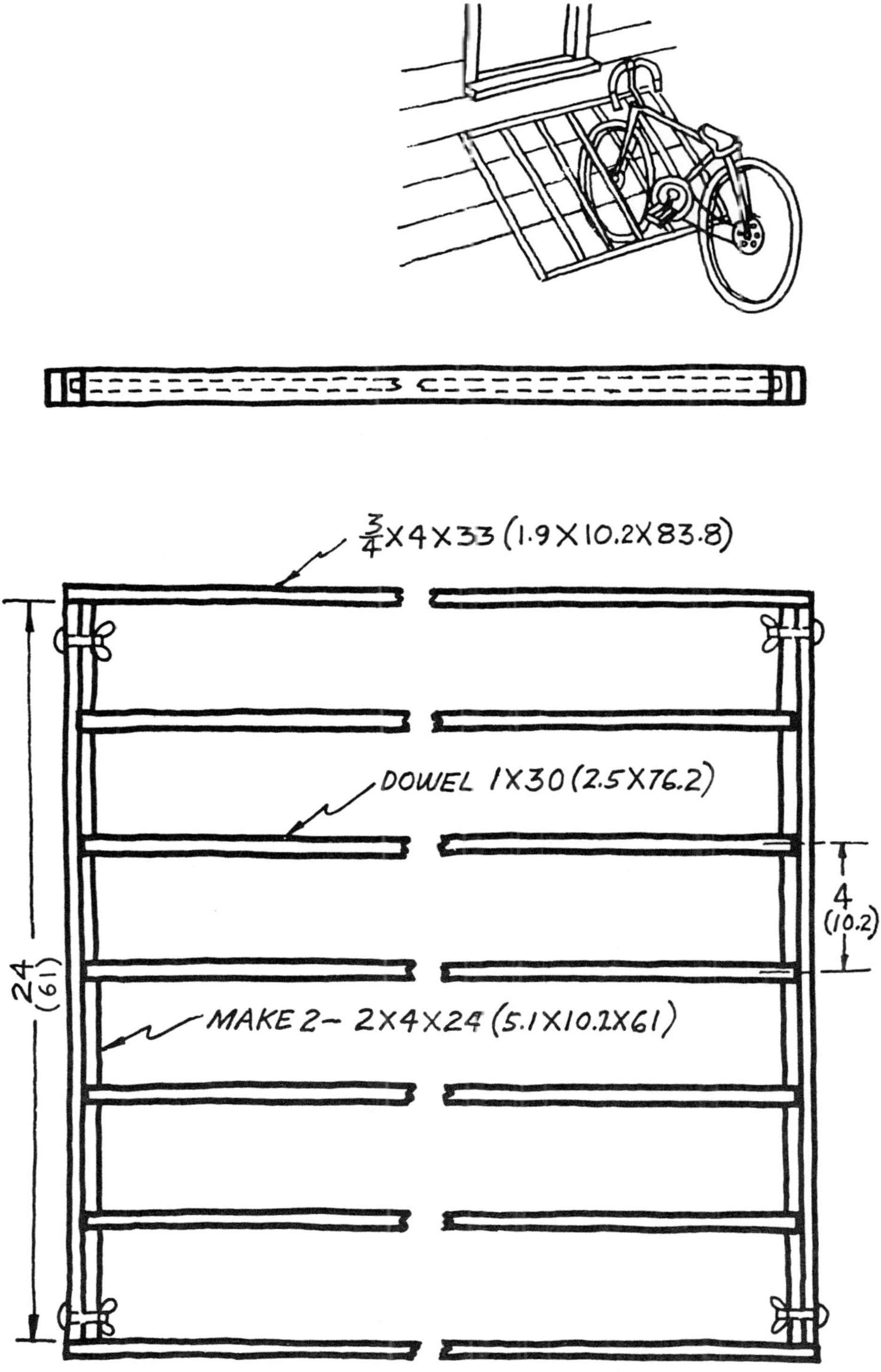

¾ X 4 X 33 (1.9 X 10.2 X 83.8)

DOWEL 1X30 (2.5 X 76.2)

MAKE 2 – 2X4X24 (5.1 X 10.2 X 61)

24 (61)

4 (10.2)

Figure 3-8. Bicycle Rack.

proof glue. Assemble the second set in the same way. Apply glue to the ends of the dowels and position them in one of the assembled sets of 2 × 4's. Fasten the other ends of the dowels to the other 2 × 4 assembly in the same manner. Be sure the entire assembly is squared up while the glue dries.

When the assembly has fully dried, turn it on its side and fasten the two side rails. Use brass wood screws as well as waterproof glue.

When all the glued joints have set, coat the entire assembly with a wood preservative, such as Woodlife. You can paint the rack after the preservative was dried.

You can now mount the rack wherever it is convenient. It was made for leaning, but if you have nothing to lean it on, make a simple stand that sticks out about 2' on either side.

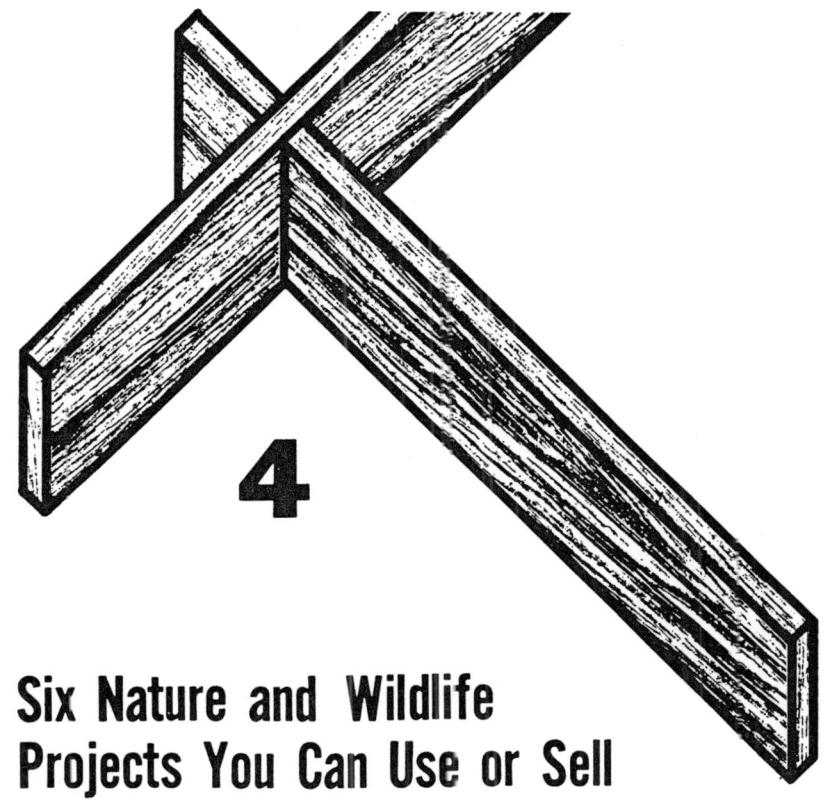

4

Six Nature and Wildlife Projects You Can Use or Sell

CAGE FOR SMALL ANIMALS

Whether the animal is just visiting, as might be a baby bunny, or is a permanent guest in the form of a guinea pig, this cage will serve you well. There are a few features that make this animal home more comfortable for its occupants, as well as for the owner. A screen mesh on the floor makes it easy to keep clean, and there is plenty of visibility for you and your small friend.

Here's What You'll Need:

- Sides—2 pcs ¼ × 23¾ × 22 high (exterior plywood) (.6 × 60.3 × 55.9)
- Roof—1 pc ½ × 36 × 36 (exterior plywood) (1.3 × 91.4 × 91.4)
- Back—1 pc ¼ × 18 × 36 (exterior plywood) (.6 × 45.7 × 91.4)
- Front stretcher—1 pc 1 × 2 × 36 (2.5 × 5.1 × 91.4)
- Rear stretcher—1 pc 1 × 2 × 32 (2.5 × 5.1 × 81.3)
- Corner—2 pcs 1 × 2 × 16 (2.5 × 5.1 × 40.6)
- Floor—2 pcs 1 × 2 × 36 (2.5 × 5.1 × 91.4)
- Floor—4 pcs 1 × 2 × 22½ (2.5 × 5.1 × 57.2)

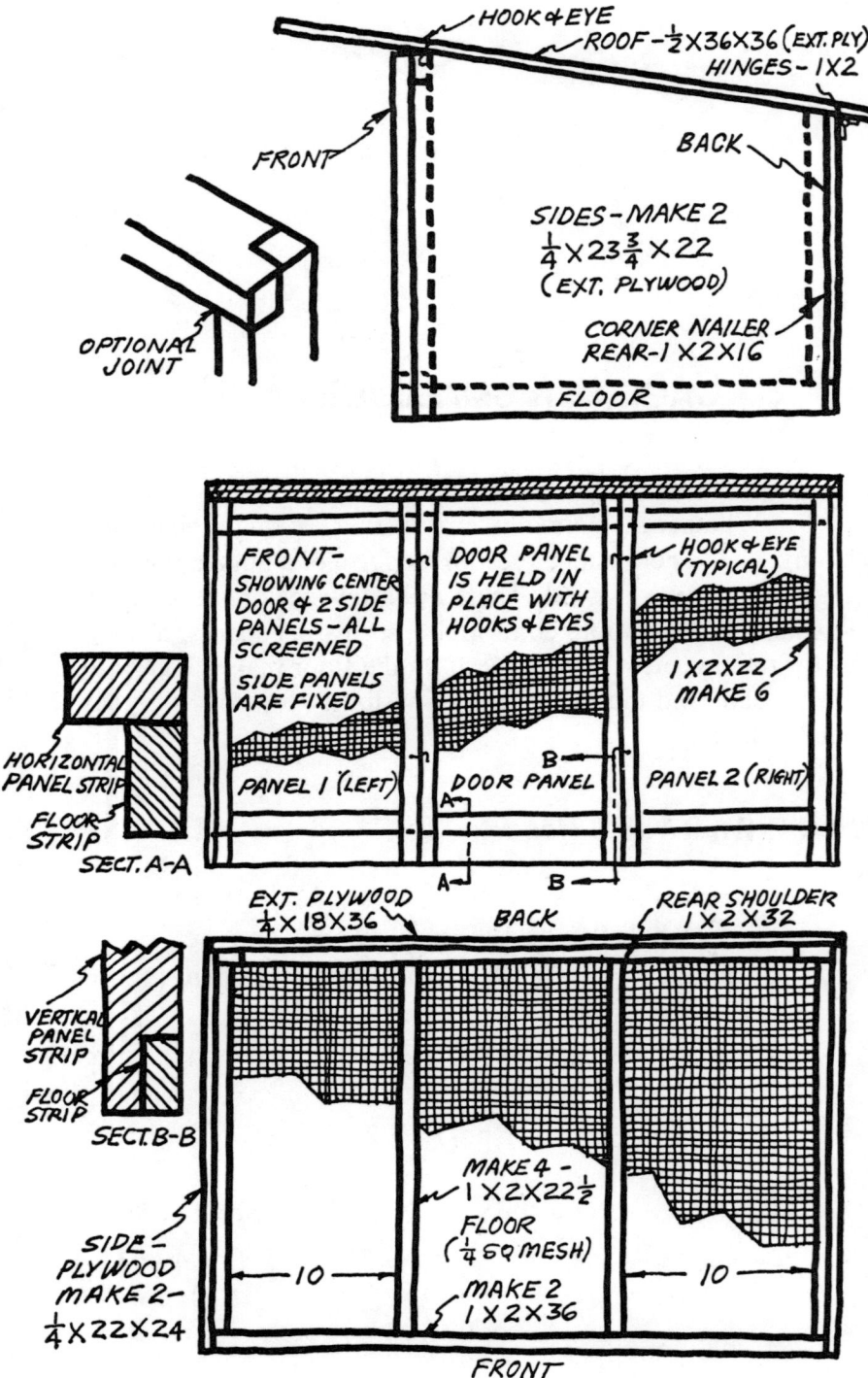

Figure 4-1. Cage for Small Animals.

- Front—6 pcs 1 × 2 × 22 (2.5 × 5.1 × 55.9)
- Front—6 pcs 1 × 2 × 5 (2.5 × 5.1 × 12.7)
- Screening—1 pc 24 × 26 (¼ sq. mesh galvanized) (61 × 66)
- Screening—3 pcs 22 × 36 (¼ sq. mesh galvanized) (55.9 × 91.4)
- Hook and eyes—4 sets
- Waterproof resorcinol glue, galvanized nails, one pair of 1 × 2 hinges with screws

Here's How to Make It:

There are a lot of parts to be bought and made for this project. We suggest that you have all parts on hand before you begin any of the construction.

Cut all pieces to size. To avoid confusion as the building progresses, it might be a good idea to label each piece as you make it. This will avoid having to measure pieces to identify them. Let's begin the assembly with the floor.

Floor

Assemble, nail and glue the strips as shown in Figure 4-1. Use resorcinol waterproof glue and clamp the sections until they have firmly bonded. A good waterproof glue is important. The weather and the water you use to clean the cage can weaken the structure if a poor glue is used.

Position the mesh screen across the floor and nail it in place. Be sure to use aluminum or galvanized nails or staples for the job. You can make the bottom even firmer by adding glue to the perimeter of the screen where it meets the frame.

Sides and rear

Glue and nail the plywood sides and back together. Note the way the pieces tie into one another to provide better nailing surfaces and appearance.

Use glue and nails to fasten the vertical corner nailers. Clamp the glued joints until they have bonded firmly.

Next, fasten the front and rear stretchers in place. The rear stretcher may be glued and nailed to the back. The front stretcher, however, fastens to the plywood side pieces only at the ends.

Front

The front is made in three sections to provide visibility and easy access without the need to lift the roof. Assemble the sections as shown in Figure 4-1. Before you begin building, study Figure 4-1, sections A-A and B-B; they will show you how the panels sit on the floor strip and rest against the top front stretcher.

When you have nailed and glued the panels, tack the mesh on the inside. Adding glue around the perimeter between the screen and the frame will further strengthen the panels. Be sure to flatten all loose ends of the wire mesh to protect your animals. If you apply the glue at the very edge of the mesh and lay on a heavy bead, you will be sure that the animals will not be hurt by loose ends of wire in the mesh. Allow enough clearance on the top, bottom and sides for the panels to slide in place.

Fasten the left and right panels permanently in place with glue and nails. Use hooks and eyes to fasten the center panel so that it can be removed for access to the cage.

Six Nature and Wildlife Projects

Roof

See the drawing for the position of the hinges and the hooks and eyes. Mount this hardware and then position the roof. Nothing more has to be done to the roof, but you can dress it up with spare shingles, contact adhesive or just a coat of paint.

Finishing

If you used exterior plywood, you don't have to finish the cage, but we do recommend at least a coat of polyurethane varnish to keep it looking natural. You can use deck paint, but we don't recommend it. Little animals like to chew on things, and paint is not high on the list of nutritious foods for animals!

CONTEMPORARY DOGHOUSE

This doghouse has style—it's not the usual saltbox that most people knock together when they decide that old bowser has to live outside. We don't know whether your dog will fully appreciate the esthetic thought that has gone into this, but your neighbors surely will.

And, we have given a lot of thought to comfort—that of your dog and yourself. As you probably know, dogs are avid collectors of anything they can get their paws on. When enough old bones have been dragged into a doghouse, it usually becomes unpleasant to be near it, especially on warm summer days. Therefore, we have designed this house so you can empty it from the top, you won't have to grope around through the door for your friend's collection; the roof lifts off.

As you probably realize, dogs come in different sizes. To make sure your dog can get in and out easily, check this table before you go any further.

Dog Shoulder Height

- *More than 25" (65 cm)*
  German Shepherd, Wolfhound, Great Dane, St. Bernard, Newfoundland
- *20 to 25" (50 to 55 cm)*
  Airdale, Boxer, Collie, Dalmation, Doberman, Retriever, Sheep Dog
- *15 to 20" (38 to 50 cm)*
  Cocker Spaniel, Fox Terrier
- *10 to 15" (25 to 38 cm)*
  Beagle, Poodle, Scottish Terrier

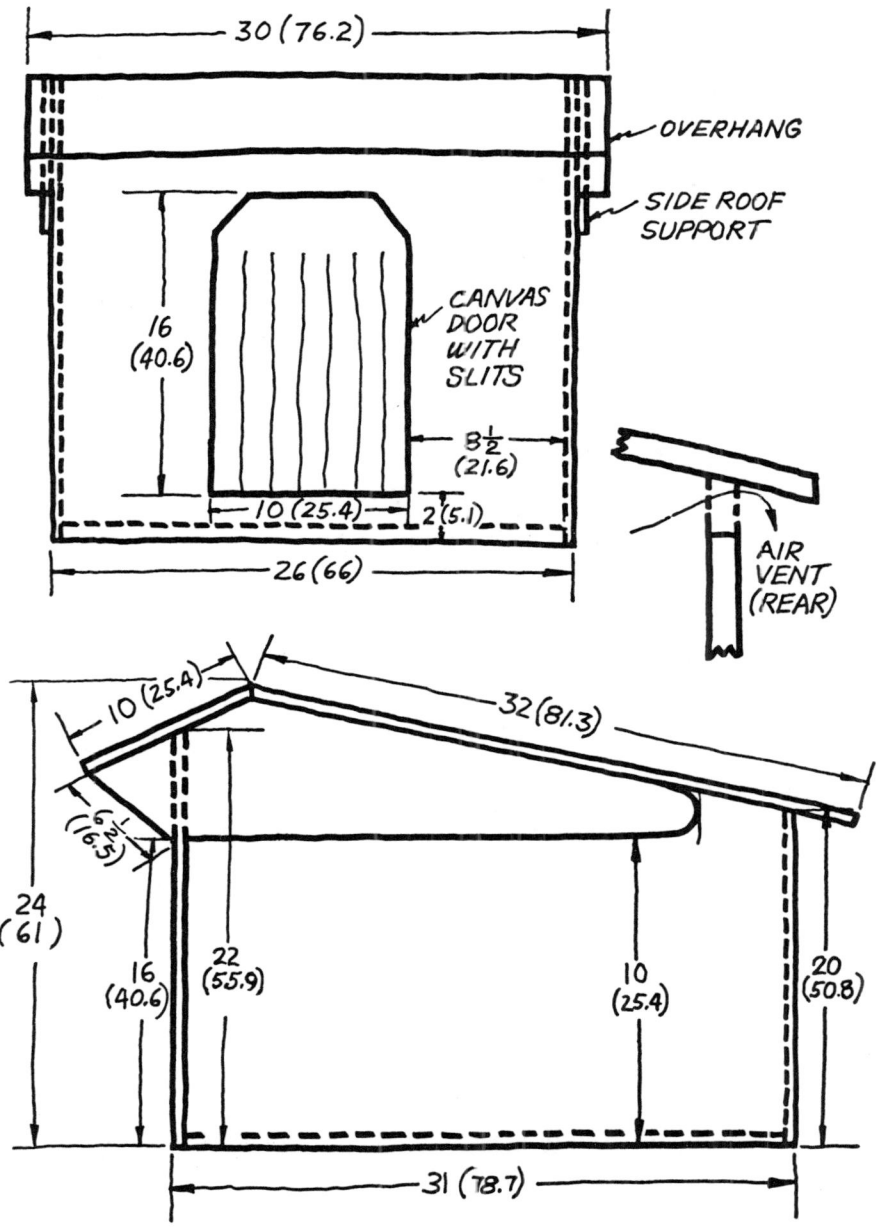

Figure 4-2. Contemporary Doghouse.

Make adjustments in the doghouse (and door) measurements if your dog is too large for the one shown here.

Here's What You'll Need:

- Sides—2 pcs ½ × 24 × 32 exterior plywood (1.3 × 61 × 81.3)
- Front—1 pc ½ × 22 × 27 exterior plywood (1.3 × 55.9 × 68.6)
- Rear—1 pc ½ × 20 × 27 exterior plywood (1.3 × 50.8 × 68.6)
- Roof front—1 pc ½ × 10 × 30 (1.3 × 25.4 × 76.2)
- Roof rear—1 pc ½ × 30 × 32 (1.3 × 76.2 × 81.3)
- Side roof supports—2 pcs ½ × 8 × 36 (1.3 × 20.3 × 91.4)
- Floor—1 pc ¾ × 26 × 31 exterior plywood (1.8 × 66 × 78.7)
- Canvas for door, roofing paper or plastic adhesive covering, nails, waterproof glue, 8 concrete half-blocks, stain and varnish or paint

Here's How to Make It:

Cut the base to size. Be sure to cut it to full size because the sides will rest on it. Cut all the other parts to size and shape.

Measure your dog and cut the appropriate dog opening.

Use nails and waterproof glue to fasten the sides, rear and front to the upper surface of the base.

When the glue has dried, lay out the roof and side supports. The support not only ties the roof together, it also

Six Nature and Wildlife Projects

adds a dashing touch to this contemporary doghouse. When the roof has been assembled, it is just set in place—not nailed or fastened in any way. That way you can lift the roof to clean bowser's palace any time you want.

Here are some hints to help you assemble the roof.

1. Tack the roof supports in place on the sides of the house, but slip a piece of shirt cardboard between the supports and the sides to assure clearance.
2. Place the front roof section in position and mark the location.
3. Do the same for the rear section, after planing the front edge to butt evenly against the rear of the front section.
4. Remove the temporary assembly and turn the roof unit upside down. Glue and nail all of the parts, and then test the roof on the house for a fit.
5. When you know the roof fits, you can add the roof covering. If you have any old shingles, you can add color and protection by nailing them in place. Caution: If you do this, make absolutely sure that the roofing nails do not protrude through the roof into the dog's living space. If this is unavoidable, turn the roof over, and bend and flatten all of the nail points against the inside of the roof.

Even though air will enter through the curtained door, you should cut a few notches at the top of the rear wall. This will allow for some air flow, insuring that your pet will always have fresh air. No rain or snow will enter the house through these vents because of the roof overhang.

You can make the protective door by cutting a piece of polyethylene or canvas to a size several inches larger than the door. Make vertical slits about an inch apart starting from the bottom and running to within 2 or 3" of the top. Tack the door inside the doghouse.

You can finish the doghouse any way you want. If you paint, be sure to apply a good primer before you use two coats of exterior water or oil paint. You can stain and varnish it, if you like.

Rather than rest the doghouse right on the ground, we suggest that you make a foundation by laying the half-blocks together.

BIRDHOUSE

What book on woodworking projects would be complete without the obligatory birdhouse? We almost did not include a birdhouse, but when we saw the pleasure it gave some neighborhood kids, we decided it must have its place. Watching a pair of birds build a nest and raise a family is an experience no one should be denied. And, without a means to attract birds to a closer viewing point, the drama is usually missed.

Rather than give you any ordinary birdhouse, we designed one that can be cleaned easily after the summer tenants have flown south for the winter. Despite all their beauty, birds can leave a birdhouse a mess. With our trap door cleaning is made simple, and you can have the house ready for the return of your friends in the spring.

Here's What You'll Need:

- Front and rear—2 pcs ½ × 7 × 8½ (1.3 × 17.8 × 21.6)
- Sides—2 pcs ½ × 5 × 9 (1.3 × 12.7 × 22.9)
- Base—1 pc ½ × 7 × 10 (1.3 × 17.8 × 25.4)
- Roof (a)—1 pc ½ × 7 × 12 (1.3 × 17.8 × 30.5) (b)—1 pc ½ × 6½ × 12 (1.3 × 16.5 × 30.5)
- Perch—1 pc ¼ dia × 3 dowel (.6 × 7.6)
- Waterproof glue, nails, 1 pair of ½" or 1" hinges, brass screws, 2 hook and eye sets, and paint

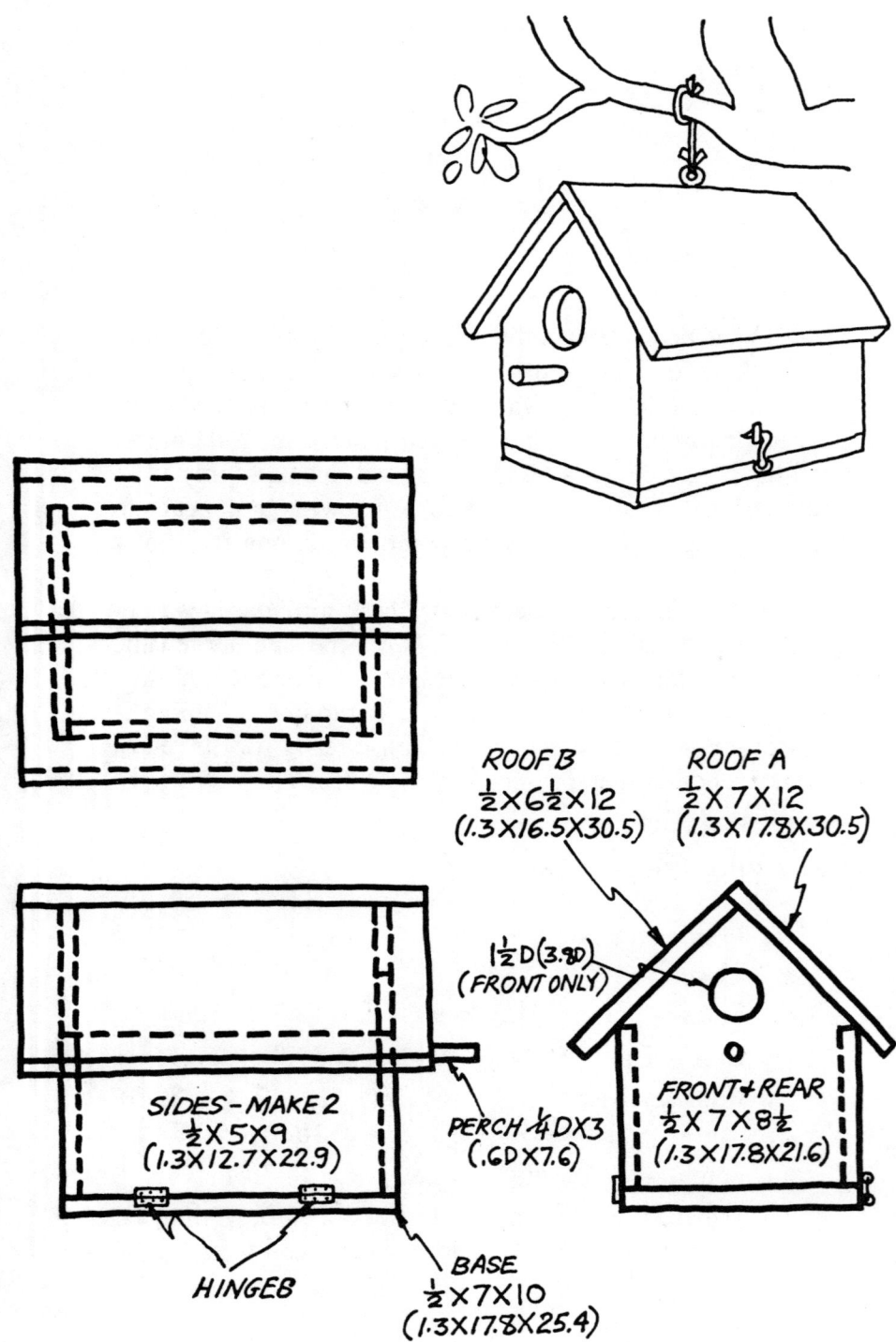

Figure 4-3. Birdhouse.

Six Nature and Wildlife Projects

Here's How to Make It:

Cut all pieces to size. The sizes are shown *finished* to allow you to prepare the roof for a good fit, at 90°. (See Figure 4-3.)

Glue and nail the roof together, and allow it to set while you are working on the rest of the project.

Lay out the location for the entrance and the perch hole. If you have an expansive bit, use it to make the round door. But, if you don't have such a bit, you can do the job with a smaller drill and a coping saw. Drill a pilot hole in the waste, and then insert a coping saw blade through the hole. Attach the blade to a saw frame and cut the hole.

Next, drill the hole for the perch. See the sketch for the position of the hole.

Drill several ¼" holes through the upper part of the back section to provide some ventilation.

Drill two or three ¼" holes in the base to allow for drainage.

Now, assemble all of the pieces as shown in Figure 4-3. Use waterproof glue and nails to assemble the birdhouse. The bottom is hinged, and held in place on the opposite side by a hook and eye. Glue the perch in the hole that was drilled for it.

You can paint the birdhouse any color you want, but the birds are more likely to select a house that doesn't stand out too much. After all, they are concerned with protection, and a flashy red birdhouse that may look well in your yard may have little appeal to the prospective parents of tiny birds.

RABBIT CASTLE

If some of the monstrosities turned out by home builders can be called colonial simply because they lack any clearly identifiable characteristics, we can call this rabbit hutch a castle. And that's just what we've done. Of course, it's up to the rabbits who will live in the castle to make their own decision, but if you match two properly, they will be happy wherever they live.

On a more practical note, the mesh on the bottom will allow your long-eared friends to live comfortably without the accumulation that often makes the inside of a rabbit castle so unattractive. Simply place the castle on a stand, or across two saw horses, and you will have a rabbit residence that is almost self-cleaning.

Here's What You'll Need:

- Top—1 pc ½ × 32 × 36 exterior plywood (1.3 × 81.3 × 91.4)
- Sides—2 pcs ½ × 24 × 24½ exterior plywood (1.3 × 61 × 62.2)
- Rear—1 pc ½ × 24½ × 25 exterior plywood (1.3 × 62.2 × 63.5)
- Shelves—2 pcs ½ × 12 × 24 exterior plywood (1.3 × 30.5 × 61)
- Shelf supports—2 pcs ¾ × 1½ × 7½ pine (1.9 × 3.8 × 19.1)
- Cross brace—1 pc 1 × 2 × 24 pine (2.5 × 5.1 × 61)

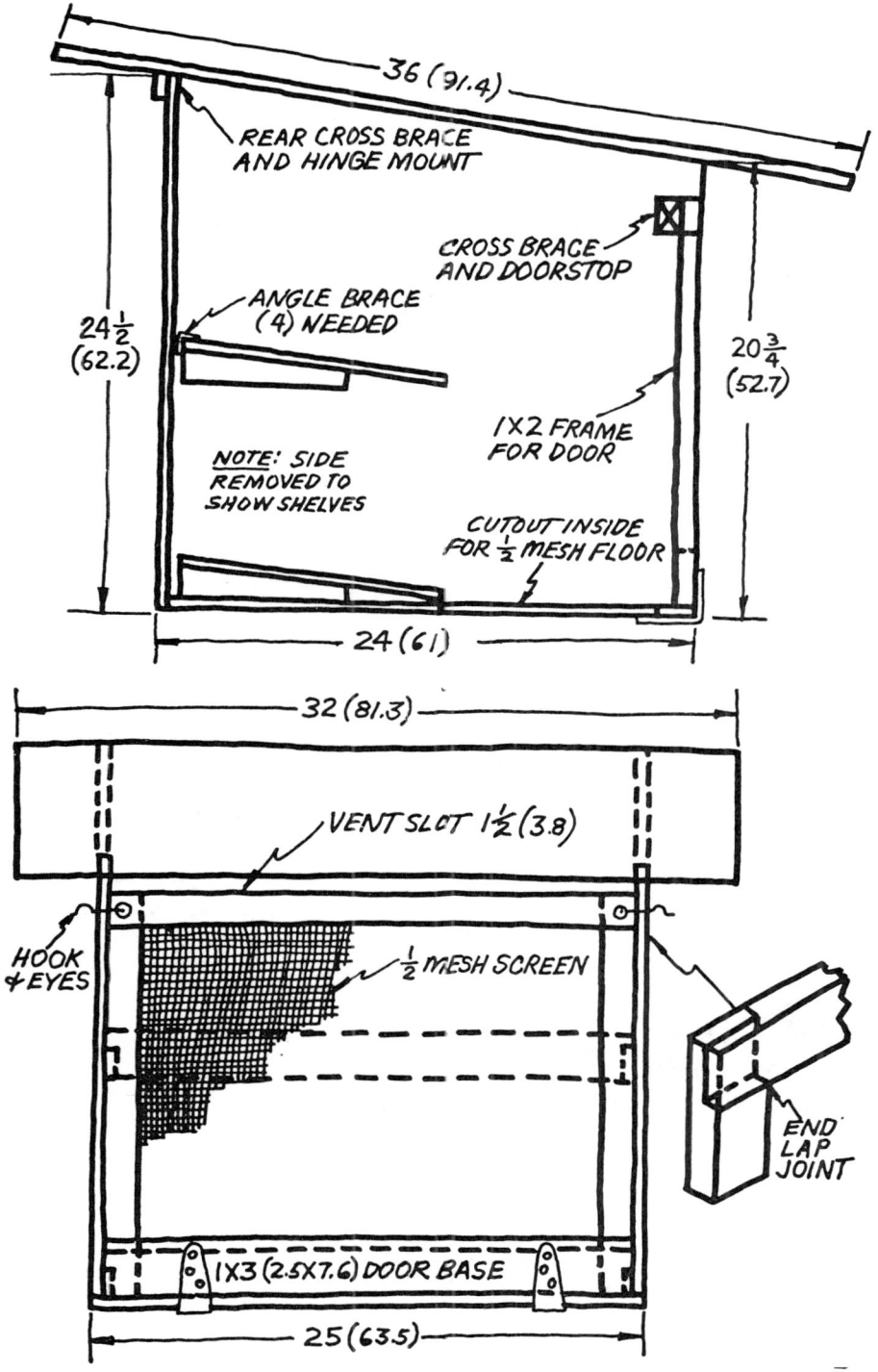

Figure 4-4. Rabbit Castle.

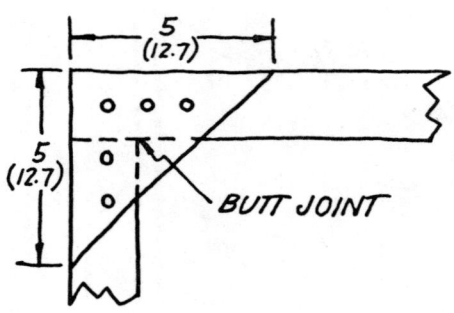

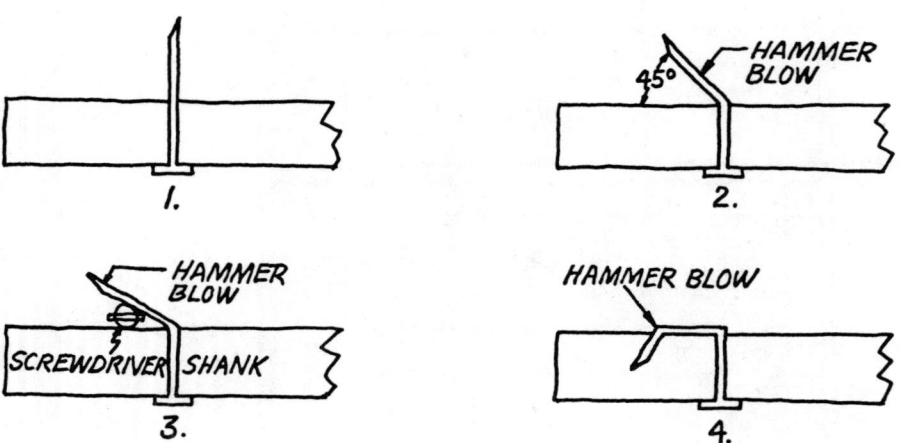

Figure 4-4 (A)

- Door base—1 pc 1 × 3 × 24 (2.5 × 7.6 × 61)
- Door sides—2 pcs 1 × 2 × 18½ (2.5 × 5.1 × 47)
- Door top—1 pc 1 × 2 × 24 (2.5 × 5.1 × 61)
- 2 hooks and eyes
- ½" square galvanized steel mesh 18 × 24 (45.7 × 61)
- ½" square galvanized steel mesh 12 × 24 (30.5 × 61)
- Angle braces 4 pcs galvanized steel 1 × 1 (2.5 × 2.5)
- Angle braces 8 pcs galvanized steel 2 × 2 (5.1 × 5.1)
- Finishing nails, staples or galvanized roofing nails

Here's How to Make It:

Begin by cutting all the plywood pieces to size. Lay out the shelf supports and fasten each in place. The upper shelf should be about 12" (30.5) above the bottom shelf support. See Figure 4-4 for the proper positioning of the bottom support. When you fasten the supports, be sure they are on opposite sides so they will be in the proper position when the castle is assembled.

Fasten the top rear hinge mounting strip in place.

Next, you can assemble the box. Because the shelves mount across the back completely, we couldn't use the corner strip system we introduced in the animal cage. For this project, fasten with screws and reinforce the corners with angle braces, as needed. Use ½" (1.3) flat head brass screws. To be absolutely certain about the corners, drill through the wood at the holes in the braces. Make each hole large enough to slip a 6-32 flat head machine screw through. Fasten the screws with washers and nuts from the inside. Screws ¾" (1.9) long should do the trick.

Fasten the cross brace across the front. Be sure it is placed below the top to provide a vent of 1½" (3.8).

Fasten the 1" (2.5) steel angle brace at each of the corners, along with edge of the shelves. The brace serves as a hook with which the shelf may be removed, cleaned and replaced.

Hinge the roof at two places.

Make up the door, as indicated in Figure 4-4. Cut the end lap joint as shown in the detailed section in Figure 4-4 and fasten with waterproof glue and nails, which can be clinched over. If you have no way to cut the joints (with a back saw or a table saw), you can make a butt joint. Make up 8 pieces of ¼" plywood in 5 × 5 triangles, and nail them across the joints, inside and out. This type of joint is used frequently to reinforce theatrical flats used for scenery. It's surprisingly strong, despite its deceiving simplicity.

If you make this joint, it's best to use nails that are twice the thickness of the wood and clinch them over. Clinching is not just flattening a protruding nail, it's a technique that adds considerable strength to a joint. A clinched nail, in effect, acts like a combined nail and staple. To clinch a nail, tap it on the side with the hammer until it bends from the surface of the wood at the 45° angle. Then, place a screwdriver shank under the nail and bend the point of the nail to a right angle. Remove the screwdriver shank and drive the point in as you would a staple.

Fit the door into the space so it will open from the top rather loosely, to allow for swelling as weather conditions change. Fasten the strap hinges and hooks and eyes. Fit and fasten the roof and the hinges to the rear of the cross brace.

The roof can be shingled, covered with roll roofing, or otherwise protected with whatever you might have available. The castle is now assembled, and all that remains is to finish it with either stain and varnish or a coat of paint.

BIRD FEEDING BOX

Not everyone is a bonafide bird watcher. But there is hardly a person who won't sit in a warm house on a cold winter day and watch a flock of birds having their breakfast. And if you can arrange it so the birds are within range of your favorite lens, you will have the pleasure of taking pictures of birds when they are most active and interesting.

If you are serious about taking pictures of birds, position the feeder to catch your favorite light. Birds tend to feed early in the morning, when the light is best for such pictures, so turn it to meet the morning sun and you'll never tire of the pictures you can get.

From a more practical point of view, this feeder holds a lot of food, but dispenses it only as fast as the birds can eat it. This means that you load enough to last quite a while without having to brave the weather to refill it.

Here's What You'll Need:

- Back—1 pc ½ × 8 × 20 (1.3 × 20.3 × 50.8)
- Hinged top—1 pc ½ × 10 × 12 (1.3 × 25.4 × 30.5)
- Sides—2 pcs ½ × 3½ × 14 (1.3 × 8.9 × 35.5)
- Tray base—1 pc ¾ × 8 × 8 (1.9 × 20.3 × 20.3)
- Front ledge—1 pc ½ × 2 × 9 (1.3 × 5.1 × 22.9)
- Side ledge—2 pcs ½ × 2½ × 8½ (1.3 × 6.3 × 21.6)
- Front—1 pc ⅛ × 8 × 14 glass or clear plastic (.3 × 20.3 × 35.5)
- 1 pair of brass hinges 1 × 1 with screws

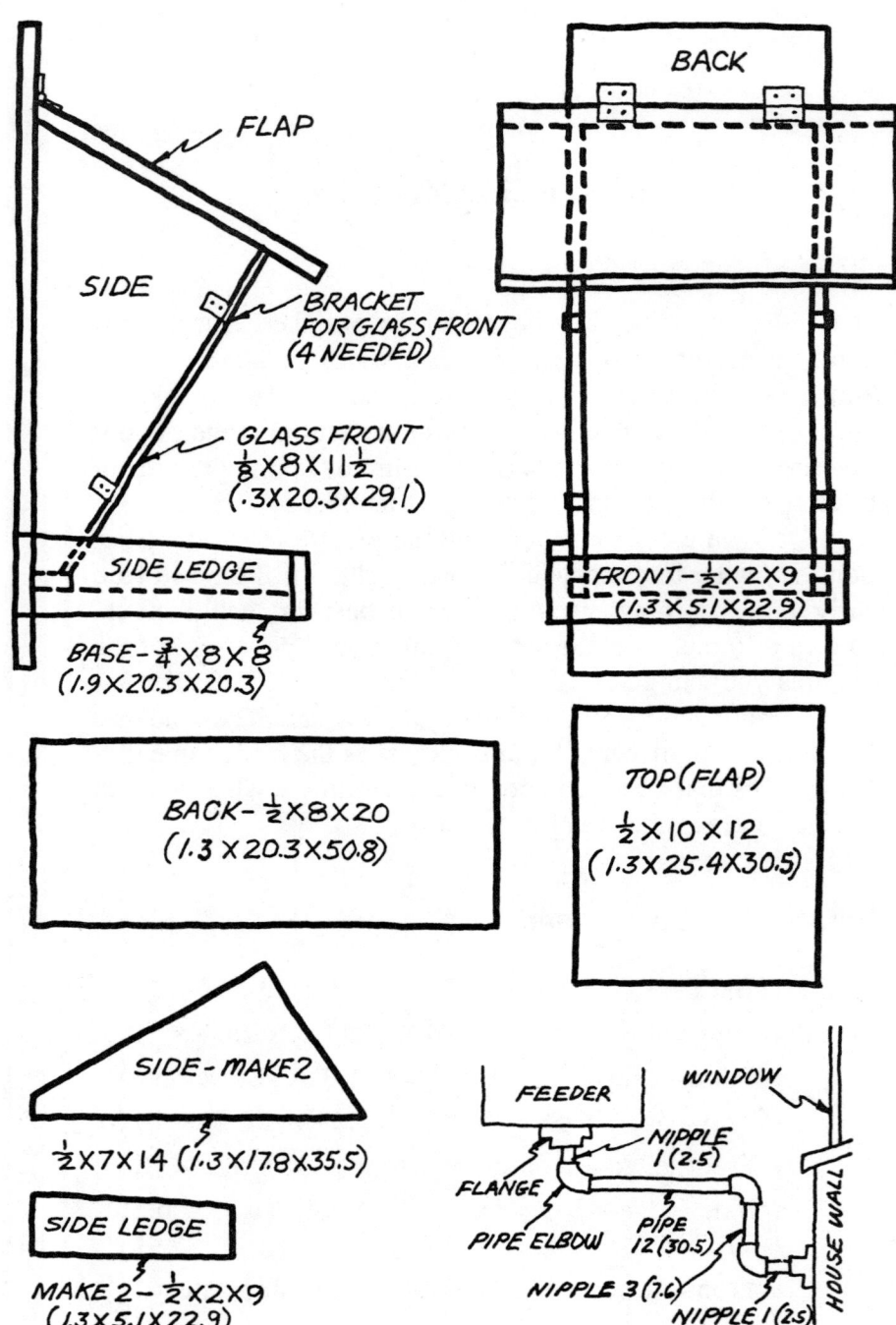

Figure 4-5. Bird Feeding Box.

Six Nature and Wildlife Projects 109

- Pipe for swinging, turning, anti-squirrel bracket ⅜" pipe (1 cm) or nearest size
- Pipe flanges 2 pcs, same size
- Pipe elbows 90°—3 pcs, same size
- Threaded pipe—1 pc 12" (threaded on ends) (30.5)
- Nipple—1 pc 3" long (7.6)
- Nipples—2 pcs 1" long (2.5)
- Small right angle brackets for glass front
- Paint, or stain and varnish
- Assorted nails and screws

Here's How to Make It:

Cut all pieces to size and shape. You can save lumber by cutting sides 1 and 2 from the same piece of wood. Smooth all surfaces and edges. Plane a bevel at the top edge of the hinged roof. This will permit a more snug fit and prevent rain from getting into the stored bird food. Mount the hinges as indicated in Figure 4-5.

Next, fasten the small angle brackets to the side pieces. Position them so that the glass will fit, but can be slid in and out easily. To prevent the glass from sliding down too far and blocking the food supply, place a small block of wood or small nail at each of the extreme sides of the front ledge. Do not mount the glass at this time. If you have a router or table saw, you can cut grooves into the sides for a more finished look.

Fasten the sides to the back with small nails and waterproof glue. See Figure 4-5 for the location of parts. Make up the feed table, using the base, the front and the two sides. Slide the assembled table in place, and fasten with waterproof glue and nails. See Figure 4-5 for the location of the table.

Set the top in place so it rests on the upper edges of the

two sides. Locate the hinge holes and fasten the hinges to the back. Then fasten the other hinge leaves to the feeder top.

Stain and varnish the feeder and then slip the glass or plexiglass in place. The feeder itself is finished, but here is a convenient way of mounting it.

Make the pipe look like the one in Figure 4-5. Remove the flanges and fasten one to the bottom of the feeder tray and the other on a window frame or below the sill. Be sure the feeder is not near a window frequented by squirrels, or they will jump toward the food and chase the birds.

Tighten all the parts with a wrench, but leave the vertical nipples loosely assembled so the support can be swung by hand. This way, you will be able to reach out the window to pull the feeder close enough to fill it.

BIRDBATH WATERING HOLE

If you've ever had a birdbath and watched it turn green in the summer heat, you can appreciate the ease with which you can solve that problem with this project. The water-containing portion of this bird watering hole is a throw-away aluminum foil broiler pan. When the bottom turns green and the birds go elsewhere for their bath and refreshment, you can simply replace the dirty pan with a fresh one.

Here's What You'll Need:

- 1 pc ¼ × 9½ × 13 exterior plywood (.6 × 24.6 × 33)
- 2 pcs ½ × 1½ × 13 (1.3 × 3.8 × 33)
- 2 pcs ½ × 1½ × 8½ (1.3 × 3.8 × 21.6)
- Aluminum foil broiler pans
- 1 pc ½" half-round molding × 48 (1.3 × 121.9)
- Waterproof glue, nails and paint

Here's How to Make It:

Cut all the pieces to size, except for the half-round molding. Glue and nail the sides to the base as shown in Figure 4-6. Locate 4 holes equally spaced on the inside of the plywood base and carefully drill with ½" drill or wood bit.

Next, fit the half-round molding to the tops of the side pieces. Mitre the corners. (That is, cut the ends of the pieces at

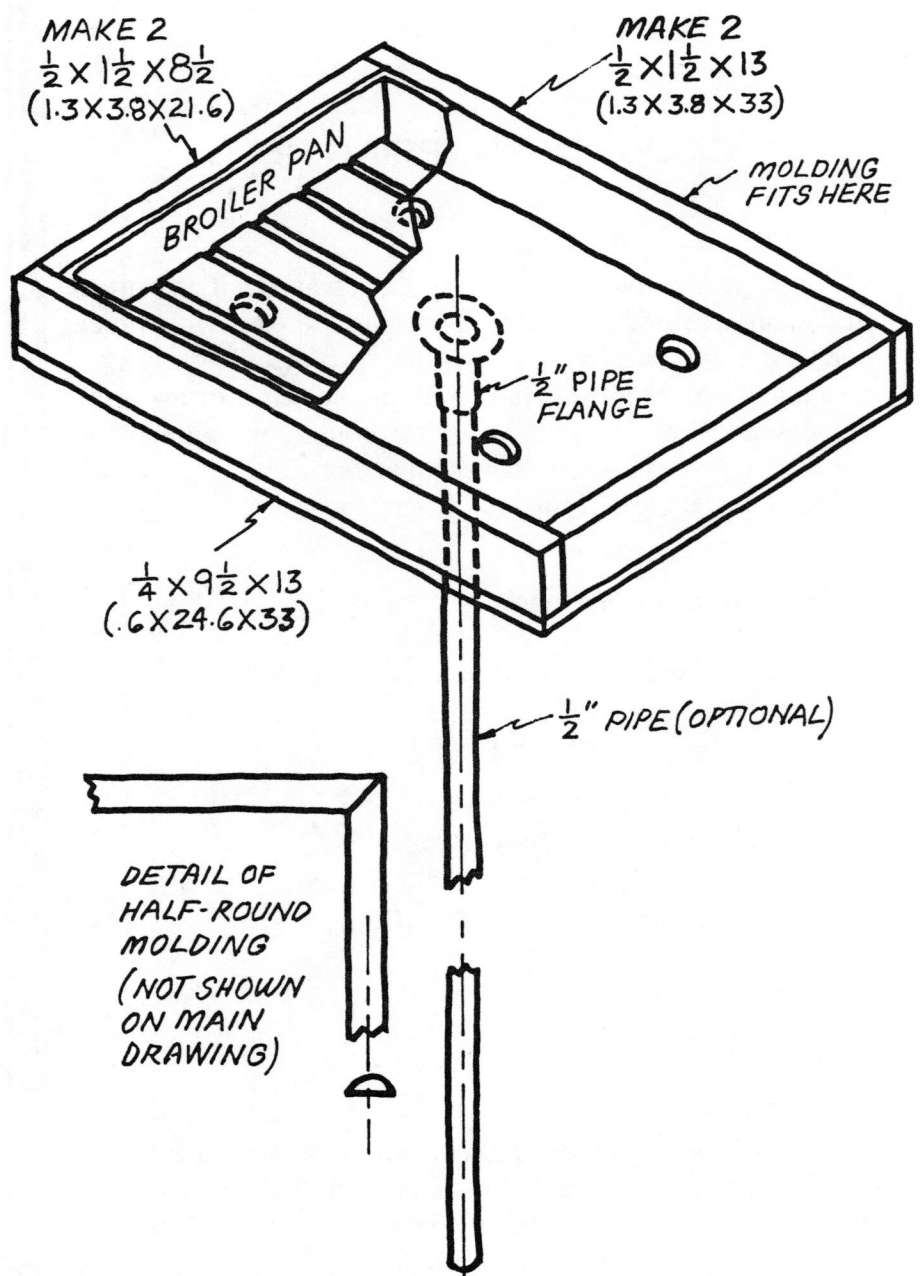

Figure 4-6. Birdbath Watering Hole.

Six Nature and Wildlife Projects 113

45° angles and join them in the same fashion as the sides of a picture frame.) Glue and nail the molding in place.

The molding does more than make the birdbath look good. It gives the birds a better place to perch when they drink, and it allows a better fit for the aluminum foil pan.

Because this birdbath will sit on the ground, it's important to prime and paint it well. Be sure that you paint the insides of the holes as well as all of the other surfaces. Give it two coats after using a good primer.

To use the birdbath, set a foil pan in place and press the edges securely in place with your fingers. Fill it with water and wait for the birds to come. When dirt and algae accumulate, don't bother to wash the foil pan out, simply replace it.

If your yard is free of cats, this system works well. But if the birds fear an attack, you might have to mount it on a pole above ground. To do this, mount a ½" pipe flange to the center of the underside of the wood frame. Then cut a piece of pipe to the length you want and fit it to the flange. When you drive the pipe into the ground, the bath will be safe from cats.

Most cats won't be able to shinny up a ½" pipe, but you might get some trouble from small squirrels. You can solve this problem by applying a little grease to the pole.

5

Ten Projects for Indoors That Everyone Wants

COLONIAL SUGAR SCOOP

Not so many people use sugar scoops these days, at least not as they were supposed to be used. But lots of people with a flair for early American decor have found that the real thing, or a good replica, can serve many practical uses around the house.

Here are a few ways that you can use our sugar scoop:

- As a note catcher.
- As a convenient place to file 3 × 5 cards.
- As a pencil holder. You can also store stamps, erasers, paper clips and other items relating to writing.
- You can even use it as a planter, if you line the bottom with a sheet of plastic to keep water from running out.
- Use it in the bathroom to store toothbrushes, nail brushes, combs, lipstick and all those other bathroom things that seem to disappear because there is no place to put them.
- How about a place to keep all those keys you have? If you're like so many others, you don't know what half of them open, but you'll never throw them away. This is an ideal item to make to solve this problem.

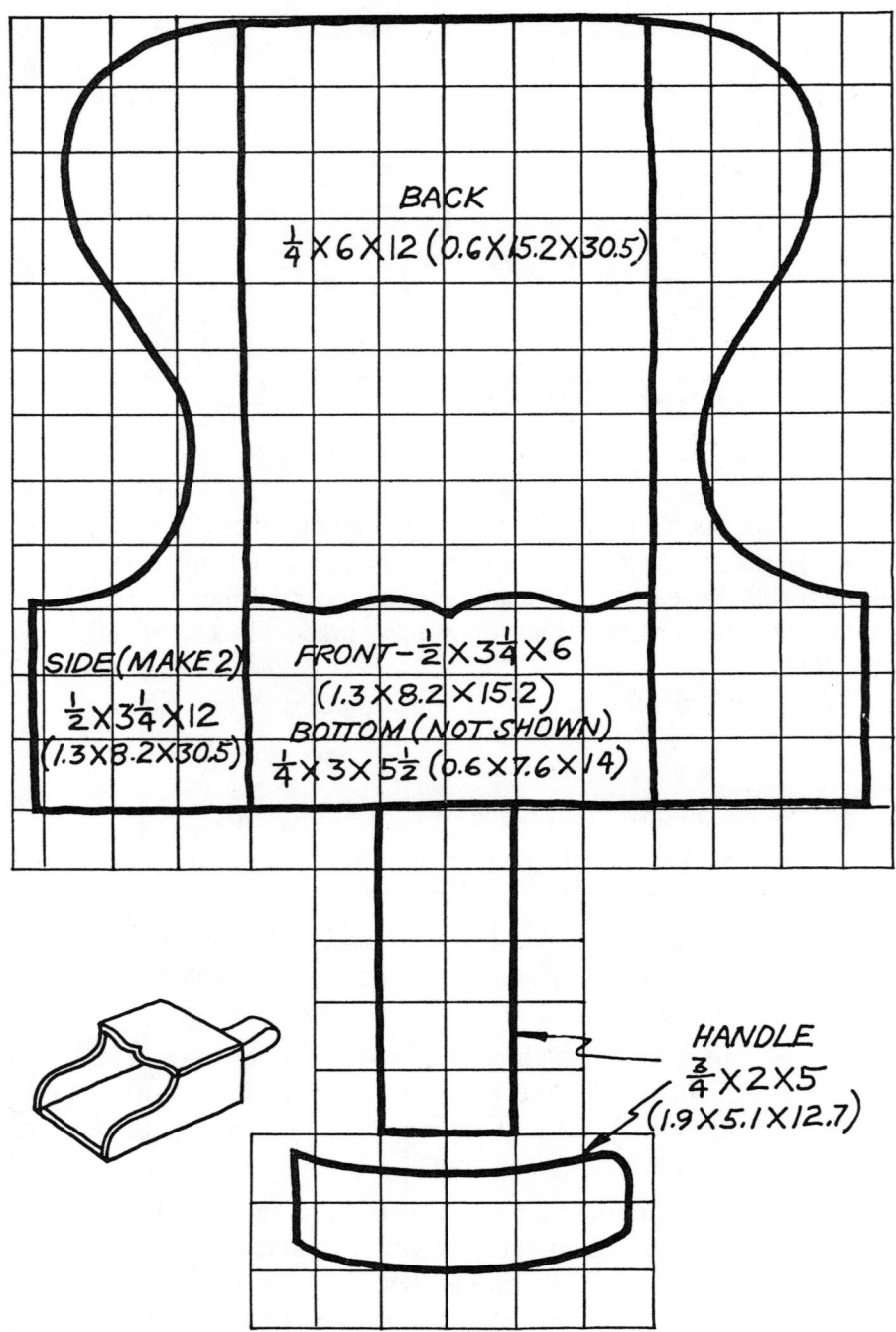

Figure 5-1. Colonial Sugar Scoop.

Here's What You'll Need:

- Back—1 pc ¼ × 6 × 12 plywood (.6 × 15.2 × 30.5)
- Sides—2 pcs ½ × 3¼ × 11 (1.3 × 8.2 × 30.5)
- Front—1 pc ½ × 3¼ × 6 (1.3 × 8.2 × 15.2)
- Bottom—1 pc ¼ × 3 × 5½ plywood (.6 × 7.6 × 14)
- Handle—1 pc ¾ × 2 × 5 (1.9 × 5.1 × 12.7)
- Finishing nails 1½" long, white resin glue, stain and varnish or paint

Here's How to Make It:

First, take a look at Figure 5-1. All the parts except the bottom can be seen, but remember that these pieces are *not* all cut from the same piece of wood.

Cut all pieces to size.

Make up the patterns full size to allow easy tracing.

Trace the pattern for the sides and transfer it to one of the blanks. Temporarily tack the two blanks together and then cut both shapes out at the same time. This will assure a perfect match.

Round off all curved edges.

Glue and nail the sides to the back. Fasten them to the face of the back, not to the edges.

Fasten the handle to the center of the bottom section. Do this with a single 1" round-head wood screw in the center of the bottom and the handle. Just before you tighten the screw, drop a dab of glue between the handle and the bottom.

Fit the bottom into the opening at the bottom of the scoop; glue and nail in place.

Drill a small hole in the back, about 1" below the top, for hanging.

This project looks good antiqued. You can paint it, or leave it as it is with just a coat of wax.

SET OF SERVING BOARDS

What can you say about a set of serving boards? We suppose that we could go on by listing everything that could be served on them, tell you how easy they are to wash and how much they will enhance your table. We might describe the fun you will have making them. We could even say that they make great presents and can be set up to be mass-produced in limited numbers. It is even possible to tell you about how they can be used for decorative purposes if you use them as a base for decoupage. We suppose that . . . and you wondered what could be said about a set of serving boards?

Here's What You'll Need:

- 3 pcs ½ × 8 × 10 hardwood (1.3 × 20.3 × 25.4)
- Vegetable oil

Here's How to Make Them:

If you make the set of three, the best way to begin is by making a stiff cardboard template. Trace the pattern on the cardboard and cut it out with scissors or a shop knife. Use sandpaper to smooth the shape of the cardboard templates.

Trace the template shape on the wood that you have chosen. Be sure that the wood grain runs *with* the handle to add strength. Use a power jig saw, band saw, or a coping saw to cut the shapes.

Use a rasp or a surface forming tool plus sandpaper to smooth the boards to a feather touch.

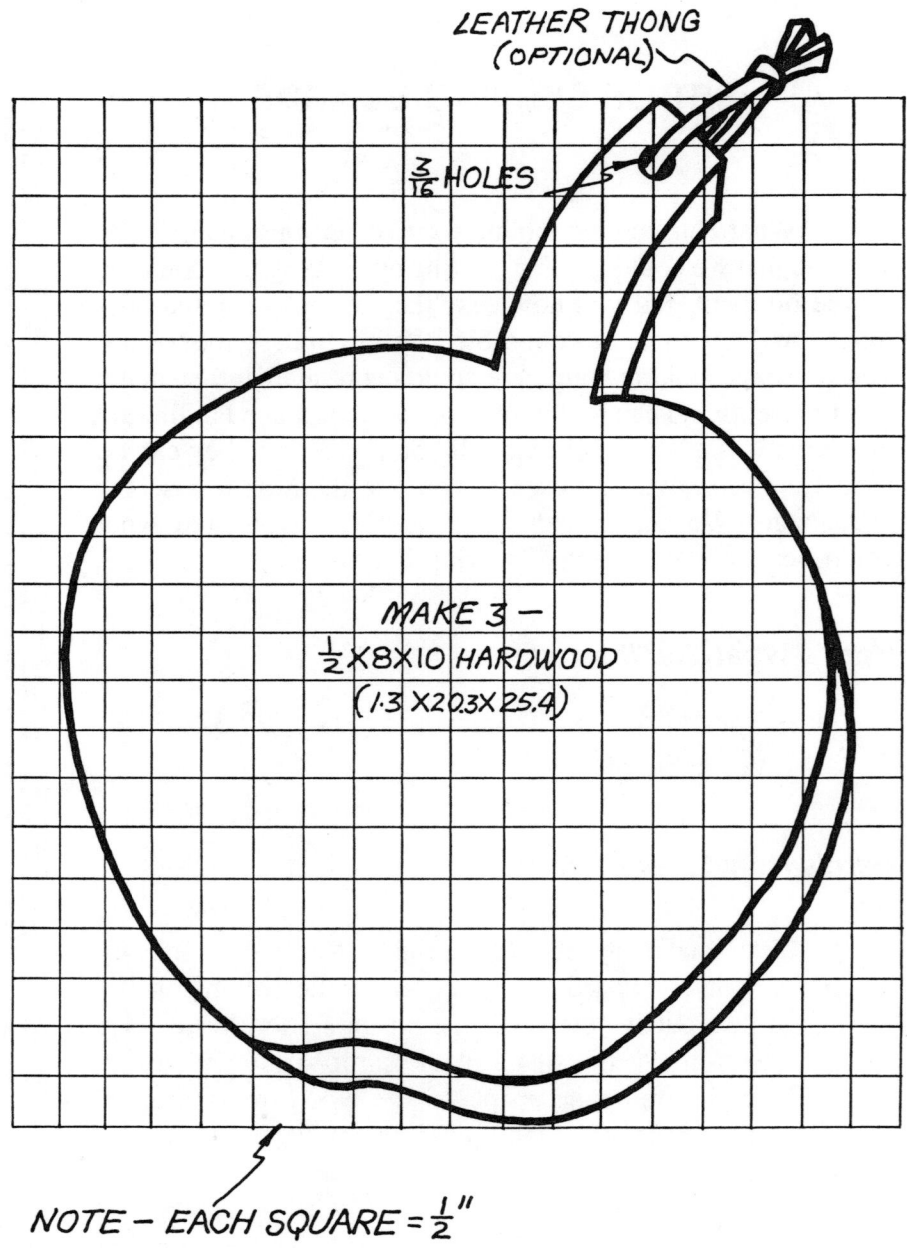

Figure 5-2. Set of Serving Boards.

Ten Projects for Indoors 123

If you are going to use them for their original purpose—serving things—soak them in vegetable oil for a few days. Let them dry, and buff them up and you will have a nice finish that will resist just about anything your sloppiest guest can spill.

If you're planning to use them for decorative purposes, skip the oil process. In fact, if you plan to decorate them (and not for serving) it's a waste to use good hardwood. Clear pine will do very nicely for this application.

FOLK TOYS

How does a toy become a folk toy? Well, the ones that are truly folk toys have been made generation after generation. Even though parts, designs and embellishments may change, the basic concept of a true folk toy stays the same.

A good case in point is the Whimmey Diddle we have included. The modern version of this toy includes a propeller as the moving part. But we're sure that this toy, which goes back thousands of years, had something other than a propeller when it was first made.

The trick pipe is not only a classic physics demonstration, it has gone through a considerable metamorphosis.

The bull roarer is just a plain noisemaker. However, the noise is subtle, not raucous. We have seen it identified by things and animals other than a bull which might have made the sound.

Can you think of any other folk toys that are made by contemporary toy makers that had their start in antiquity? How about the tap dancing figure held at the end of a stick and made to dance by bouncing it on a springboard? Any others?

The Whizzer Bull Roarer

When this toy is whirled rapidly overhead, it makes a strange noise. It's not just wind rushing past a piece of wood, it's a low roar. Try it and you'll see what we mean.

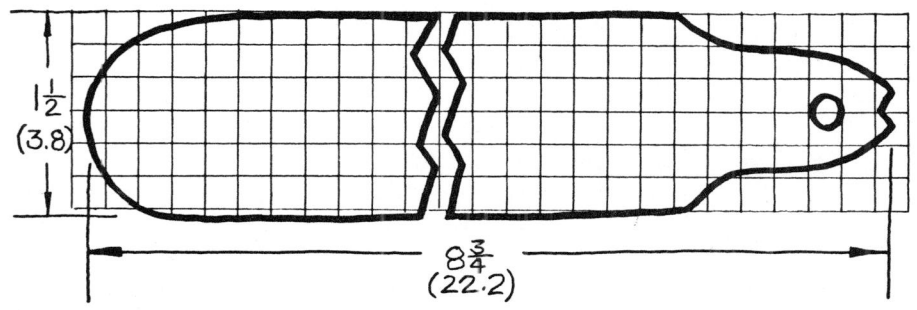

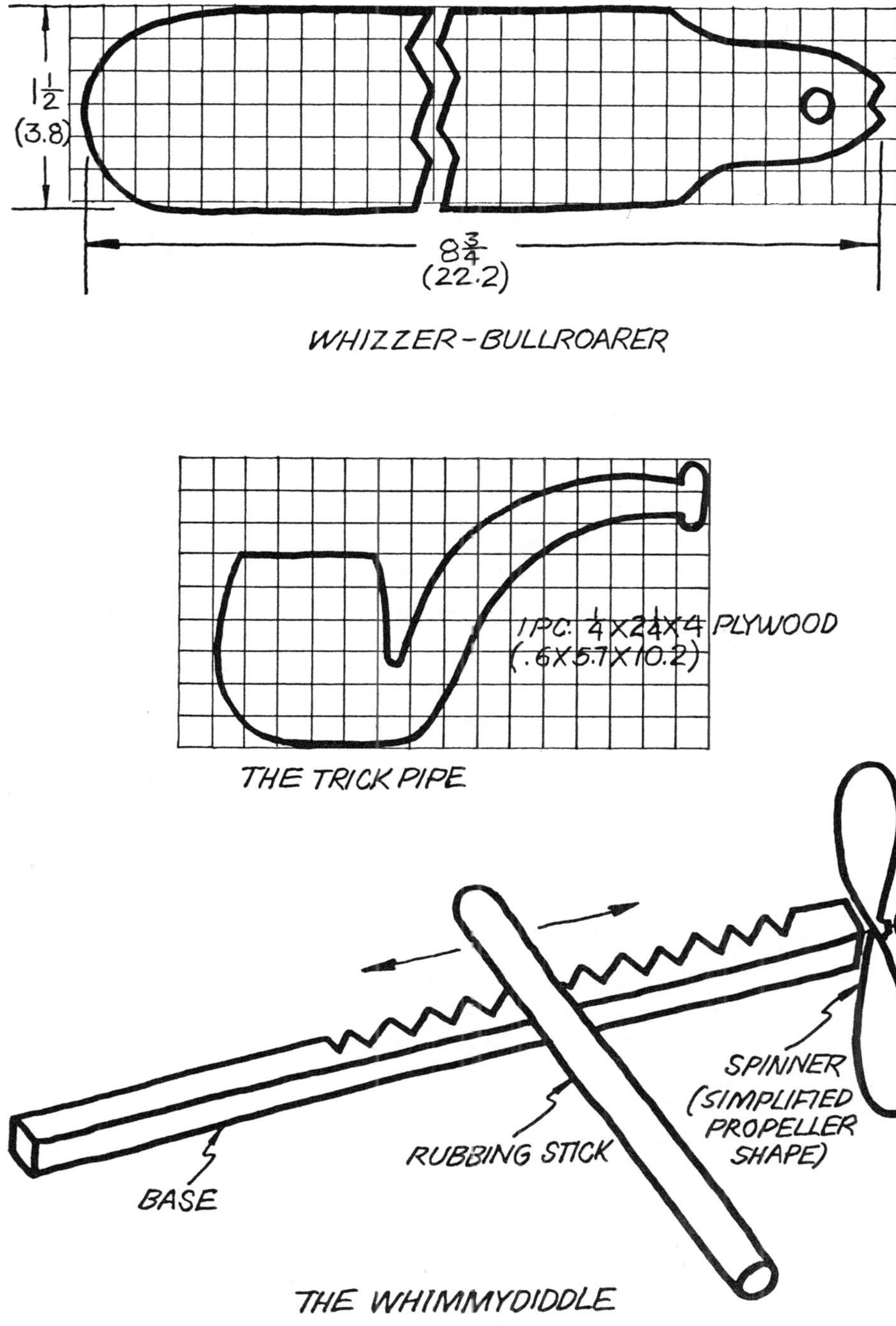

Figure 5-3. Folk Toys.

Here's What You'll Need:

- Wood—1 pc ⅛ × 1½ × 8¾ (.3 × 3.8 × 22.2)
- Length of strong string or heavy fishing line
- A fisherman's swivel, if available.
- Dowel—1 pc ½ × 10" (1.3 × 25.4)

Here's How to Make It:

Lay out the pattern and cut the shape as shown in Figure 5-3. Drill the hole in the end for the string. Sand the edges, paying particular attention to the edges of the hole. The string will get rough treatment here, and any rough edges could cut it.

Use a file to notch the end of the wood nearest the hole. Tie the string tightly in this notch. You might want to add a drop of glue on the knot as further insurance that the whizzer won't fly off.

Attach the fishing swivel to the dowel with several loops of string. Attach the other end of the long string to the swivel. Again, a drop of glue will help keep it all together.

Now, you're ready. Swing the roarer over your head and listen for the sound. It won't overpower you, but you will hear much more than the rush of air.

The Trick Pipe

When you loop a belt over this pipe and place the bit precariously at the edge of a table, this pipe mysteriously hangs on. It's all a matter of the center of gravity, but for those who don't remember high school physics or the kids who haven't taken the course yet, it can be quite entertaining.

Here's What You'll Need:

- Plywood—1 pc ¼ × 2¼ × 4

Here's How to Make It:

Trace the outline on the plywood and then cut out the shape. You can use a power jig saw or a hand coping saw.

Smooth the edges, and it's ready to use. If you're planning to give it to someone, you might want to apply a coat of paint.

Here's How to Use It:

Buckle up a firm leather belt and slip it into the notch formed by the stem and bowl of the pipe. Now, place the tip of the stem on the edge of a table and allow the belt to swing free; it will swing under the edge of the table, but the pipe will not fall. Even though the whole thing looks as though it should fall to the floor, it will simply hang on. The center of gravity is at the bottom of the belt and under the table, so the tip of the pipe will hang on to its apparently precarious perch.

The Whimmy Diddle

This is no substitute for a polluting gasoline engine, but it will turn a propeller with no more fuel than a little elbow grease. When the Whimmy Diddle is rubbed with the stick, the prop will take off. It is great for kids getting their first exposure to airplanes.

Here's What You'll Need:

Base—1 pc ⅜ × ⅜ × 10 (1 × 1 × 25.4)
Spinner—1 pc ⅛ × ¼ × 4 (.3 × .6 × 10.2) or a plastic propeller of similar dimensions used for a model airplane.
Rubbing stick—1 pc ½ × 6 dowel (.6 × 15.2)

Here's How to Make It:

Use a knife or a saw to cut a series of regular notches in one side of the base. Leave enough of the base uncut to provide a comfortable handle grip.

Mount the spinner with a brad at the end opposite the handle. Make sure the spinner turns freely.

Here's How to Use It:

Hold the slotted stick assembly in one hand and rub the dowel over the notches. Watch the prop take off.

Can you figure out how to make the prop turn in the opposite direction? Try switching from thumb pressure on the near side of the rubbing stick to pressure with your forefinger on the far side of the stick.

WALL-MOUNTED DESK

Wall-mounted desks can save a lot of space. They were not only popular in earlier times when space was at a premium, but their modern cousins can be found in such unusual places as submarines (made of metal, of course) and kids rooms where space is always cramped.

You can use just about any type of wood to make this desk, but you should consider a piece of hardwood for the top. A softwood can be marred easily for example, when you are pressing down with a ball point pen to fill out the multi-layered forms we all have to complete once in a while.

Here's What You'll Need:

- Lid—1 pc ¾ × 16¼ × 30 (1.9 × 41.2 × 76.2)
- Base—1 pc ¾ × 7½ × 28½ (1.9 × 19.1 × 72.4)
- Top— 1 pc ¾ × 6½ × 30 (1.9 × 16.5 × 76.2)
- Sides—2 pcs ¾ × 7½ × 16 (1.9 × 19.1 × 40.6)
- Nailing strip—1 pc ¾ × 1½ × 28½ (1.9 × 3.8 × 72.4)
- Shelf—1 pc ¾ × 5 × 28½ (1.9 × 12.7 × 72.4)
- Back—1 pc ⅛ or ¼ × 17 × 30 plywood or hardboard (.3 or .6 × 43.2 × 76.2)
- Piano hinge—28½ (72.4) with flat head screws to match
- Transom chain—1 length brass or galvanized steel, about 2' long

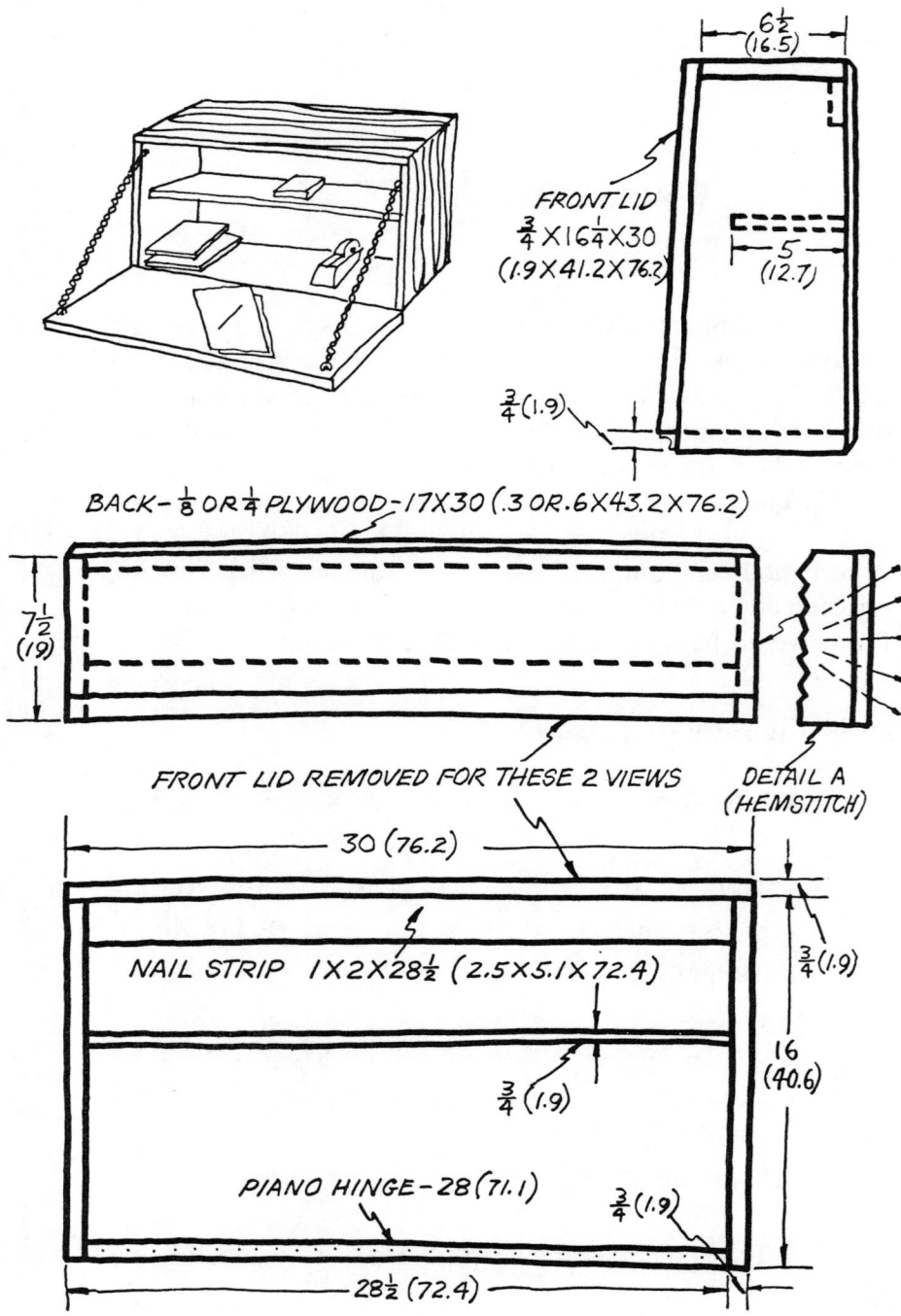

Figure 5-4. Wall-Mounted Desk.

Ten Projects for Indoors

- Anchor screws, lag screws or toggle bolts
- Magnetic cabinet latches (2)
- Screw eyes for chain
- Finishing nails, glue, paint or stain and varnish

Here's How to Make It:

Before we get into the construction details, look at the sketches and note that the top is somewhat narrower than the bottom. This was done to give the desk a little style, and make it look less like a wall-mounted box. The ends are cut according to Figure 5-4, but note that the taper cut changes angle at the bottom by ¾". This allows the hinge to work properly, insuring a horizontal writing surface when the lid is open.

Because this desk may be subject to some abuse, we suggest that you use this fastening system. Draw pencil lines along the surfaces where the nails will be driven. Drive one nail in the center so it barely penetrates the other side. On either side of this center nail, drive other nails so they sort of "hemstitich" or aim at the center nail. See detail A in Figure 5-4. The angled nails should only penetrate slightly, as does the first center nail.

Next, apply a good wood glue and clamp the pieces in place. Be sure to check for the squareness, and then drive the "hemstitch" nails in place. Drive the nails below the surface with a nail set *before* the glue dries.

This technique will not only make a virtually indestructable joint, it can also be used to secure slightly warped pieces of wood. Long finishing nails are best for this technique.

The shelf and nailing strip should be assembled and glued by the same process we just described.

Cut a bevel or chamfer on the outside edges of the

back, and then fasten it in place with nails and glue. (See Figure 5-4.) Use the same nailing and glue system on this section as well.

Make the lid by simply smoothing all the surfaces. But do not round the bottom edge; it should retain its squareness for the piano hinge.

Fasten the hinge to the lid first. Make sure the better surface faces the outside. Hold the lid in place on the box, and following Figure 5-4 for location, spot the screw holes and fasten the hinge in place.

Next, you should decide where you want to mount the wall desk. Pick a place where it will be out of the way, whether it is opened or closed.

To mount the desk, drill holes in the nailing strip to suit the following wall-mounting methods:

1. If you can find two studs, drill for long wood screws.
2. If you have plaster or wall board, use heavy toggle bolts.
3. If you have a solid masonry wall, drill for anchor shields and lag screws.

When you have your mounting finished, remove the desk from the wall and paint or stain it to suit your decorating scheme. Now is the time to mount the support chain. Cut it into two lengths, and attach it to the two sides and the lid using the screw eyes. To make sure the lid desk surface is perfectly even, use a spirit level. Position the chain and the screw eyes to be sure that you will be able to close the desk.

MEMO PAD / PENCIL HOLDER

It probably isn't necessary to tell you that a memo pad and pencil holder can help make life a lot easier in the kitchen or around the telephone. So instead, we'll tell you what a nice gift it makes, and how it can be made very easily by the junior woodworkers in your family. Furthermore, it's the kind of project that can be mass-produced, as far as the average home wood shop permits. So you might even be able to solve your Christmas present problems with a few evenings' work.

Here's What You'll Need:

- Sides—2 pcs ⅜ × 3 × 8½ (1 × 7.6 × 21.6)
- Base—1 pc ⅜ × 3¼ × 13 (1 × 8.2 × 33)
- Pencil holder—1 pc 1 × 1 × 2 (2.5 × 2.5 × 5.1)
- Roller—1 pc ⅜ × 3¼ dowel (1 × 8.3)
- Cutter bar—1 pc ⅛ × ½ × 3¼ (.3 × 1.3 × 8.2)

Here's How to Make It:

Cut blanks for the sides and base. Tack the two side blanks together, face to face in preparation for sawing the shapes. Transfer the side pattern to one of the blanks and cut the two shapes at one time.

While the two sides are still tacked together, drill a ⅜" hole for the upper paper roller.

Separate the pieces and sand all edges except the bot-

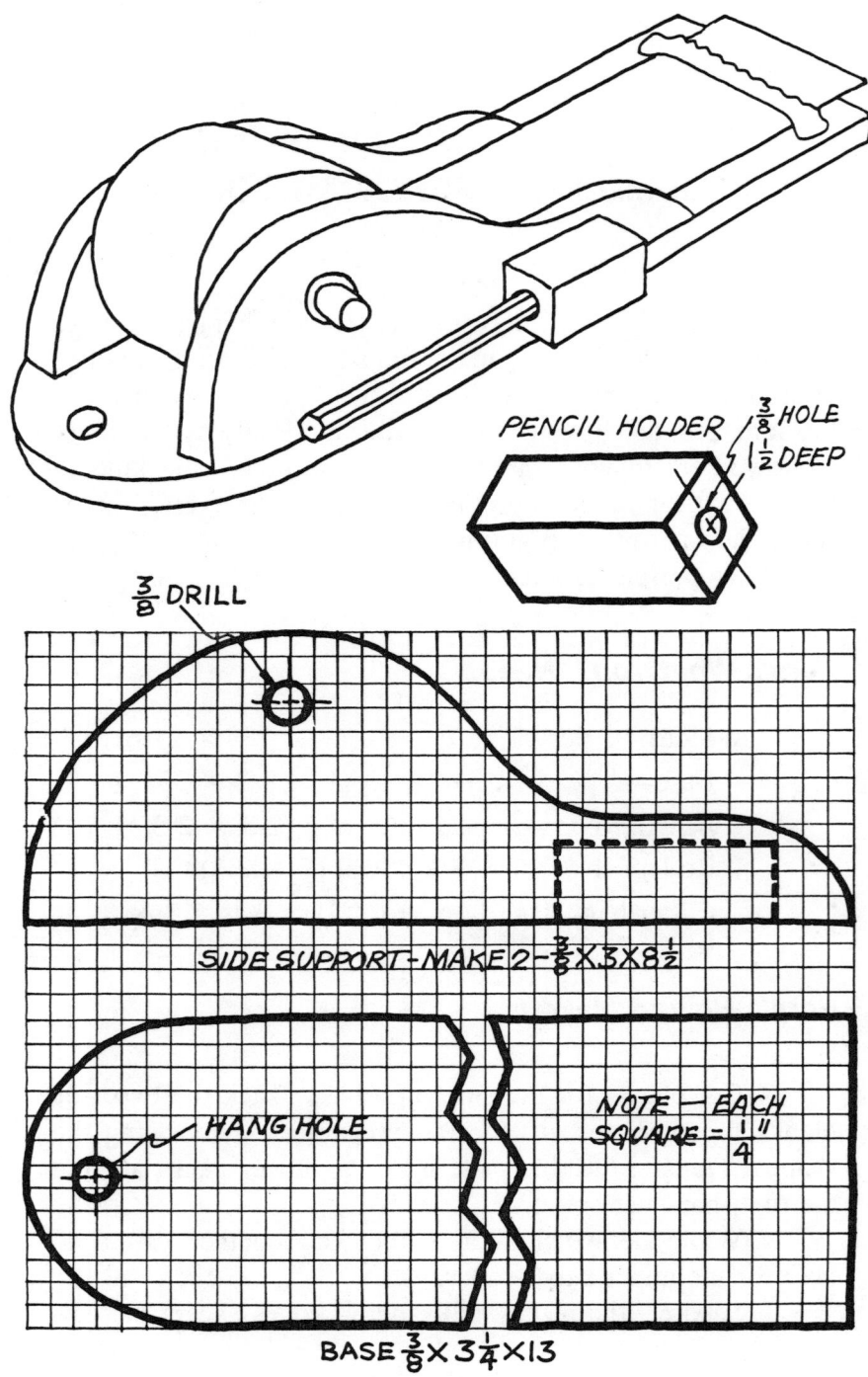

Figure 5-5. Memo Pad/Pencil Holder.

Ten Projects for Indoors

tom edge. The bottom edge must be square and straight to allow for fastening later on.

Locate the center of the block that will be the pencil holder. Drill a ⅜" hole, 1½" deep. You can use a drill gauge to limit the depth of the drill. If you don't have such a gauge, wrap a piece of masking tape one turn around the drill 1½" above the paint, and drill until you reach the lower edge of the tape.

Lay out the pattern of the top curve of the base including the hanging hole. Use a jig saw or coping saw to cut out the shape. Next, drill the hanging hole.

Glue and nail all of the parts together. Be sure that the sides are glued on *top* of the base—not alongside.

The paper cutter can be made of wood, tin plate or galvanized steel. Even a piece of an old hack-saw blade will work. In fact, it will work better than the other materials. Cut the paper cutter to size, and drill small mounting holes at either end. When you mount it, be sure to space it slightly above the base so that the paper will feed through. Don't make it too high above the base, or it will be difficult to make a clean tear. Try using shims under each mounting screw made of two or three sheets of the paper that will be rolled under it. You might have to use more because the paper will become compressed. Experiment a little until you find the right thickness to give you a clean one-handed tear.

Mount a roll of adding-machine tape by first sliding the dowel through one side of the holder, then through the core of the tape and then through the other side of the holder. You can hold the dowel in place by slipping a small plumber's "O" ring over each end.

THE FARMER'S HAT RACK

This is not the kind of hat rack you will find at most farms today. But you probably won't find too many horses on a modern farm, either. However, as a bit of nostalgia, and a very practical way to keep everyone's hats in one place, we offer the farmer's hat rack.

Here's What You'll Need:

- Long arms—4 pcs ¼ × 1⅛ × 22 lattice strip (.6 × 2.8 × 55.9)
- Short arms—4 pcs ¼ × 1⅛ × 12⅛ lattice strip (.6 × 2.8 × 30.7)
- Pegs—10 pcs ½" dowel × 4½ (1.3 × 11.5)
- Lock pins—10 pcs $^{1}/_{16}$" × 1 soft steel rod

Here's How to Make It:

First; cut all pieces to size. Then, at a length of 1⅛" from each end, centered, lay out and drill ½" holes. Do this with both the long and short pieces.

The old hat racks had pins that were turned and shaped, not only to look better, but to provide a better hold on the hats. It isn't necessary to turn the pins on a lathe; you can do a good job with a drill press, or a ½" portable electric drill. Simply chuck up each peg, and while the drill is running round, shape it with sandpaper or a file. If you are using a hand electric drill, make sure that it is safely clamped to the bench before you do any shaping.

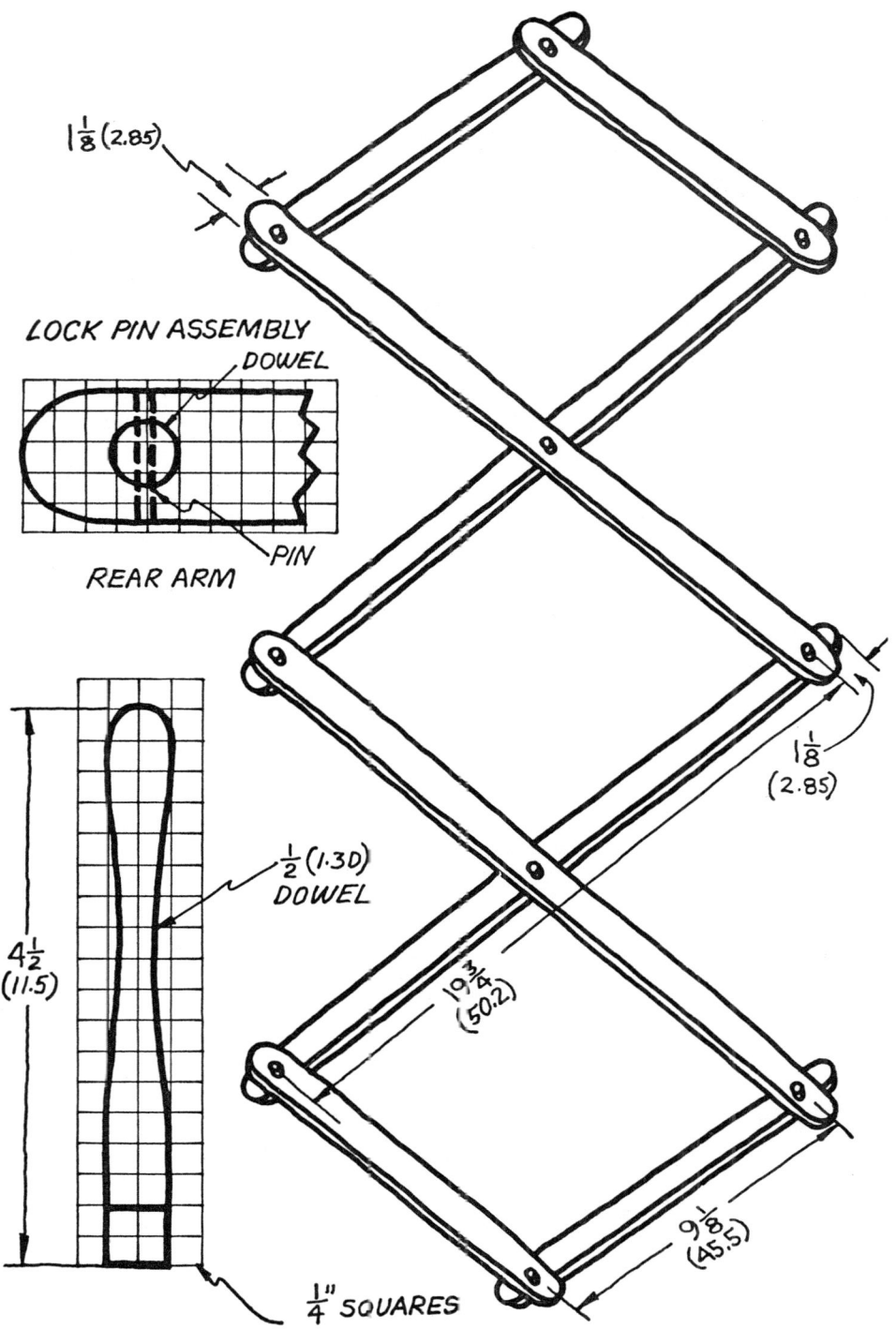

Figure 5-6. The Farmer's Hat Rack.

Next, sand all edges. You may now assemble the rack by pushing the dowels in place onto each rear strip; glue in place. Drill $1/16''$ holes into the side of the stock and into the dowel on each rear piece. Coat the pins with glue and insert them into the holes. Be sure the dowels are set squarely in the holes, and let the glue dry.

Position all the front pieces, as shown in the sketch.

This rack will look best with a medium-tone stain and a few coats of matte finish varnish. You might even want to distress the surface to make it look more like an old piece.

KEY RACK

The key to finding something is to sort out everything that doesn't look like what is lost. What better way to make sure your keys don't disappear than to make a big key rack. Corny? Possibly. But, we're willing to bet that you will seldom have to hunt for the keys again with this on your wall.

Here's What You'll Need:

- Key—1 pc ½ × 7 × 12 (1.3 × 17.8 × 30.5)
- Cup hooks—9 pcs
- Stain, varnish or paint

Here's How to Make It:

Trace the pattern on a piece of paper lined with 1" squares to give you the full-size drawing. (See Figure 5-7.) Drill the hole used to hang the rack. This is done first to reduce the possibility of splitting the wood during other operations. To be safe, drill the hole halfway through from one side, and then finish the job from the other side.

Use a coping saw, sabre saw, jig saw or hand saw to cut out the outline. Use a thin saw blade to make shallow cross-cuts at the base of the finger grip to simulate a real key. If you really want to imitate a key, clamp the wood and make shallow cuts along the key blade. Take a look at one of your own keys for an idea of how these grooves should look.

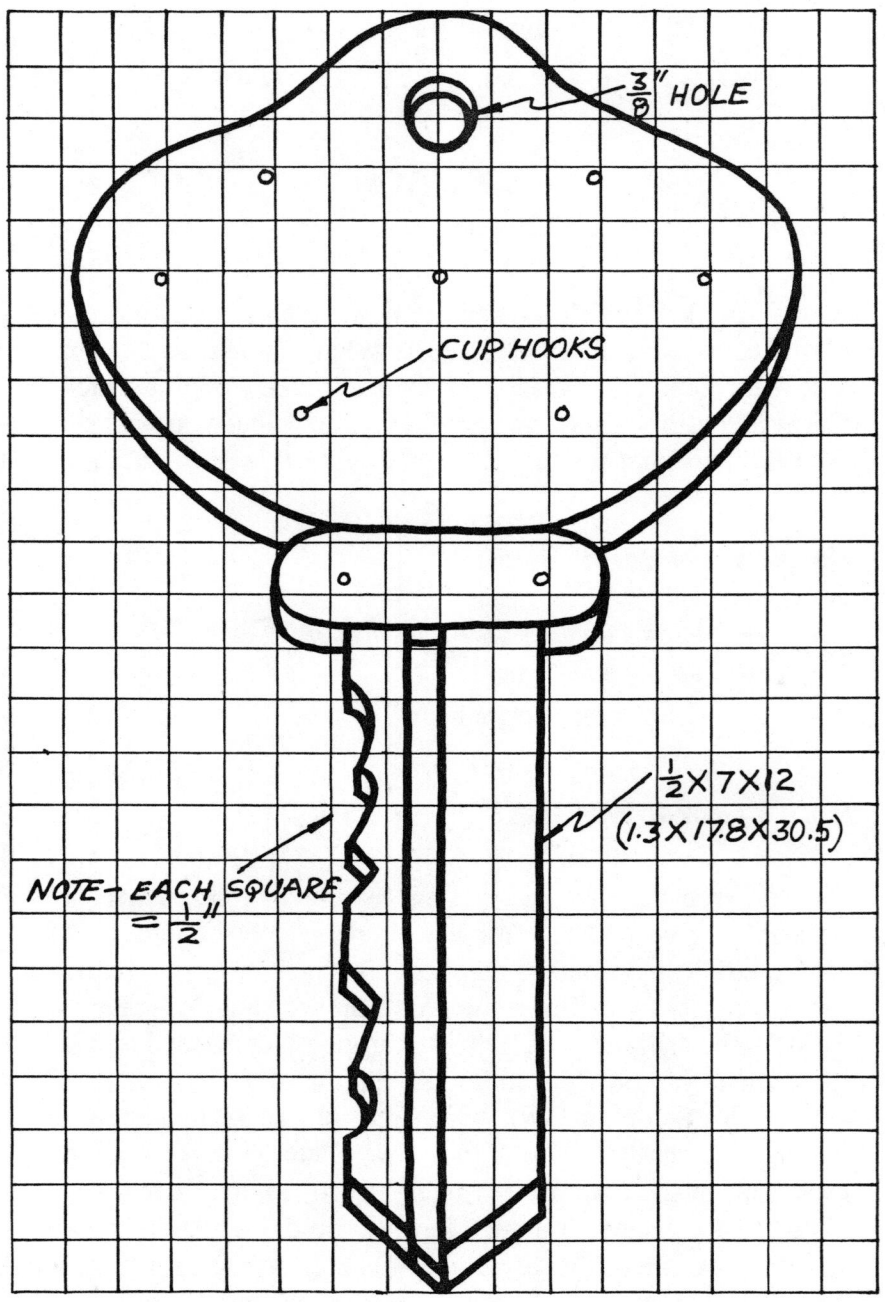

Figure 5-7. Key Rack.

Ten Projects for Indoors 141

Drill the pilot holes for the hooks, but don't mount them yet.

You're now ready to apply a finish. Use whatever will blend with your decor—paint, stain and varnish, or just a waxed wood surface.

Now you can screw in the cup hooks.

WINE GLASS RACK

When wine glasses are stored standing up in a cabinet, they fill with dust and chip when they bump each other. To solve both of these problems, we have created a simple, but very effective wine glass rack. This, incidentally, is the way wine glasses are stored in the best restaurants.

The rack, when assembled, is simply fastened to a convenient ceiling location, and the glasses are slipped in place. It can even be hung from the ceiling in a large cupboard or closet. Either way, it will save you from chipped glasses and prevent you from ruining a Chateau Lafitte with a mouthful of dust.

Here's What You'll Need:

- Separators—5 pcs 1 × 4 × 36 (2.5 × 10.2 × 91.4)
- Spacers—10 pcs ½ × 1¾ × 3 plywood (1.3 × 4.4 × 7.6)
- Cross hangers—2 pcs 1 × 2 × 26 (2.5 × 5.1 × 66)
- 10 brass bolts and nuts—F.H. 10-24 × 1½ (3.8)
- Steel screws—F.H. 1¼-8 (3.2)
- Glue, shellac, varnish

Here's How to Make It:

First, cut all pieces to size. Then sand all the separators to a very fine finish. The best way to do this is to sand with successively finer grit papers until you end with a 4/0 grade.

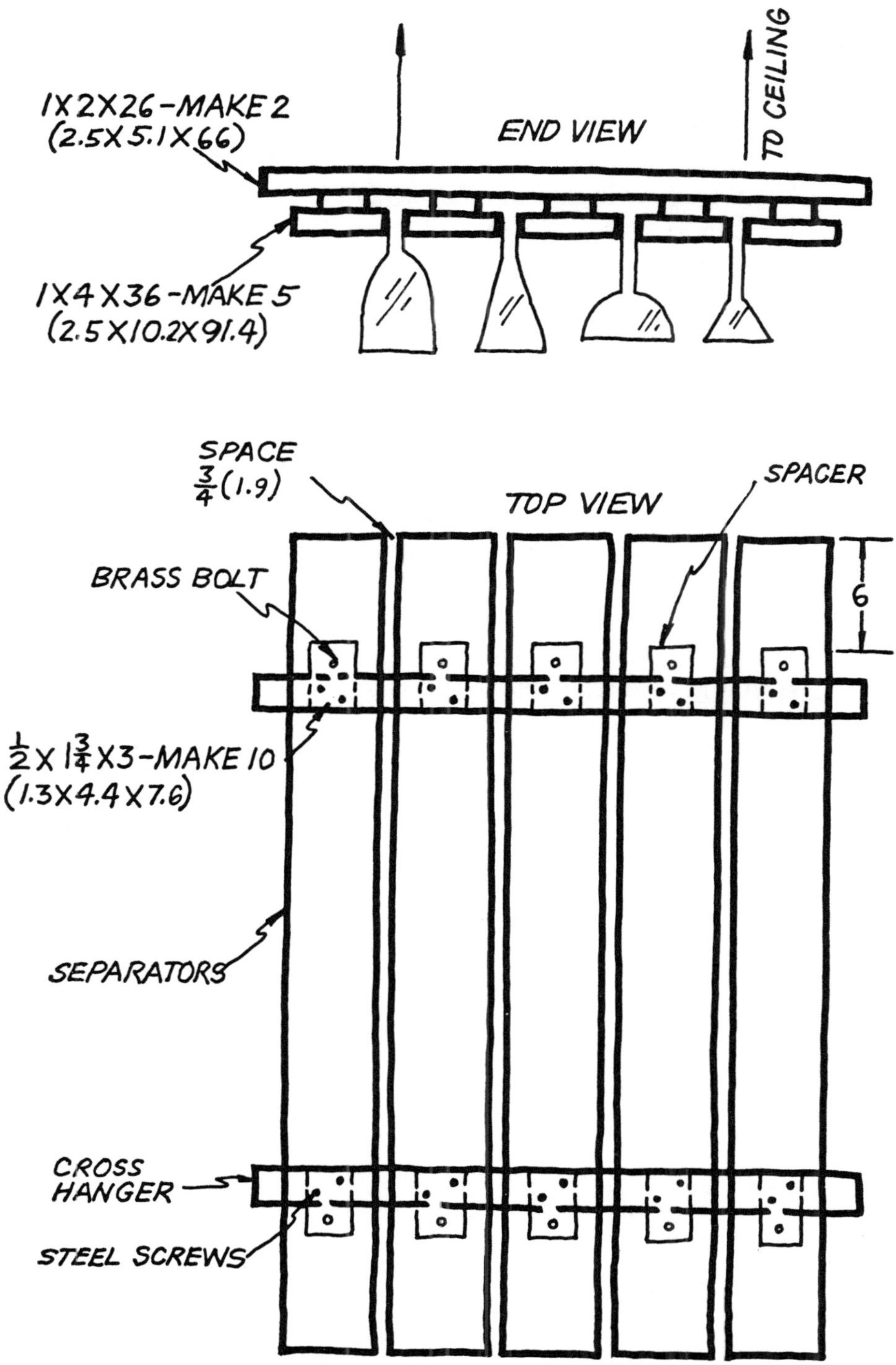

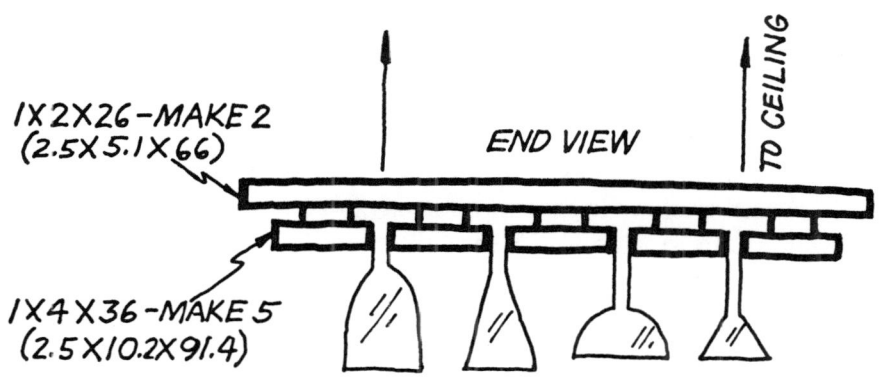

Figure 5-8. Wine Glass Rack.

Measure in 6" from the end of each separator, and mark a point in the center. Drill holes at all these points for the brass bolts. Fasten the spacer to the back of each screw hole, drilling through to fasten with the bolts and nuts. The spacers should be positioned towards the center of the glass holders.

Position all the separators so there is ¾" (1.9) space between them. Lay the cross hangers on them, as shown in Figure 5-8 and temporarily fasten the spacers to the cross hangers with finishing nails. Disconnect the spacers from the separators, turn over the cross-hanger-spacer subassembly and fasten permanently with flat head wood screws. Replace the brass bolts in proper position and you're done.

You can paint, or use stain and varnish to suit the decor of the room in which the rack will be used.

The rack can be mounted directly on the ceiling, or it can be suspended by short lengths of chain from each corner, if you have the height.

A SET OF PUZZLES

There are two kinds of puzzles—those you work out yourself and those which you must discover how someone else did it. Both are fun, and we have an example of each to test your craft-making skill and the puzzle-solving abilities of those on whom you try them.

The Tower of Benares

The Tower of Benares is a structure in a holy Hindu city in India. Legend has it that this puzzle originated there, but there are enough similar puzzles named for other ancient cities and people to suggest that the real origin of this fun puzzle is really lost in antiquity.

The problem posed by this puzzle is to move the discs which have been stacked on the left hand peg to the right hand peg—but without covering any smaller discs with larger discs on the way.

Here's What You'll Need:

- Discs, one each of the following sizes: 1, 1¼, 1½, 1¾, 2, 2½ inch diameter—quarter-inch plywood (2.5, 3.2, 3.8, 4.4, 5.1, 6.3 × .6 plywood)
- Pegs—3 pcs ¼ × 3" dowel (.6 × 7.6)
- Base—1 pc ¼ × 3 × 10 plywood (.6 × 7.6 × 25.4)
- Glue and various color paints

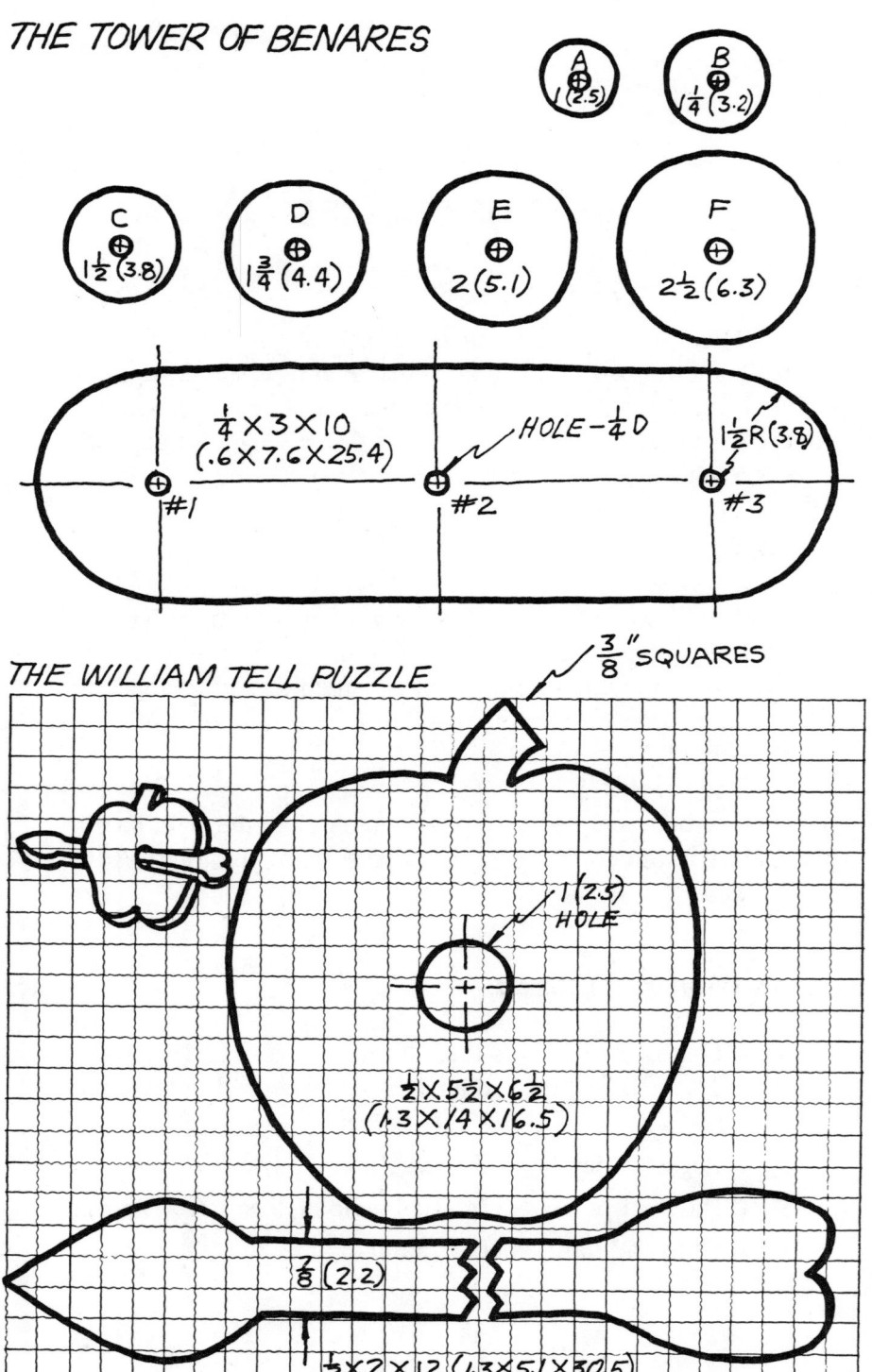

Figure 5-9. A Set of Puzzles.

Here's How to Make It:

Cut all pieces to size, and then sand all the surfaces and edges. Drill the holes in the base, as shown in Figure 5-9. Insert and glue the dowels in place. Paint each peg a different color and label them on the base, from left to right: 1, 2, 3.

Lightly pencil-in these labels on the discs, beginning with the smallest and progressing to the largest: A, B, C, D, E, F.

Paint discs A, C, and E one color.
Paint discs B, D, F, another color.

It isn't necessary for the letter markings to remain visible after the discs have been painted. It's easy enough to identify them (when you use the following instructions) simply by remembering that they go from A to F, starting with the smallest.

Here's how to do it. Discs A, C and E move from left to right, and discs B, D, and F move from right to left in rotation, except for disc A which is moved from left to right, every other turn. Follow this sequence:

A to 2, B to 3, A to 3, C to 2, A to 1, B to 2, A to 2, etc.

The William Tell Puzzle

There is a large arrow, right through a small hole in the apple. The head and the fletching are much too big to fit through the hole, but there it is. How was it done? The first answer is that the entire assembly was carved from a single piece of wood. Although possible, it would be a very difficult job. We have an easier way:

Here's What You'll Need:

- Arrow—1 pc ½ × 2 × 12 basswood. (1.3 × 5.1 × 30.5)
- Apple—1 pc ½ × 5½ × 6½ basswood (1.3 × 14 × 16.5)

Here's How to Make It:

Cut both pieces to size and shape. The sizes are not critical as long as the head and fletching of the arrow are a bit bigger that the hole you will drill in the apple. Shape the arrow; that is, sand the edges of the arrowhead and fletching, and round the shaft.

Soak the arrow in water overnight. In the morning, gently squeeze the arrowhead, either with your hands or in a wood vise. As you squeeze, slide the arrowhead through the hole in the apple. Continue squeezing and sliding until the head passes through the hole completely. Let the assembly dry.

Soak the arrowhead once more and give it a chance to swell. After it has swollen and dried, you can use a knife or chisel to nick the head to make it look like flint, and as though it had been carved from one piece of wood.

Now, puzzle your friends.

KITCHEN SLATE REMINDER

If you've ever forgotten anything, this project is just what you need. It fits with any decor, and can be decorated to compliment a dominant motif. It's fun to make, and once something is written on it, it will be impossible to say, "I forgot."

There was a time when you could go into a lumber yard and order blackboard frame molding. Yes, there actually was a type of molding made just for this purpose. And, believe it or not, you could even buy chalk-trough molding, made just for blackboards. You may still be able to buy it, but we haven't seen it in a long time. Anyway, whether you can get this molding or not, you can still make a very handy wall reminder with wood that is readily available.

Here's What You'll Need:

- Slate—1 pc. tempered hardboard ¼ × 12 × 18 (.6 × 30.5 × 45.7)
- Frame—1 pc ¾ × 1¾ × 8 ft blackboard molding If unavailable, get ¾ × 1¾ strip molding (1.9 × 4.4)
- Pegs—1 pc ⅛" × 6" dowel (.3 × 15.2) cut into three equal pieces
- Bin—Back—¼ × 3 × 10½ (.6 × 7.6 × 26.7)
  Bottom—¼ × 3 × 10½ (.6 × 7.6 × 26.7)
  Front—¼ × 3 × 10½ (.6 × 7.6 × 26.7)
  Ends—2 pcs ¼ × 3 × 3½ (.6 × 7.6 × 8.9)
- Finishing nails, white glue, chalkboard paint, stain, varnish

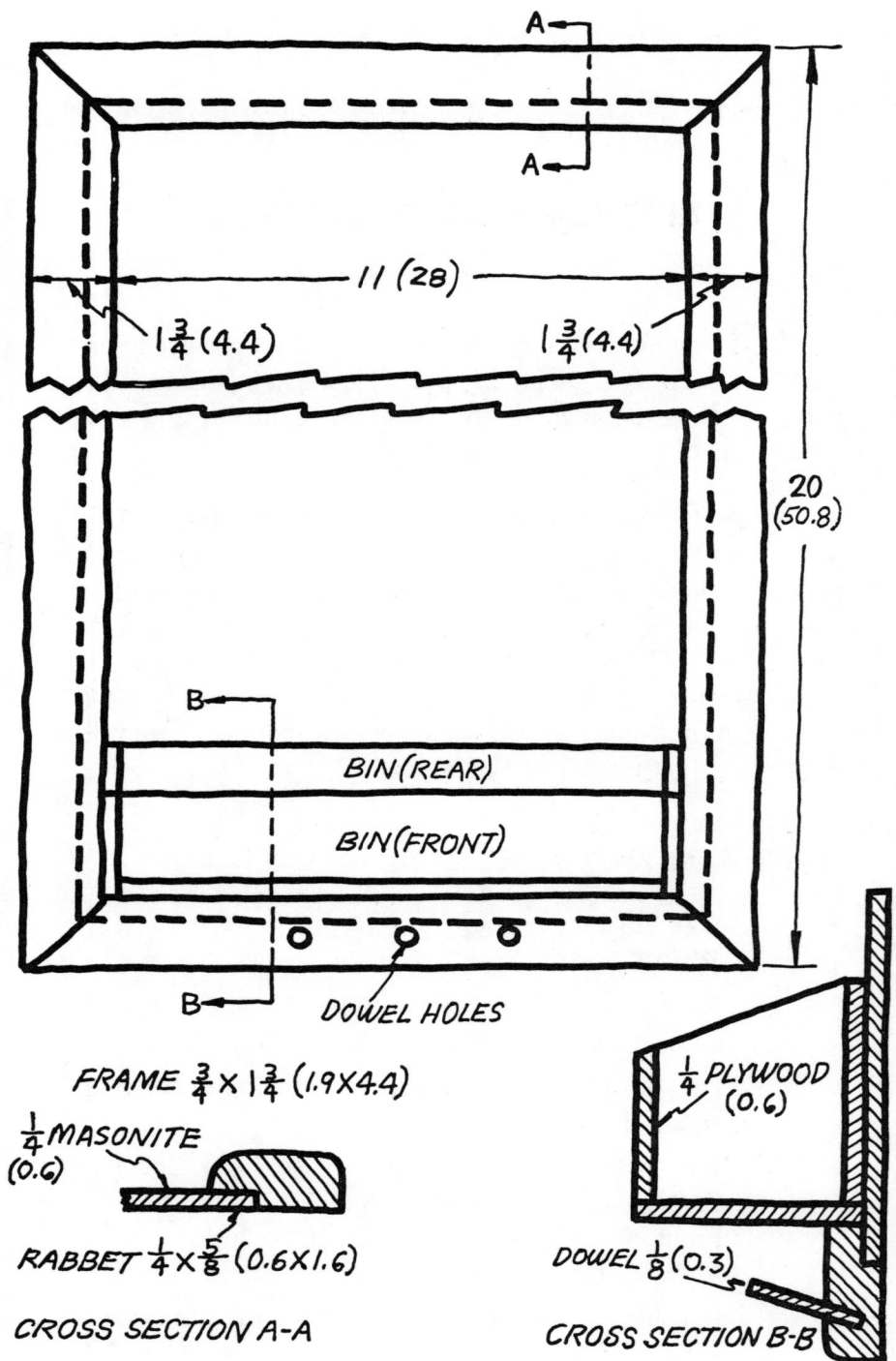

Figure 5-10. Kitchen Slate Reminder.

Ten Projects for Indoors

Here's How to Make It:

If you were able to buy the blackboard molding, begin by cutting 45° miters so the longest lengths of the pieces are 14 and 18" apart, respectively.

If you are working with strip molding, rather than blackboard molding, cut a rabbet along one edge, as shown in cross section A-A in Figure 5-10. When you have the frame sections cut, round the edges with a Surform tool, rasp, file, router or a shaper. Next, cut 45° miters so the longest lengths are 14 and 18" apart, respectively.

If you have a picture-framing device, it will help in the next step. But if you don't, take a little extra care as you fit, glue and nail the corners to assemble the frame. Be sure that the frame is *flat* as well as *square* before you leave the glue to dry on the assembly.

To make the chalk bin, cut all the pieces to size. Assemble the rear, bottom and front sections as shown in cross section B-B in Figure 5-10. Use glue and finishing nails, and be sure to check the squareness of this assembly as well. Fasten the two end pieces with glue and finishing nails, after the glued assembly has dried.

To assemble the reminder board, first fit the hardboard into the frame. Make a trial fit of the box to the frame. (See Figure 5-10, cross section B-B). With the box in place, draw a line on the hardboard at the top of the box. This line will be the border for the blackboard paint.

When you have the line drawn, remove the board, and apply several coats of blackboard paint to the line. You can get green board paint which has a less harsh look than flat black.

Drill the holes at a slight angle as indicated on the frame drawing and on cross section B-B in Figure 5-10, and put the three well-sanded dowels in place.

Sand the frames and box well, in preparation for paint or stain. If you plan to stain the unit, you should apply a coat of shellac or varnish over the stain. You can get matte or gloss varnish finishes to compliment your decorating sheme.

Fasten the painted hardboard board to the frame. First, be sure to predrill nail holes in the hardboard. You should use glue as well as finishing nails to hold the board in place.

Next, use small brads or wood screws and glue to fasten the bin in place. See cross section B-B (Figure 5-10) for the details.

The reminder blackboard can be mounted in a wall using conventional picture-hanging techniques, but that method is not too stable. You are better off using separate hooks and eyes on each side of the frame. It's a lot easier to write on the board when it is stable than when it hangs loosely. Use the dowels to hang such things as pot holders, keys or recipes.

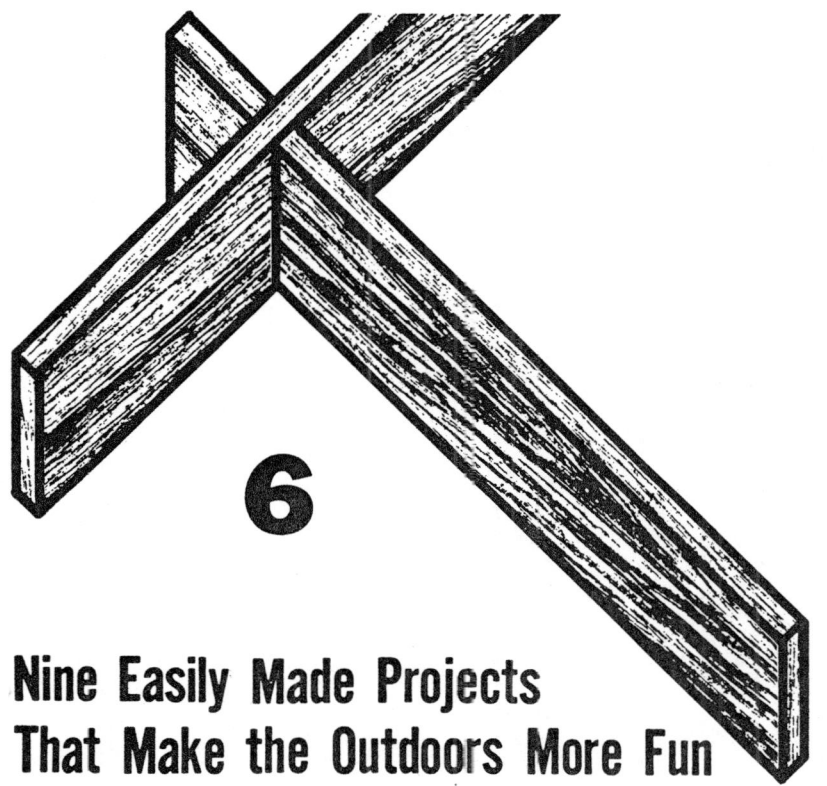

6

Nine Easily Made Projects
That Make the Outdoors More Fun

COMBINATION PICNIC BOX/TABLETOP

There are two things that can take the fun out of a picnic—ants and eating off a tablecloth laid on bumpy grass. There isn't anything we can do about the ants, but we can solve the bumpy table problem with this box. And we can solve the problem of what to do with all of the dishes and cutlery that must be carried. Everything can be stored right in this multipurpose picnic project.

Here's What You'll Need:

- Covers—2 pcs ¼ × 10 × 20 plywood (.6 × 25.4 × 50.8)
- Sides—4 pcs 1 × 3 × 20 (2.5 × 7.6 × 50.8)
- Ends—4 pcs 1 × 3 × 8½ (2.5 × 7.6 × 21.6)
- Stiffeners—2 pcs ¼ × 2½ × 9 plywood (.6 × 6.3 × 22.9)
- 1 continuous hinge 18 (45.7) long
- 2 valise locks with screws to fit
- 1 small garage door type handle with screws to fit
- Lock strips 2 pcs $^{1}/_{16}$ × ½ × 6 soft steel with 4-½ × 3 RH woodscrews (.15 × 1.3 × 15.2)

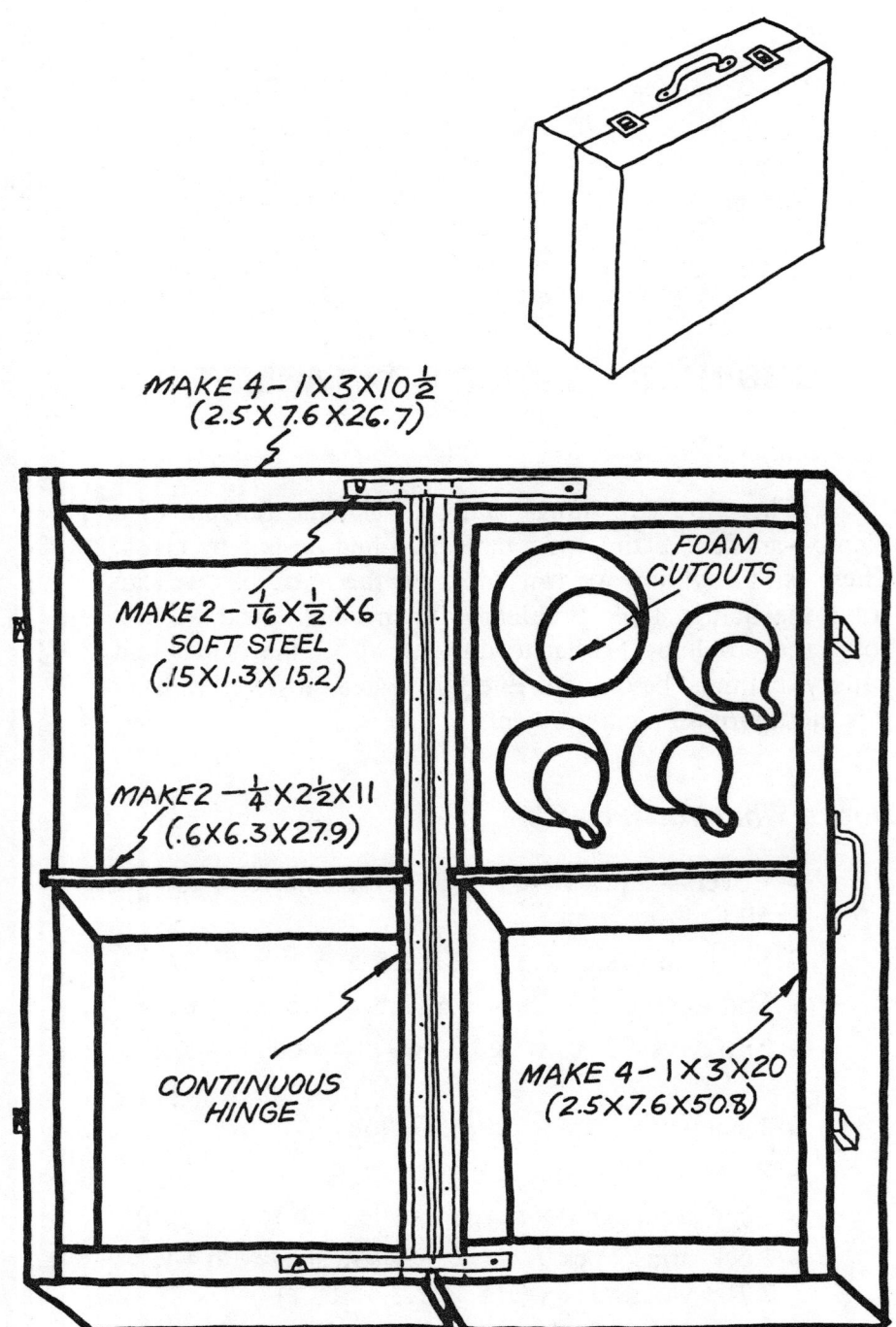

Figure 6-1. Combination Picnic Box/Tabletop.

Nine Easily Made Outdoor Projects 157

- 2 pcs polyfoam ½ to 1 × 8½ × 18½ (1.3 to 2.5 × 21.6 × 47)
- 2 pcs polyfoam 1½ to 2 × 8½ × 18½ (3.7 to 5.1 × 21.6 × 47)
- Finishing nails, glue, paint or stain and varnish

Here's How to Make It:

Cut the plywood and side pieces to size. In the center of each sidepiece, cut a ¼" groove ¼" deep. Cut the end pieces to size. Assemble the box by gluing and nailing the side pieces to the plywood with the slots facing each other. Before the glue sets, set in the end pieces and glue and nail in place. Drive a few nails across the side pieces into the ends. Be sure to glue the ends and side pieces, too. Clamp the glued assembly in place to assure a square and straight box.

When the glue has set, insert and glue the stiffeners in place. When they are positioned correctly, the bottoms of the stiffeners will be glued directly to the covers, and will remain slightly below the top edges.

Clean and smooth all edges and surfaces. Next, mount the hinge on both halves of the box. If necessary, recess one side piece so that the box closes completely. Look at any door to a room and you'll see what we mean.

Make up the lock strip by drilling two holes ¼" from each end of steel strips. At one end of each, file a "V" shaped opening into the hole, as shown in Figure 6-1.

Position the lock strips so that they, too, will be recessed when the box is closed. It will be necessary to recess only the side with the pivots. Allow the screws to protrude, but recess the opposite end piece to provide the needed clearance when the box is closed. Note that the steel straps are offset from the center so that you can do this.

Mount the carrying handle and the valise locks and then test for smooth operation. If any points bind, you can clear them with a file or some sandpaper.

Cut the thinner foam to fit in the bottom of each section of the box. Glue the sheets of trimmed foam in place in both halves of the box.

Next you can use the thicker foam to make permanent stacking for your picnic items or you can simply pack what you want for each picnic and insulate everything against damage and rattle by packing foam in the spaces. We suggest that whichever way you go, use plastic (not china) plates and cups, and that you carry aluminum cooking pots because they are the lightest.

If you want to make permanent foam mountings, first prepare templates of the stacked items that will be stored in each section and cut out openings in the thicker foam to accommodate them. When you have all the foam pieces cut to shape, and you are sure that they fit and hold the items in place snugly, you can join them with glue, and then glue the assemblies in place in the box.

Sand and finish the box with either stain and varnish or a coat of paint.

You can turn the box upside down, after you have removed all the dishes, and use it as a table right on the ground. Or, you can lay it on a camp chair to insure that you will not have to share your lunch with the ants.

COMPOST COLLECTOR

It's tempting to grow some of your own food. Unfortunately, the cost to produce your own vegetables can often amount to as much as you pay for the food you buy in a store— if you account for all expenses, including your own labor. Perhaps one of the biggest costs is that of fertilizer, whether it's organic or chemical in origin. But you can make your own compost from much of what you now pay the garbage man to haul away. To do this you need a collector, and that's what you can build if you follow these instructions.

Compost is made of organic waste from the kitchen and the garden laid in layers in your collector. The process of making it useable in the garden is aided by the addition of readily available enzymes. After a season of bacterial activity, you will have a back yard fertilizer plant that will make better plant food than you can buy. And . . . the price is right!

For details on just how to make the best compost, check in any good gardening book. For information on how to make the best compost collector, read on.

Here's What You'll Need:

- Front—2 pcs ¾ × 12 × 48 exterior plywood (1.9 × 30.5 × 121.9)
- Rear—1 pc ¾ × 24 × 48 exterior plywood (1.9 × 61 × 121.9)
- Sides—2 pcs ¾ × 24 × 48 exterior plywood (1.9 × 61 × 121.9)
- Corner posts—2 pcs 2 × 4 × 24 (5.1 × 10.2 × 61)

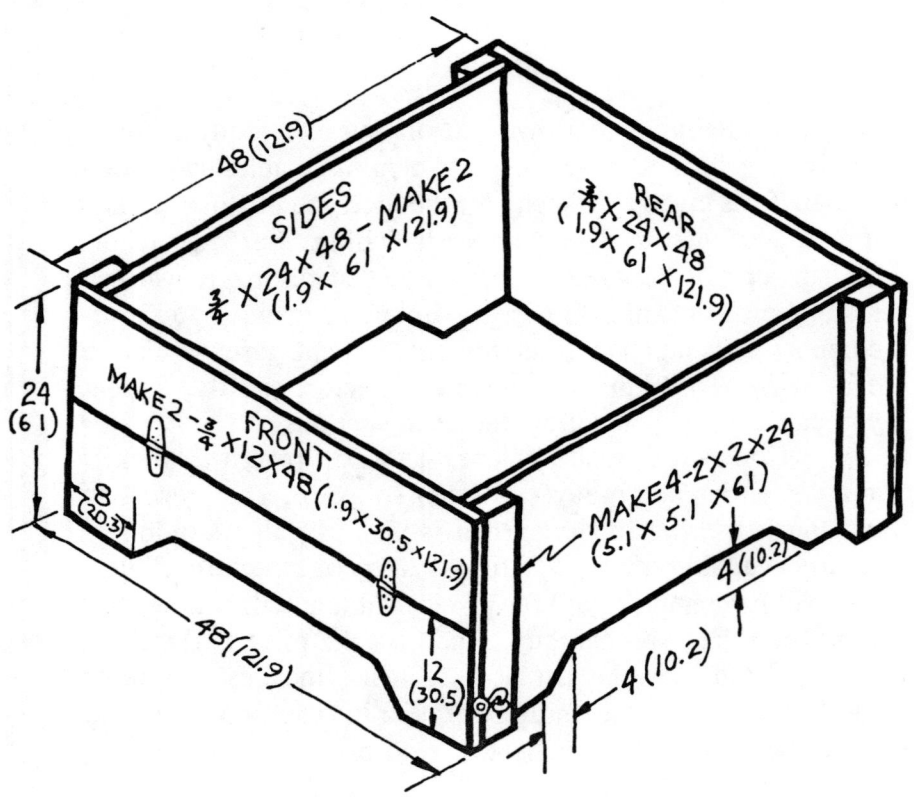

Figure 6-2. Compost Collector.

Nine Easily Made Outdoor Projects 161

- Aluminum or galvanized nails
- 1 pair 3″ strap hinges, galvanized (7.6)
- 2 hooks and eyes

The wood you use must be able to withstand nature. Redwood, cedar, cypress and teak will take whatever is dished out, but these woods are expensive. You can get just about as much mileage from wood that has been treated with any of the wood preservatives made from pentachlorophenol. Lumber can be bought pretreated, or you can do the job yourself. If you choose to treat the wood yourself, be very careful not to get the material on your skin. Be especially careful to protect your eyes when you work with wood preservatives. If you prefer it, you can simply coat the wood with creosote or paint after assembly. (Not both!)

Here's How to Make It:

Cut all pieces to size, and then lay out the drainage cutouts on the front piece and the two sides. There is no drainage cutout on the rear piece. Cut the drainage openings and then smooth all edges.

Nail the vertical supports at the ends of each of the two sides. Do your nailing from the inside into the support. Fasten the rear piece by nailing into both of the 2 × 4's (5.1 × 10.2) and into the end boards for greater strength.

Nail the upper front piece (without cutout) to the upper edge of the end pieces. Nail through the front piece into the 2 × 4's (5.1 × 10.2).

Attach the hinges to the upper front piece with galvanized or brass screws and then attach the notched lower piece to the hinges. Next, install the hooks and eyes on either side of the hinged lower front piece. When the compost collector is in use, you will unhook the lower section in order to scoop out the fertilizer that is ready to use. Because the collector is loaded from the top and emptied from the bottom, you will have a complete natural cycle taking place as the organic matter you load turns to rich plant food at the bottom.

THE JET BOAT

Here's a project that's a lot of fun for everyone to use. You can make it and just enjoy tinkering with different "fuel" mixtures or hull design changes to get maximum speed, or you can build a few of them and challenge your friends to a race in everything from a bathtub to a local pond.

Here's What You'll Need:

- Hull—1 pc ½ × 4 × 10 balsa or 2 pcs ¼ × 4 × 10 (1.3 × 10.2 × 25.4)
- Keel—1 pc ⅛ × ¾ × 8 balsa or pine (.3 × 1.8 × 20.3)
- Cradle—scraps of soft ½" wood (1.3)
- Jet—plastic squeeze bottle
- Plastic tubing
- Glue
- Some Alka-Seltzer tablets

Here's How to Make It:

Cut the hull to size. If you are using two ¼" pieces, cut them both to size and glue them together.

Draw lines down the middle of the top as well as the underside of the hull. Cut the keel and glue it in place, using one center line as a guide.

Make a cradle to suit the plastic power bottle you have selected and glue it in place. If the bottom has little or no neck,

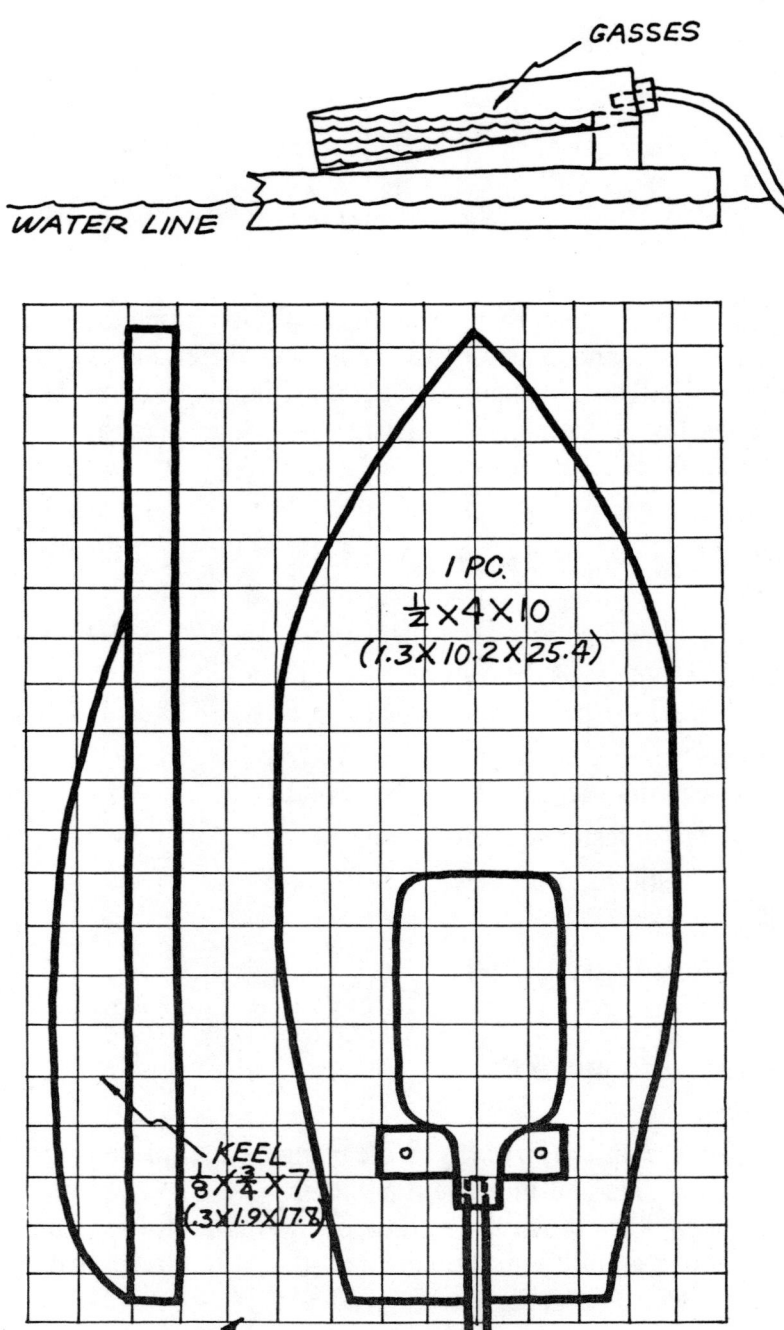

Figure 6-3. The Jet Boat.

Nine Easily Made Outdoor Projects

it will have to tilt as shown in Figure 6-3. A bottle with a neck smaller than the diameter of the bottle can lie almost flat on the top of the hull. The idea is to be able to have water in the bottle, but have the outlet for the jet hose above the water level. See Figure 6-3.

Attach the exhaust tube to the nozzle on the squeeze bottle and position it so that the other end will be below the waterline and pointing straight aft of the hull. You can hold the bottle in place with a rubber band. If you use flexible tubing, another band can be used to keep the jet end of the tube over the side.

Sand and paint or varnish the hull.

To get under way, put enough water in the bottle so that it will be about half full, yet leave the hose connection above the water in the bottle when it is positioned on deck. Break up an Alka-Seltzer tablet and drop it in the bottle. Secure the cap and hose quickly and put the boat in the water. The gas generated by the tablet and the water in the bottle will move the boat forward.

You can experiment with different water and seltzer mixtures for maximum speed, and the course of the boat can be changed by repositioning the jet end of the tube in the water.

PATHWAY LAMP

Here's a lamp that you can use to light a driveway, footpath, or just as an accent for your plantings. It can be set up with permanent outside wiring, or you can make it a portable to light up anything you want with the aid of an outdoor extension cord.

We have not included any electrical details, or specified any type of electrical fixture. This lamp is adaptable to just about anything you have around. But, we would like to suggest that you use the new low-voltage power system with this lamp. It's to be used outside, and when you have a transformer between you and ground, such as you have in the low-voltage systems, you will greatly reduce the possibility of an electric shock.

If you are going to have several of them on one line, such as you might on an outside pathway, be sure to wire them in parallel, not in series.

Here's What You'll Need:

- Top A—2 pcs 1 × 4 × 16 (2.5 × 10.2 × 40.6)
  B—2 pcs 1 × 4 × 16 (2.5 × 10.2 × 40.6)
  C—2 pcs 1 × 2 × 8 (2.5 × 5.1 × 20.3)
- Legs D—4 pcs 1 × 2 × 18 (2.5 × 5.1 × 45.7)
- Plastic—4 pcs ⅛ × 12 × 12 (.3 × 30.5 × 30.5)
- Plastic top—1 pc ⅛ × 9 × 16 (.3 × 22.9 × 40.6)

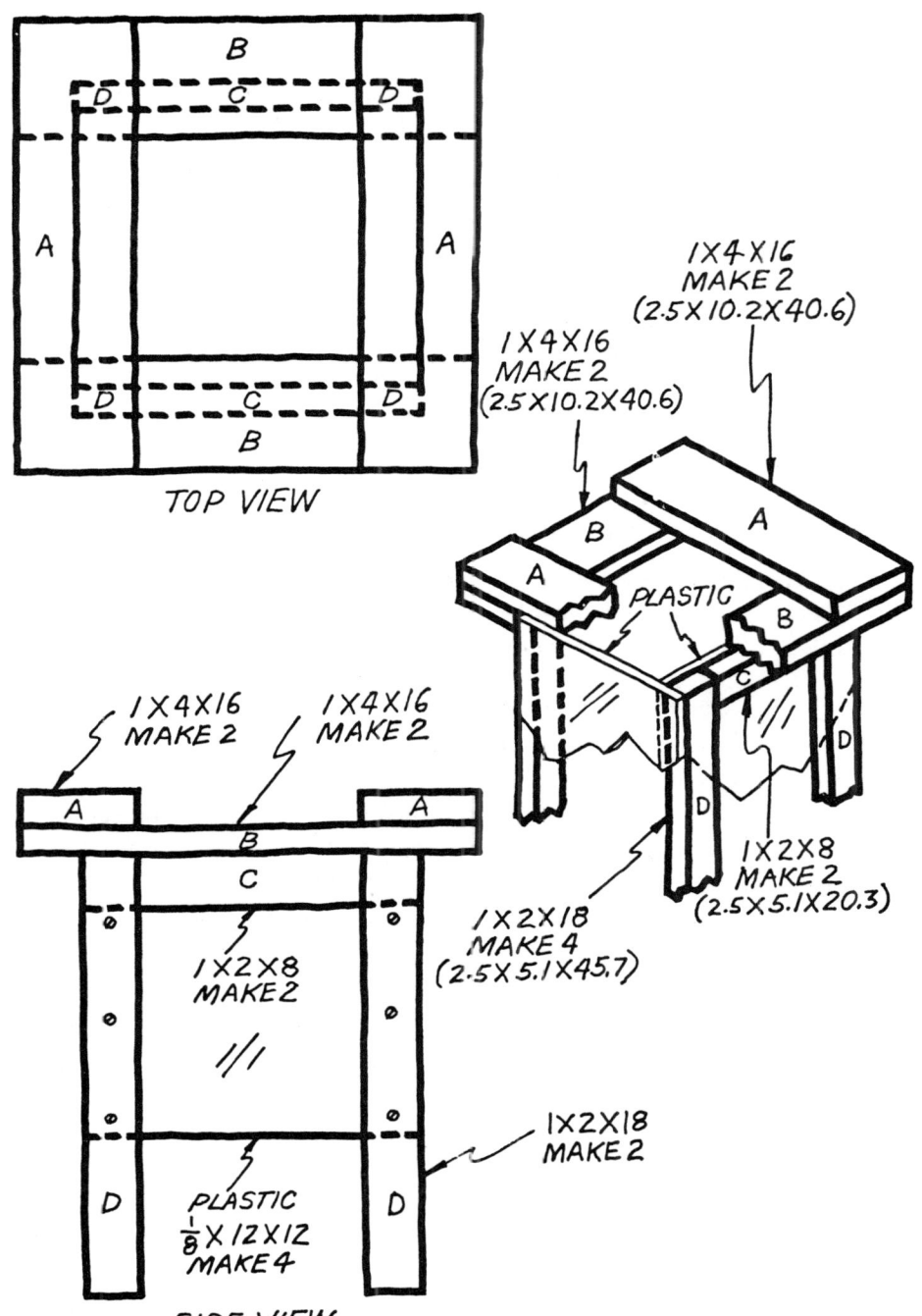

Figure 6-4. Pathway Lamp.

- Nails, small round head screws—1/2-3" will do nicely.
- Suitable electrical fixture and wiring

Here's How to Make It:

Cut all pieces to size and label them with very light pencil marks. Smooth all edges, ends and surfaces before you begin assembly.

NOTE: If you expect to finish the lamp with a stain or paint, do this before assembly or the plastic coverings will prevent covering all the wood. On the other hand, if you intend to leave the wood alone, then ignore this note.

Make two sides first.

Place the plastic atop the faces of the two D pieces.

Locate and drill three equidistant holes for the small screws in the plastic. (Drill the holes a bit larger than the screw size.) Fasten them to the flat sides of D. Repeat this for the opposite side.

Locate and drill holes for the 3rd and 4th plastic walls so that they serve to make a kind of plastic box with the four D pieces at the corners.

Make up wood pieces A and B as shown in Figure 6-4. Nail together. Turn upside down. Place newly made plastic box upside down and centered on the A and B block. Set in the two locking pieces labeled C. Clamp C to B, remove the plastic box and fasten C to B permanently.

The remaining plastic piece is now fastened atop B between the two A pieces.

What have we so far? A plastic box to surround the lamp bulb and a decorative cover to be somewhat weather-

Nine Easily Made Outdoor Projects

proof and clear to allow light through and which can be lifted off when needed.

Lamps and sockets can be hung from the top unit or mounted on a block of wood which would fit at the bottom of the plastic walls between the *D*. corners.

If finishing with a stain, wait until the stain is dry, when cover with a clear polyurethane varnish to protect the wood from the elements. For a solid color, apply a coat of primer or undercoat, and complete the job with a porch and deck paint.

LAWN CHAIR

When we were kids, everybody called them Adirondack chairs. These chairs are still seen in furniture stores, but it's been a long time since anyone has used that name. They seem to be called different names by different manufacturers, but to us they will still be Adirondack chairs. There is only one difference between ours and the oldie; the back and seat of ours is made of solid wood and the original was made of slats. Actually ours is more comfortable because of the solid construction.

Here's What You'll Need:

- Back—1 pc ¾ × 22 × 36 exterior plywood (1.9 × 55.9 × 91.4)
- Seat—1 pc ¾ × 18 × 22 exterior plywood (1.9 × 45.7 × 55.9)
- Front legs—2 pcs 1 × 4 × 22 (2.5 × 10.2 × 55.9)
- Rear legs—2 pcs 1 × 5 × 40 (2.5 × 12.7 × 101.6)
- Arms—2 pcs 1 × 8 × 28 (2.5 × 20.3 × 71.1)
- Braces—2 pcs 1 × 4 × 8 (2.5 × 10.2 × 20.3)
- Top rear support—1 pc 1 × 4 × 25 (2.5 × 10.2 × 63.5)
- Lower rear support—1 pc 1 × 4 × 22 (2.5 × 10.2 × 55.9)
- Front support—1 pc 1 × 6 × 22 (2.5 × 15.2 × 55.9)

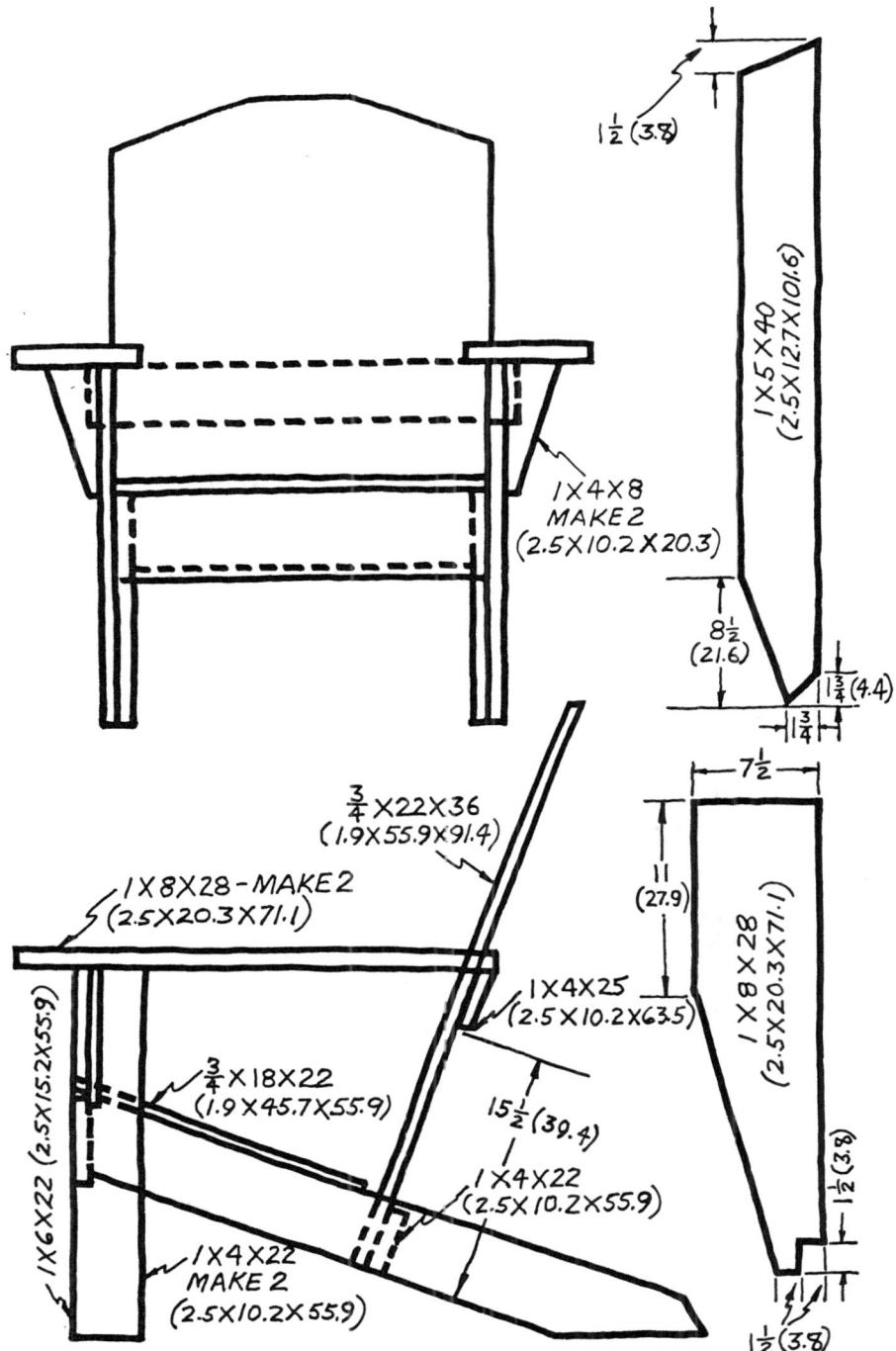

Figure 6-5. Lawn Chair.

- Flat head wood screws—1 ½-10 galvanized or brass
- Paint

Here's How to Make It:

If you plan to leave the chair outdoors a lot, you should make it from a rot-resistant wood such as redwood. You can also use cedar, cypress or any pressure-treated lumber.

Cut all pieces to size, and do all the cutouts. We have left the top edge of the back of the chair plain, but you can do anything you want with it. Think of some embellishment that will be in keeping with a dominant theme outside your house.

Clean up all edges and surfaces with a plane, a file and sandpaper.

Fasten the rear supports to the back of the seat. Be sure that all parts are square.

Lay out one set of legs against a framing square or against some boards positioned as a right triangle. Place the legs in position so that the front leg is vertical.

Clamp the two legs together.

Repeat the process for the other side, making sure that the position of the two legs is reversed, thus making a pair.

Fasten the parts of the leg sets with only one screw, to allow for late adjustments if needed.

Drill preparatory holes in the seat sides before setting the seat into place as shown in Figure 6-5.

Fasten the seat into place along the top of the slant legs.

Allowing about ¾" space behind the seat, set the back into place so that it is at a right angle to the slant leg. Fasten lightly into place. Use screws in the back and also in the lower rear support.

Lay the arms into place atop the vertical leg and the

Nine Easily Made Outdoor Projects

rear resting on the upper rear support. Fasten both into place so that they are approximately horizontal, although this is not really critical.

Set the braces into place. Now do all your permanent fastening using screws and a strong glue, while clamping the entire chair together into perfect position.

When the glue is dry, remove clamps, sand all surfaces and slightly chamfer all edges to eliminate the possibility of splinters.

Leave natural, or paint with a good undercoat followed by one or two coats of porch and deck paint. You can also finish with a clear polyurethane finish.

PICNIC SALAD SET

You can't have a picnic without a salad, and you can't serve a picnic salad with just any old spoon and fork. When you make this set, you will have solved the salad tossing problem and you will have done more than just cut out a few shapes. This project is actually a basic exercise in woodcarving. You will have to use gouges and chisels—tools that are used nowhere else in this book. If you haven't used similar tools, we suggest that you do a little practicing with them on some hardwood scraps before you dig into this project. Try some simple gouging to produce the bowl-like effect we have shown in the shape of the spoon and fork. (See Figure 6-6). When you feel confident with the tools and the wood, go ahead with the set.

Here's What You'll Need:

- 2 pieces of ¾ × 4 × 14½ (1.9 × 10.2 × 36.8) finished size ash, oak, mahogany, walnut or teak.

Here's How to Make It:

Do *not* cut the pieces to shape yet. The scoops should be carved while the wood is intact. You will need the strength of the entire blank while working with the gouges.

Lay out the face of the implements as though both are to be spoons. Clamp the wood in a vise by the waste, and

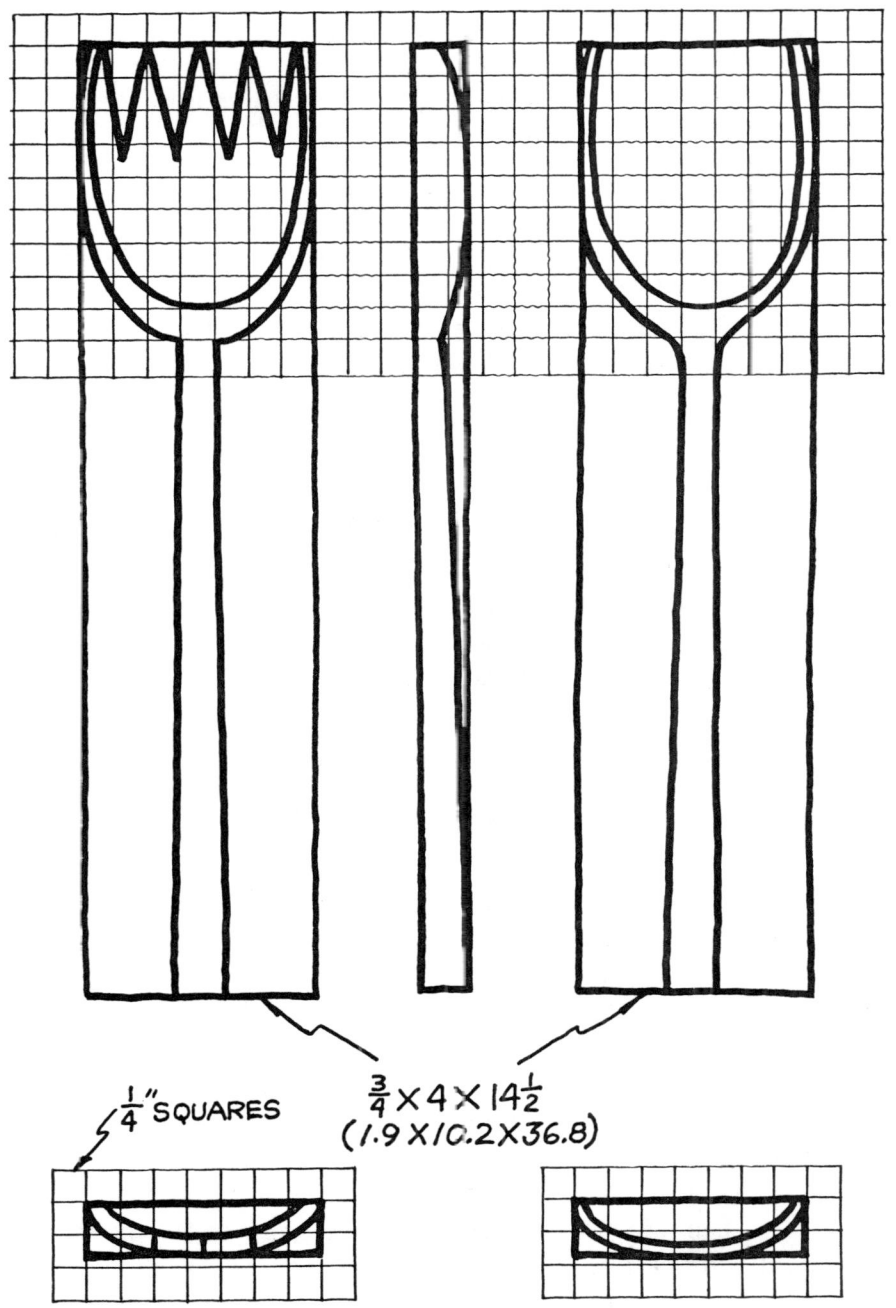

Figure 6-6. Picnic Salad Set.

begin carving the scoops. Here are a few important hints to follow when using chisels and gouges:

1. Always keep both hands *behind* the cutting edge.
2. Always work the chisel or gouge *away* from your body.
3. When using a chisel or gouge to remove wood, work with the bevel *down*.
4. For this project, the best tools to use are gouges with curved cross sections with the bevel on the convex side of the curve.
5. Take your time; you can't replace a gouged-out mistake.
6. Keep tools very sharp. Whetting them every 15 minutes during steady work is not too often. Most problems are caused by dull edges.
7. As you work closer to the finished edges, work more slowly and remove smaller pieces of wood.

With these points in mind, and with a little practice you should have very little difficulty turning out a beautiful set of salad servers. Now, on to the steps required to finish the job.

After you have gouged the two shapes, cut out the blanks with a coping saw or power jig saw. Now clamp the shapes with the back facing up and carve the backs to conform to the shape you just gouged out. You can do this with a rasp, or a surface forming tool and a file. When the scoops have been properly shaped, do a thorough finishing job with progressively finer grades of sandpaper until you have a perfectly smooth finish. Work with the grain whenever you can.

Cut the fork tines with a jeweler's saw or a coping saw fitted with a fine-tooth blade. The tine edges should be rounded, but do not use anything as bulky and potentially

Nine Easily Made Outdoor Projects

damaging as a file. Strips of sandpaper used as you would use a rag to shine a shoe will do the job.

When you have the shape and finish you want, all that is required is a coating of vegetable oil. When the oil soaks in, you will have a nice finish that will be safe for your food.

If you want to dress up this set a bit, you might consider attaching a leather thong to the end of each handle. Just drill a hole large enough to accommodate the thong through the ends of the handles. Thread the thong through and tie a snug square knot.

OLD-FASHIONED WAGON RACER

When we made racers as kids, oranges still came in crates—not cardboard boxes. There was hardly a fruit store owner who wasn't happy to have kids raid his yard for wood. But today it's another story. There is very little scrap wood around, at least the kind that can be used to make a good racer or delivery cart. But there is now first-rate plywood, and that's what this project uses. Wheels for the cart can be bought or salvaged from an old baby carriage or someone else's racer. They're usually not too hard to find.

Here's What You'll Need:

- Main base—1 pc ¾ × 21 × 60 plywood (1.8 × 53.3 × 152.4)
- Axle hangers—2 pcs 2 × 4 × 22 (5.1 × 10.2 × 55.9)
- Sides—2 pcs ¾ × 12 × 24 plywood (1.9 × 30.5 × 61)
- Back—1 pc ¾ × 11½ × 22 plywood (1.9 × 29.1 × 55.9)
- Wheels—4 pcs 10" dia. with 30" axles to match (25.4 dia. wheels with 76.2 axles to match)
- Axle holders—8 screw eyes that fit loosely over axles
- 4 cotter pins for axles
- 8 washers to fit axle on either sides of each wheel
- Carriage bolt ⅜—4 with 4 washers (1.9 × 10.2)
- Steering rings—2 screw eyes

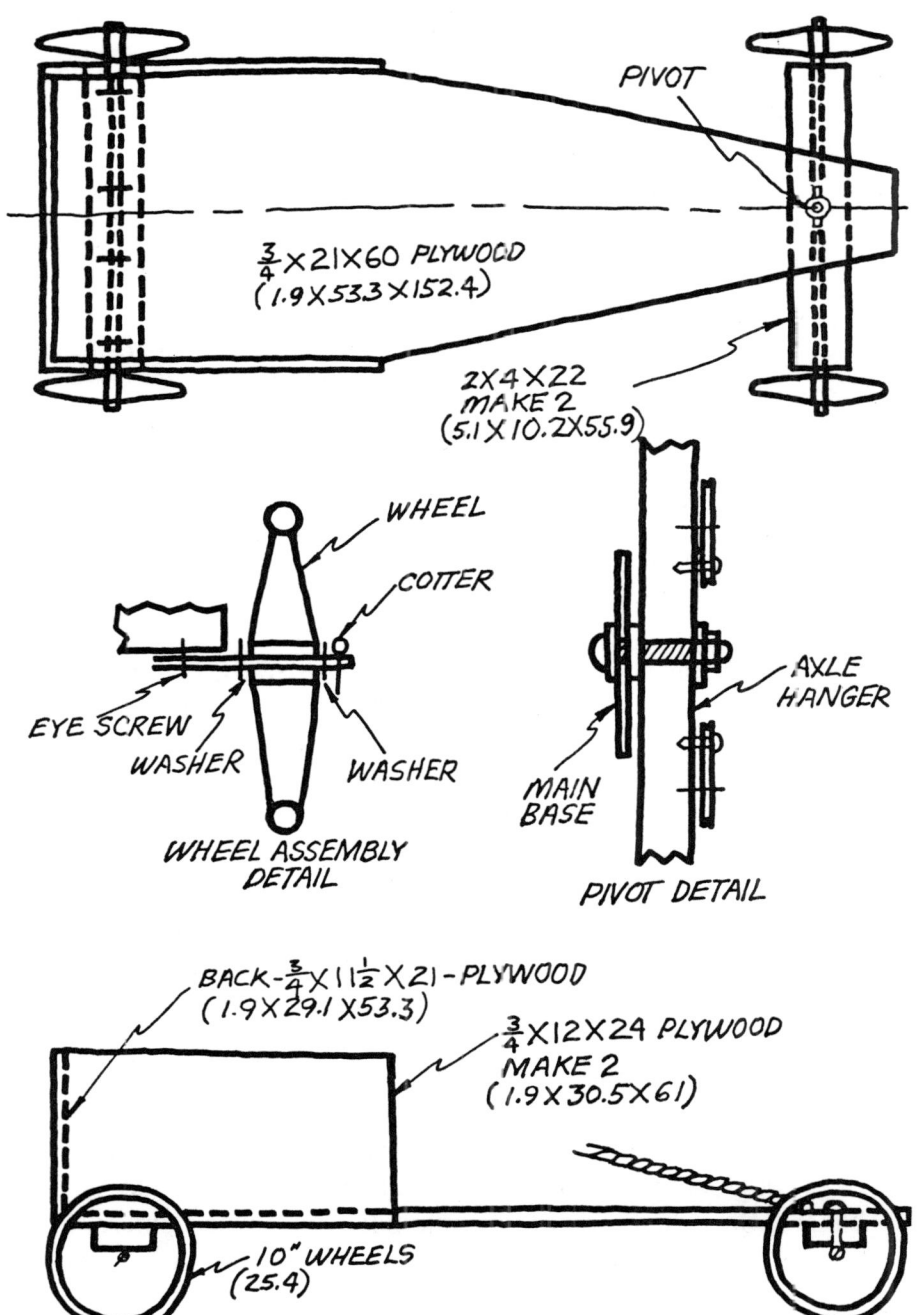

Figure 6-7. Old-Fashioned Wagon Racer.

Here's How to Make It:

Before you begin any of the woodwork, get the wheels and axles. If you are unable to find parts of the size we suggest, you can change the measurements to suit. But you should have this squared away before you cut any expensive wood. May we suggest that you try to find wheels and axles before you buy a set. There is always someone with an old baby carriage rusting in a garage, or a retired kid's wagon that can be stripped. Maybe we are making more of finding wheels than we should, but when we were kids, this was *the* challenge. A good set of wheels to a 10-year-old meant as much as a good set of wheels seems to mean to a teen-age car driver today.

If the axle you find isn't already drilled for cotter pins on each end, do it now. See Figure 6-7 for details of the wheel assembly.

Now you're ready to cut all pieces to size. Drill a ⅜" hole 5" from the front end of the base. This will hold the carriage bolt later.

Assemble the rest of the cab. Note that the sides are fastened on the outside and the back, and that the back sits inside and on top of the base. To add a sleek touch, and possibly some comfort, you can position the back at a slant, rather than vertically as we have shown it.

Lay out the rear axle hanger as shown in Figure 6-7. Make sure that you position the hanger at a perfect right angle to the center line of the base. Mount the axle hanger by nailing or driving screws from the inside of the cart down into the hanger. Sink the heads and fill the holes with wood putty. If you nail from the underside, you might have a few nail points in an uncomfortable place for the driver.

Line up the screw eyes on the rear axle hanger. Set one

at each end, 1″ from the ends. The other two are positioned 7″ from the first. Test the position of the eyes by sliding the axle in place. It need not be loose, but it shouldn't bind.

Before you mount the front axle hanger on the base, mount the axle on the hanger. This is mounted in essentially the same fashion as the rear axle, except that it must be cut so there are a few inches in the middle for the pivot bolt. You can cut out a 2 or 3″ section with a hack saw. It will be necessary to drill holes at each end of the axle and to drive screws through the holes into the hangers to keep the axle in place. Use the screw eyes in the same way described for the rear axle.

Drill a hole through the front axle hanger and fasten the assembly to the base with a bolt, nut and washers as shown in Figure 6-7. If you can get a lock nut, you will prevent the front wheel assembly from coming off without having to tighten it so much that the wheels are difficult to turn.

Mount the wheels as shown in Figure 6-7. Be sure to use washers on both sides of the wheel to assure free turning.

This cart can be steered by feet, but it's a good idea to include a rope for pulling. Mount screw eyes at each end of the front axle hanger and attach a rope of a convenient length.

No go-cart is complete without a flashy coat of paint and a number. You might even give it a racing stripe, just like a sports car.

HOUSE NUMBER SIGNBOARD

Some people, we think, intentionally hide the number of their house. Perhaps they are trying to duck a bill collector or a bothersome relative. But for those who would like to have friends find them, this number signboard is just the thing.

Here's What You'll Need:

- Sign—1 pc 1 × 8 × 18 (2.5 × 20.3 × 45.7)
- Roof sides—2 pcs ½ × 8 × 18 (1.3 × 20.3 × 45.7)
- Roof ends—2 pcs ½ × 8 × 8 (1.3 × 20.3 × 20.3)
- Top—1 pc ½ × 5 × 18 (1.3 × 12.7 × 45.7)
- Post—1 pc 4 × 4 × 6' (Cedar, redwood, cypress, or treated fir (10.2 × 10.2 × 182.8)
- 2 waterproof electrical sockets with bulbs
- 2-⅛" pipe nipples, or 2-⅛" pipe flanges to hold socket
- Wire (to suit, see text)
- Aluminum nails, or non-rusting screws
- Outdoor varnish or paint
- Numbers, as needed

Here's How to Make It:

Cut all pieces to size.
Drill ⅜" holes in the end pieces. Fasten the sides and ends to the top, to form the light canopy. Use nails and glue.

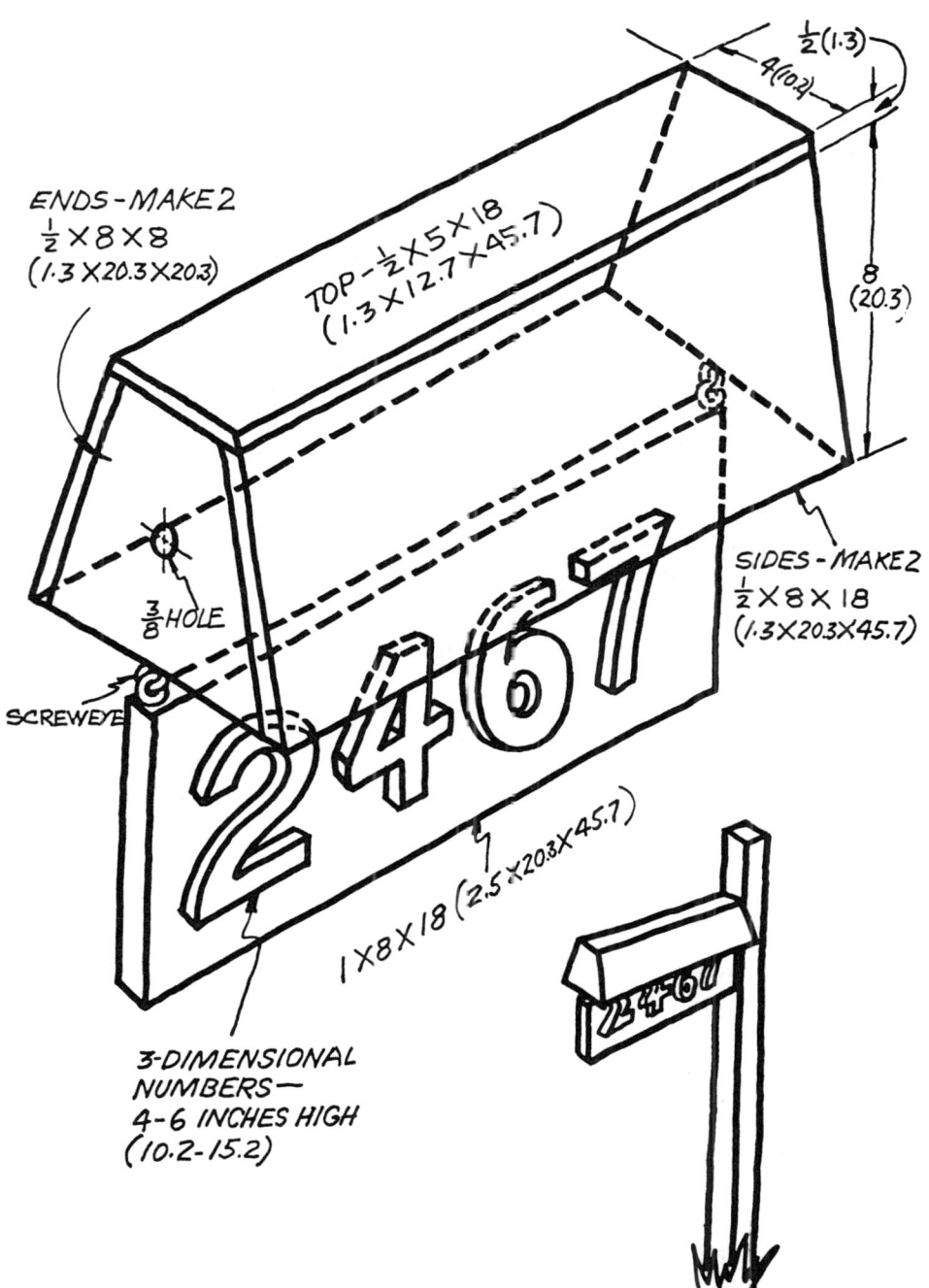

Figure 6-8. House Number Signboard.

Plane and sand all edges and surfaces. Paint the inside with several coats of glossy white paint.

You are now ready to fasten the lamp sockets inside the canopy. But, before you do this, be sure to check your local electrical codes to make sure that the job will meet outdoor standards. It may be necessary to run a special underground cable to the house for power and switch control. Be sure that you meet the codes—not only to comply with the law, but to make sure that you don't start an electrical fire or electrocute someone.

Because there are so many different types of electrical fixtures, we can't tell you how to mount the sockets. However, mounting steps are usually included with the fixtures you buy, and many of them are quite easy to install.

Attach one end of the lamp canopy to the sign post. Use wood screws and some waterproof glue. Position the assembly so that when the board is hung under it, the numbers can be seen from either direction. To make this a sturdy installation, you should sink the post in some concrete which you have poured in a 1' hole with a diameter that is about the width of a shovel blade.

If underground wiring is to be installed, be sure that you have it in place before you sink the post.

Mount the three-dimensional numbers on both sides of the signboard by following the manufacturer's directions. But if all that will hold them is some adhesive backing, it's best to add some holding power in the form of one or two small brass screws in each number. Heat and cold does nasty things to most of the adhesives that are made for this purpose. If you're going to paint the signboard, do it before you attach the numbers. But be sure that the numbers stand out in strong contrast to the background. Paint the canopy and then, using hooks and eyes, attach the board to the canopy, as shown.

GARDEN CADDY

Garden tools are like wire coat hangers. Grab for one and you'll have no trouble, but as soon as you must handle two or more, you have a Chinese puzzle. This project won't solve your coat hanger problems, but it will sure make gardening a lot easier. You can use the garden caddy to carry tools to and from the garden and to store everything in one convenient place.

And to solve your garage storage space problem, we designed this handy tool to hang vertically against a wall. It sticks out from the wall only a little over 1'. We've even included an automatic third leg pivot near the handle. Now you really have no excuse not to get out there and do a job.

Here's What You'll Need:

- Back—1 pc ¼ × 30 × 60 perforated hardboard (tempered) (.6 × 76.2 × 152.4)
- Frame sides—2 pcs 2 × 2 × 60 (5.1 × 5.1 × 152.4)
- Frame back—1 pc 2 × 2 × 27 (5.1 × 5.1 × 68.6)
- Frame bottom—1 pc 1 × 7½ × 33½ (2.5 × 19 × 85.1)
- Box front—1 pc 1 × 7½ × 31½ (2.5 × 19.1 × 80)
- Wheel supports—2 pcs 1 × 6¾ × 10½ (2.5 × 17.1 × 26.7)
- Hinge support—1 pc 1 × 2 × 10 (2.5 × 5.1 × 25.4)
- Handles—2 heavy-duty garage door pulls
- Wheels—1 pr 7" diameter (18)

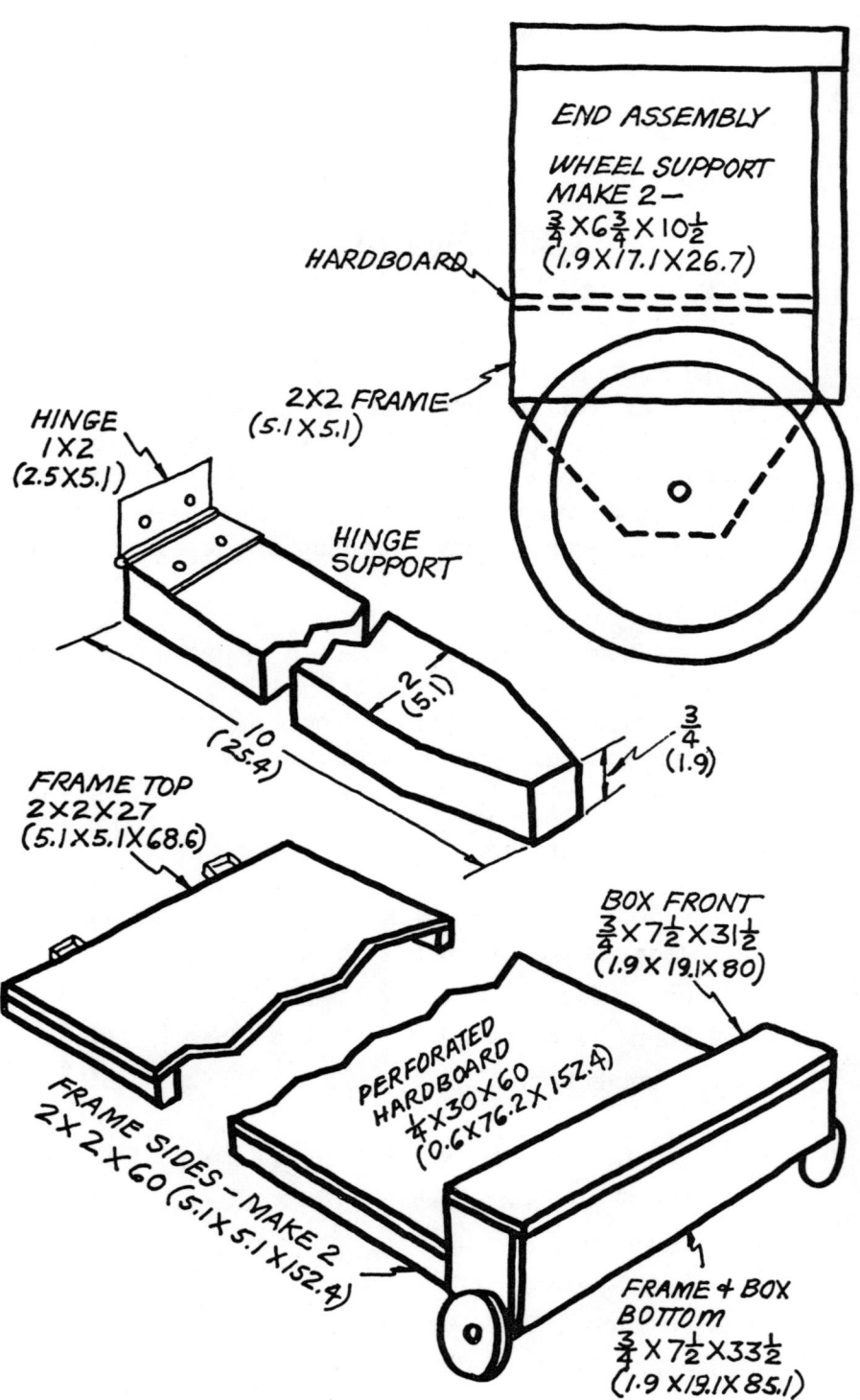

Figure 6-9. Garden Caddy.

Nine Easily Made Outdoor Projects

- Axle—to match above wheels × 36″ long (91.4)
- Waterproof glue, screws, nails, friction nuts, exterior varnish or paint, hinge, washers, and assorted perforated hardboard accessories holders

Here's How to Make It:

Begin by cutting all pieces to size and shape. Fasten the frame sides and top to the pegboard with 1 ¼-9 round-head screws and washers. It's best to space the screws every 6 to 8″.

Drill holes in the wheel supports for the axles. To assure alignment, tack or clamp the two supports together and drill them simultaneously.

Assemble the bottom box by using the frame bottom, box top and wheel supports. Use nails or screws and waterproof glue. When the box has been made, slide it on the bottom of the pegboard and fasten it securely with screws.

Slide the axle in place, and slip a few washers on at both ends. The washers will protect the wood from the wheel. Mount a wheel on each end of the axle, position a washer after each wheel and secure the assembly with the press-on friction nuts.

Next, you should attach the handles on the frame top. These should be positioned wherever they are most comfortable.

After you have attached a hinge at the end of the dropleg, locate a spot near the top in the center of the pegboard. Fasten the hinge so that it lies flat when the caddy is standing or hanging vertically, and drops down when it is lowered.

Next, finish all the surfaces with anything that will provide good protection—exterior paint, spar varnish or shellac.

Locate the pegboard holders to suit the tools you will store and use with the caddy.

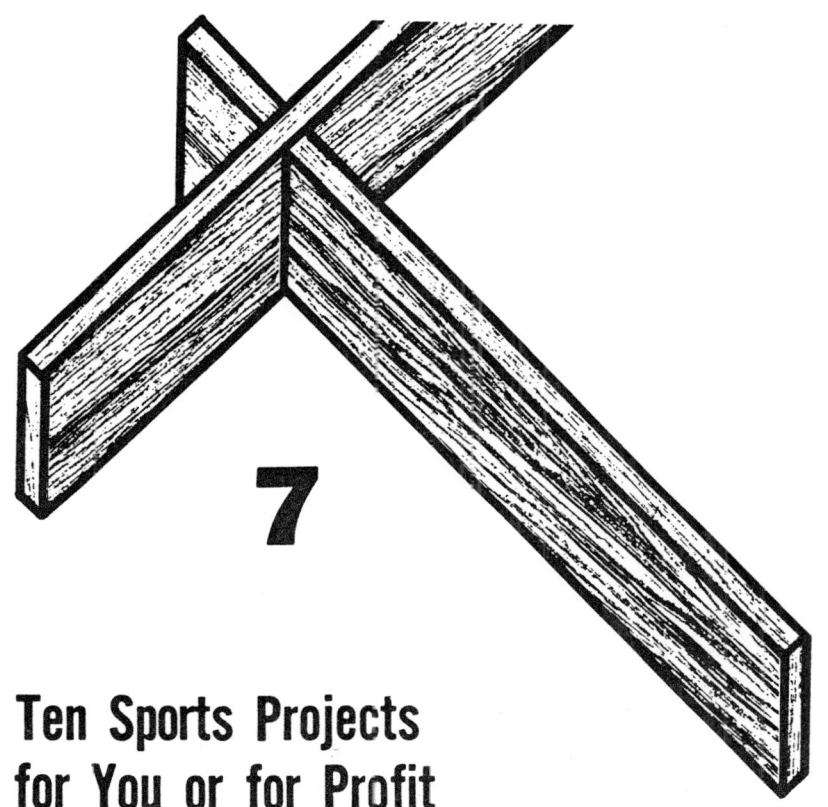

7

Ten Sports Projects for You or for Profit

BEACH CLOGS

Why pay $10 or more for a pair of clogs when you can make your own for much less money. And you can probably do a better job when it comes to shaping and styling. You can even choose any color strap you want—something you can't do if you buy a pair of beach clogs.

Here's What You'll Need:

- 2 pcs—1⅜ × 6 × 12 clear pine, birch or maple (3.5 × 15.2 × 30.5)
- 2 pcs of canvas webbing 3 × 12 (7.6 × 30.5)
- 16 upholstery tacks
- 1 quart of boiled linseed oil

NOTE: If you can't find a piece of wood 1⅜" thick, buy a couple of pieces that can be glued together to give approximately the same thickness.

Here's How to Make Them:

Begin by making a template of your foot on a piece of paper. You will want to have your full weight on the paper as

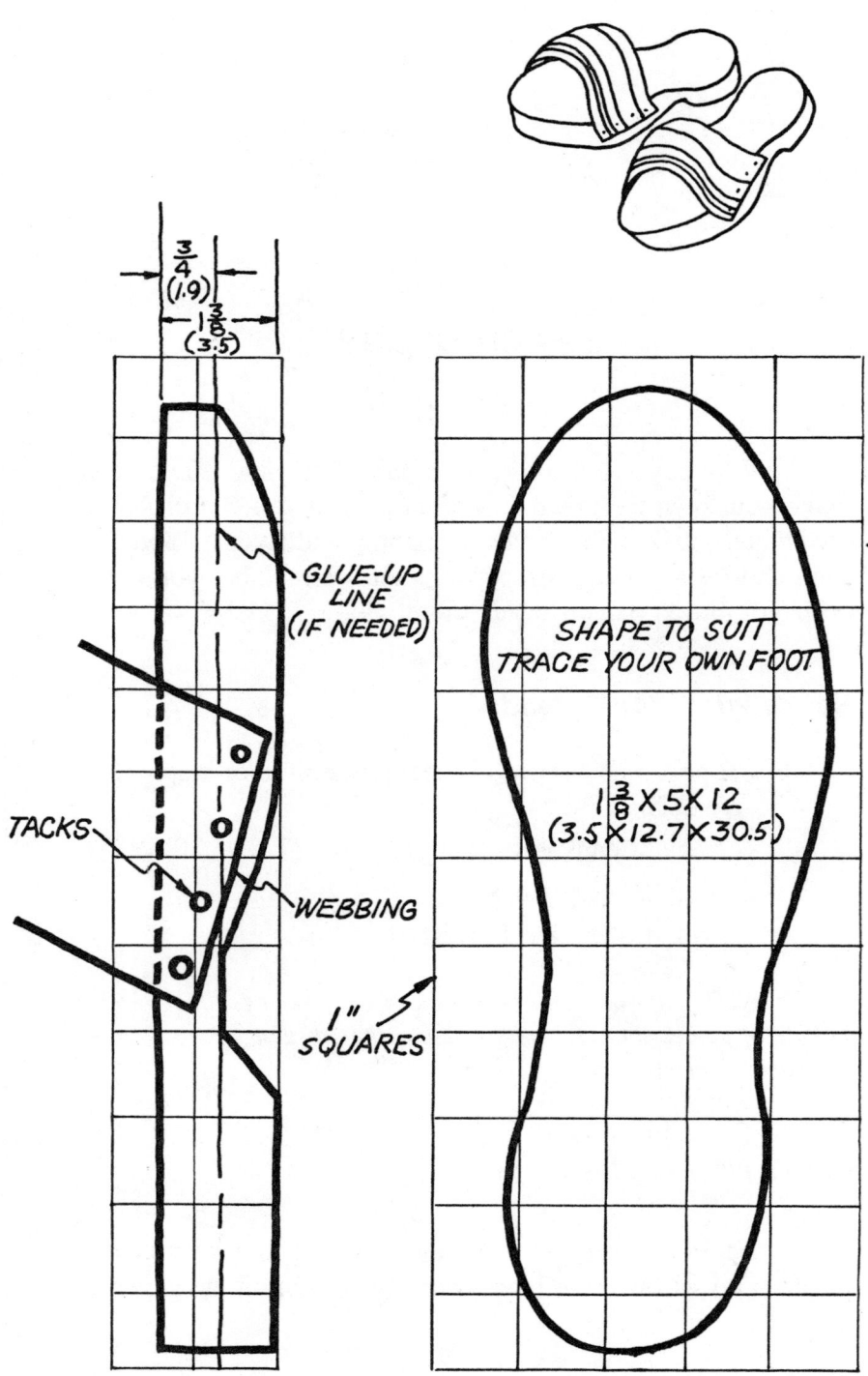

Figure 7-1. Beach Clogs.

Ten Sports Projects

the foot is traced, so it will probably be easier to have a friend do the tracing while you are standing. Make patterns of both feet. When you have two outlines, smooth them so they look like the sole of a shoe. You should add about a ½" in front to protect your toes. Transfer the patterns to the blocks of wood.

Before you cut these shapes you should cut the profiles of the bottoms. Make sure that the arch corresponds to the pattern you have traced on the surface of each block. You can prepare the arch profile with a rasp, or surface forming tool. The bottom is prepared first to make it easier to hold the work in a vise. If you had cut the shape of the foot first, it would have been difficult to hold in a vise.

Next, cut out the patterns with a jig, coping or band saw. Trim and smooth the edges. You can use a file, or the surface forming tool.

Sandpaper all surfaces until they are very smooth, and then soak the clogs in boiled linseed oil for 2 or 3 days. They should be left to dry for at least 4 or 5 days.

When the wood is no longer sticky, you can make the strap. Place your foot on the clog and measure the proper length by using the webbing. This should not fit tightly; the canvas may shrink when it gets wet. When you are sure that you have the right length, add about 1" to each end and cut the strap from the stock length. Fold a ½" hem and tack one side, as shown in Figure 7-1. Then place your foot on the clog and position the strap over your foot. Fold the hem and make a mark on the other side as a reference for the tacking. Tack the other side and you have a custom-fitted clog. Do the same thing with the other and you will have a pair, just what's needed for the beach.

TWO KITES AND A KITE REEL

Inside every adult there is a little kid who would like to play with a kite. If you don't believe this, have you ever been able to watch a child with a kite in the air without remembering the fun you had at the end of a kite string when you were that age? Even if you aren't willing to own up to it, you can make some nice kites for the smaller people in your life.

We have included two basic kite designs here. The bow kite is fun to fly. It's a little unpredictable in the air, which means that you will have to develop your skill in handling it. But when you do, you will be well rewarded for your efforts.

The box kite is the more stable of the two kites. With a little breeze and a long string, it will go up and fly forever. It isn't as playful in the wind, but the chances are that shifts in the wind won't leave you holding the end of an empty string.

The Bow Kite

Here's What You'll Need:

- Upright—1 pc ¼ × ¼ × 36 pine, spruce, ash or boxwood (.6 × .6 ×91.4)
- Bow—1 pc ¼ × ¼ × 32 same material (.6 × .6 × 81.3)
- Thin fabric (polyester, cotton or nylon) 1 yard square (1 meter)
- Twine—#10 fishing line will do very well.

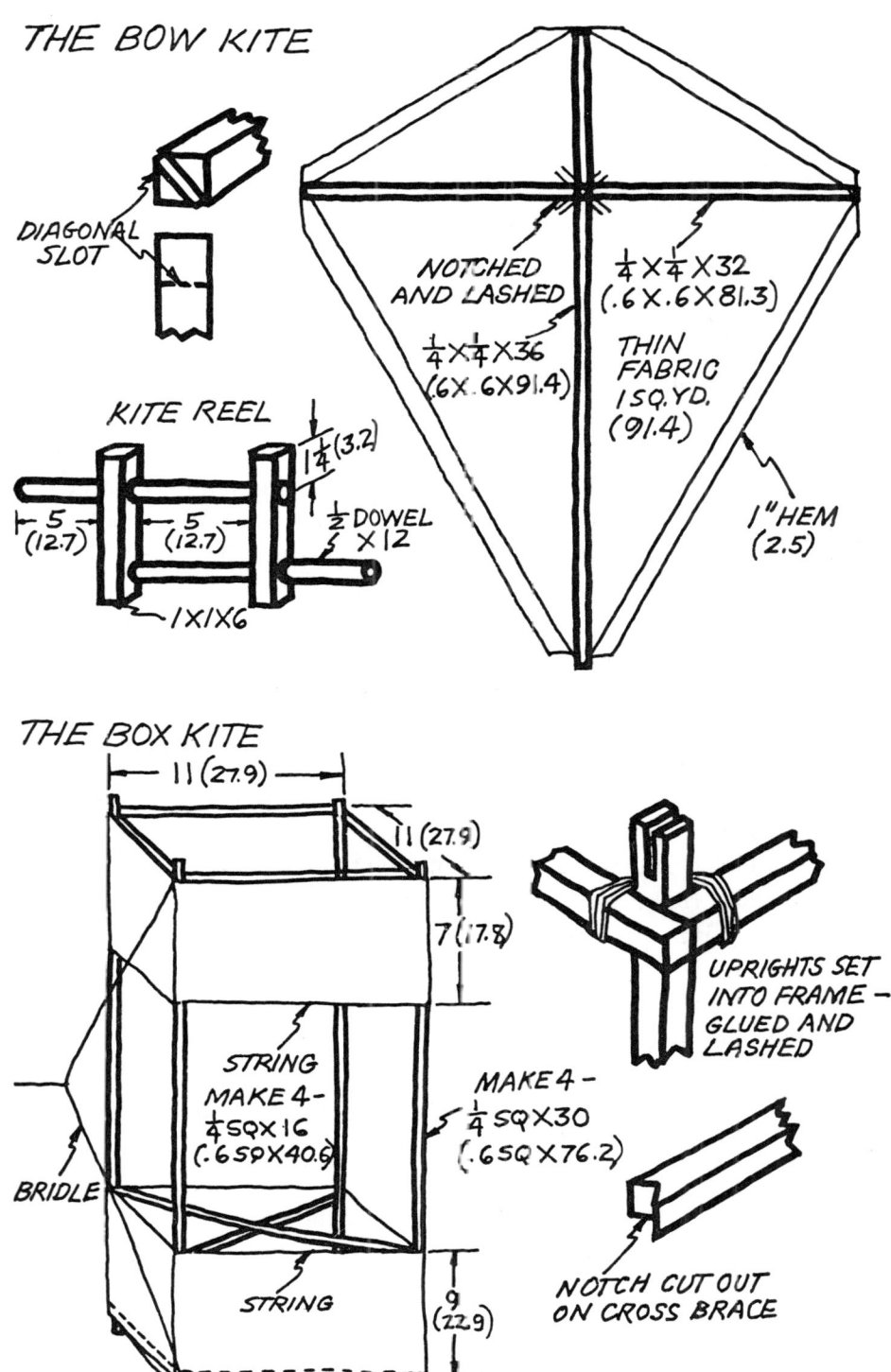

Figure 7-2. Two Kites and a Kite Reel.

- Shellac
- Household cement

Here's How to Make It:

Cut the wood pieces to length.

Cut notches across the diagonal cross section about ¼" down on both strips. In the center of the shorter strip and 9" down on the upright, notch out for a cross lap joint. Don't cut this notch any more than ¼ of the thickness of the wood!

Glue the two struts together at the cross lap joint. Lash the joint with a few tight turns of twine to make the joint even more secure. Before the glue begins to dry, place the frame on a flat surface and string the frame with the line. Tie the cord securely after it has been snugly tensioned. Apply a dab of cement to each slot, and allow the entire assembly to dry.

When the glue is dry, place the assembly on the fabric you have chosen and cut the shape of the kite, leaving a 1" hem all around. Fold the hem over the string which forms the perimeter of the kite and fasten it on the back of the cloth with shellac. Make sure that the cloth hems from the outside in.

When the shellac has dried, make marks on the front center, 5" down (12.7) and 8" up (20.3) from the bottom. Punch small holes at each mark. Tie one end of a 36" string to the spar, after passing it through the upper hole. Pass the other end of the string through the lower hole and secure it to the spar. It's a good idea to dab a little glue on each knot for security. A dab of glue over the string and spar will keep the string from slipping during flight.

The towing point will vary with the weight of your kite, but begin by tying the flying line to the bridle about 10" (25.4) down from the top hole. You will have to experiment a little, but you will know when you have the right spot by the

Ten Sports Projects

ease with which the kite will take off and handle once it's in the air.

Bow kites often fly better with a tail made of strips of cloth tied together. Again, it's best to experiment with different lengths. Start with two strips tied together, each 12" long, and add foot-long strips until you find the length that will provide the greatest stability for your kite.

The Box Kite

Here's What You'll Need:

- Uprights—4 pcs ¼ square × 30 (.6 sq. × 76.2)
- End frames—8 pcs ¼ square × 11 (.6 sq. × 27.9)
- Cross braces—4 pcs ¼ square × 16 (.6 sq. × 40.6)
- Cloth—1 pc 9 × 48 (22.9 × 121.9) (cotton, nylon, polyester, etc.)—1 pc 11 × 48 (27.9 × 121.9)
- Twine
- Household cement
- Shellac

Here's How to Make It:

Cut all pieces to size, and then cut ½" slots in the ends of the long uprights.

Assemble the square frames on a sheet of wax paper (to prevent glue from sticking) and glue together. Check each frame with a square before the glue sets.

When the glue holding the frames has set, place the uprights at each corner of each frame to form the box shape. The ends of the uprights should protrude from the top and bottom frame ½" (1.3). Lash the joints with twine and glue the assembly together. Check the entire construction for squareness before the glue sets.

Cut a corner notch into the ends of all the cross braces. When the box frame glue has set, fit the braces across the diagonal at the points which where the cloth will end; 7" (17.8) at one end and 9" (22.9) at the other. The braces should fit snugly in order to make the box frame quite rigid. If they are too long, trim small amounts from one end until they fit. Cement the joints and lash the cross pieces together with twine.

Wrap twine around the frame at the points 7" from one end and 9" from the other at the cross braces. Make sure the string is taut. Cement the knots and cement the string where it touches each upright.

Lay one piece of cloth on the floor, and cut it to include hems 1" wider that the distance between the string and frame at each end. Fold the hems over the string and frame, and fix with shellac. Cut away cloth at the corners so that it fits smoothly on the string. Be sure to pull the cloth snug when you fold and shellac the hem. Repeat this process on the other end.

Tie a bridle to each end of one of the uprights and you are ready for a flight test. You may have to shift the position of the flying line attachment, but start by hooking it slightly off center. When you find the place where the kite flies well and is stable in rough air, mark it for future flying.

Kite Reel

This handy device will allow you to fly your kite with a minimum of problems. It will reduce the possibility of snags that can occur if you just wrap string on a stick, and it will reduce the possibility of the string wearing out, leaving you holding a line—without a kite at the other end.

Here's What You'll Need:

- Reel—2 pcs ½" dowel × 12 (1.3 dia. × 30.5)
- Supports—2 pcs 1 × 1 × 6 (2.5 × 2.5 × 15.2)
- Glue

Here's How to Make It:

Drill ½" holes in each 1 × 1, both 1¼" (3.2) in from the ends.

Assemble the dowels and supports as shown in Figure 7-2. Glue the dowels in place and allow the assembly to dry. After the glue has set, sand the entire unit with fine paper. You want to be sure that there are no burrs to fray the kite string. Give the reel a coat of varnish, and the job is done. To use it, just tie the end of the flying line to one of the dowels between the supports, and wind on the string with a hand over hand action. Try to wind the string so that you get an even layer.

STORABLE PING-PONG TABLE

Have you priced commercially made ping-pong tables recently? Pretty expensive, aren't they? And when you get a store-bought model, there is nothing you can do with it but play ping-pong. You can make our model for a fraction of the cost, and you can use it, or parts of it from many other things. The supports can be used as saw horses, and you can even use half of the table when more people than you expected show up for dinner.

Here's What You'll Need:

- Table top—1 pc ½ × 60 × 108 plywood (1.3 × 152.4 × 274.2)
- Frame—4 pcs 1 × 2 × 60 (2.5 × 5.1 × 152.4)—4 pcs 1 × 2 × 52½ (2.5 × 5.1 × 133.3)
- Legs—8 pcs 2 × 4 × 32 (5.1 × 10.2 × 81.3)
- Supports—8 pcs 1 × 6 × 8 (2.5 × 15.2 × 20.3)—8 pcs 1 × 4 × 18 (2.5 × 10.2 × 45.7)
- Bar—2 pcs 2 × 4 × 96 (5.1 × 10.2 × 243.6)
- Bar braces—16 pcs 1 × 4 × 24 (2.5 × 10.2 × 61)
- 1 pair loose pin hinges 3" long with screws (7.6)
- Nails, screws
- Paint, green and white

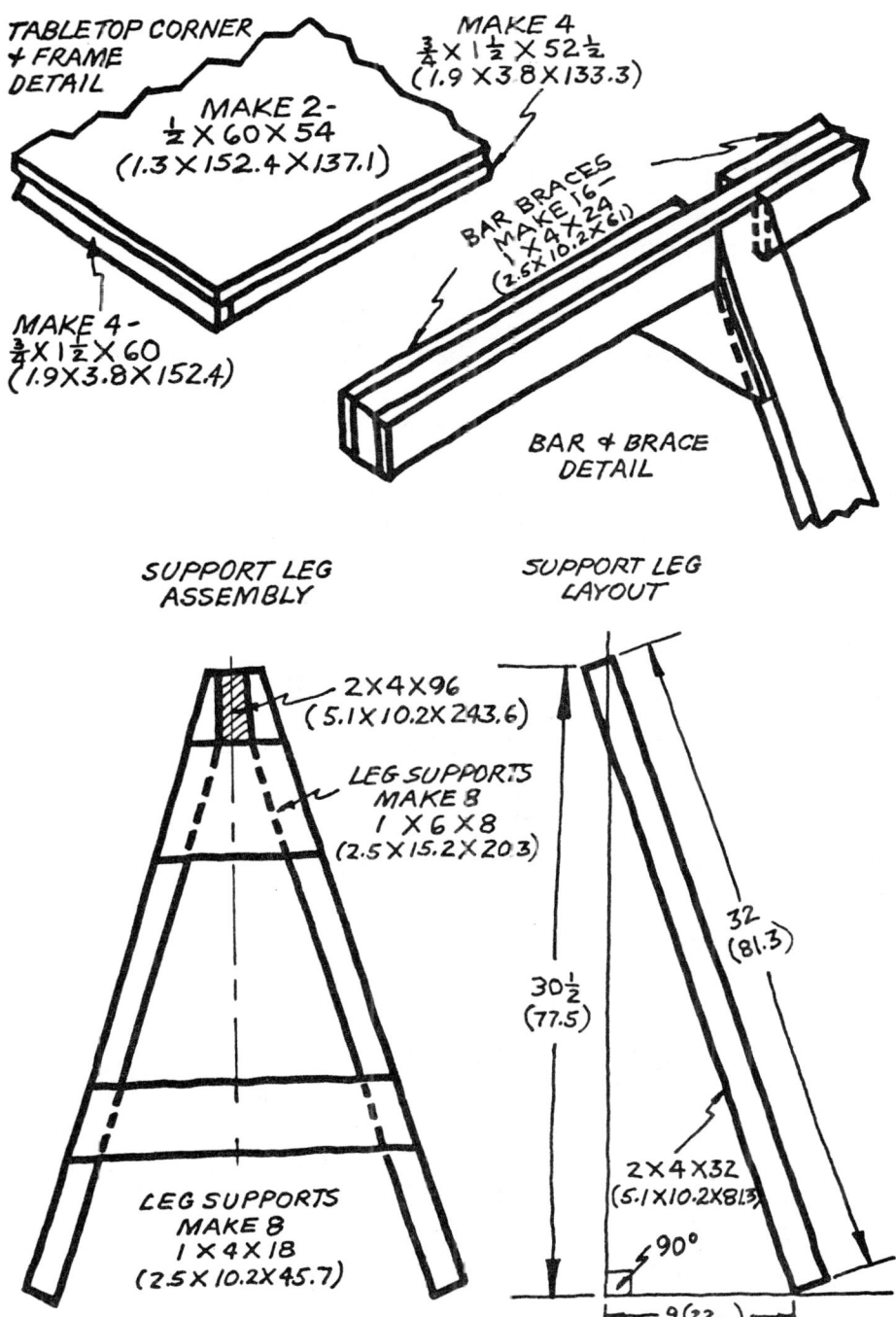

Figure 7-3. Storable Ping-Pong Table.

Here's How to Make It:

Regulation ping-pong tables are 5 × 9' (152.4 × 274.2). Cut the board in half so that each piece will be 5' (152.4) by 4½' (137.1). Cut the frame pieces that will be used to support and strengthen the top. Next, glue and screw the frame securely.

Temporarily rejoin the two halves of the top. Now lay out and install a set of hinges.

Paint the top of the table surface with several coats of flat green paint. Then paint a white stripe down the middle. The stripe should be about ½" (1.3) wide. Then stripe the edges of the table at the same width. The white paint should also be used to cover the edges of the table as the stripe is painted. You can be assured a perfect striping job if you use masking tape.

Your table top is ready, but you must have something on which to stand it. It is possible to buy standard saw horses, but it's more fun to make your own. And it's a lot less expensive.

Here's How to Make Them:

Cut all the pieces to size. Then, lay a piece of wrapping paper on the floor and draw a right triangle, as shown in Figure 7-3 (drawing 1). Lay out the 2 × 4 on edge so that the lower corner touches a line 9" (22.9) in from the 90° angle. On the upper end, draw a ½" line along the *outside*. This is the line which should line up with the long vertical line of your pattern. The angle formed by this line should be transferred to the 2 × 4. This will give you the proper leg spread for good support.

Temporarily clamp a short piece of 2 × 4 in place. While the two legs are still on the floor, screw in the supports on the top and bottom. See Figure 7-4 (drawing 2) for the details.

The long 8' bar is prevented from slipping and tipping by nailing the bar braces to the bar on both sides of the leg. This prevents wobbling, and will allow you to disassemble everything for easy storage.

You can make the saw horses do multiple duty by cutting additional bars to whatever length you want. When you label the parts you will then have a very efficient kit of table supports.

INDOOR TETHER BALL

What do you do when it's raining and the kids can't play outside? Apart from hoping they will be invited to a friend's house, you plan games that will keep them active, yet not destroy your house.

Our indoor tether ball is such a game. It's played just like outside tether ball. Two players face each other on opposite sides of the pole, and by hitting the ball with ping-pong paddles try to wrap the tether line so the ball winds up at the pole. One player hits right, the other left. If this turns out to be too easy, wrap a piece of colored tape about a foot below the top of the pole and change the rules so that all of the cord must be wrapped above the tape to win.

Here's What You'll Need:

- Base—1 pc ¾ × 36 × 36 plywood or particleboard (1.9 × 91.4 × 91.4)
- Support—3 pcs ¾ × 12 × 12 plywood (1.9 × 30.5 × 30.5)
- Post—1 pc 1⁵/₁₆ × 6 ft closet pole (3.3D × 182.8)
- Tether—1 length of Nylon cord ⅛" D
- Ball—3" diameter hard plastic ball
- Screw-eye, paint, ping-pong paddles.

NOTE: You can cut all of the wood for the base and support from one sheet of ¾" plywood or particle board.

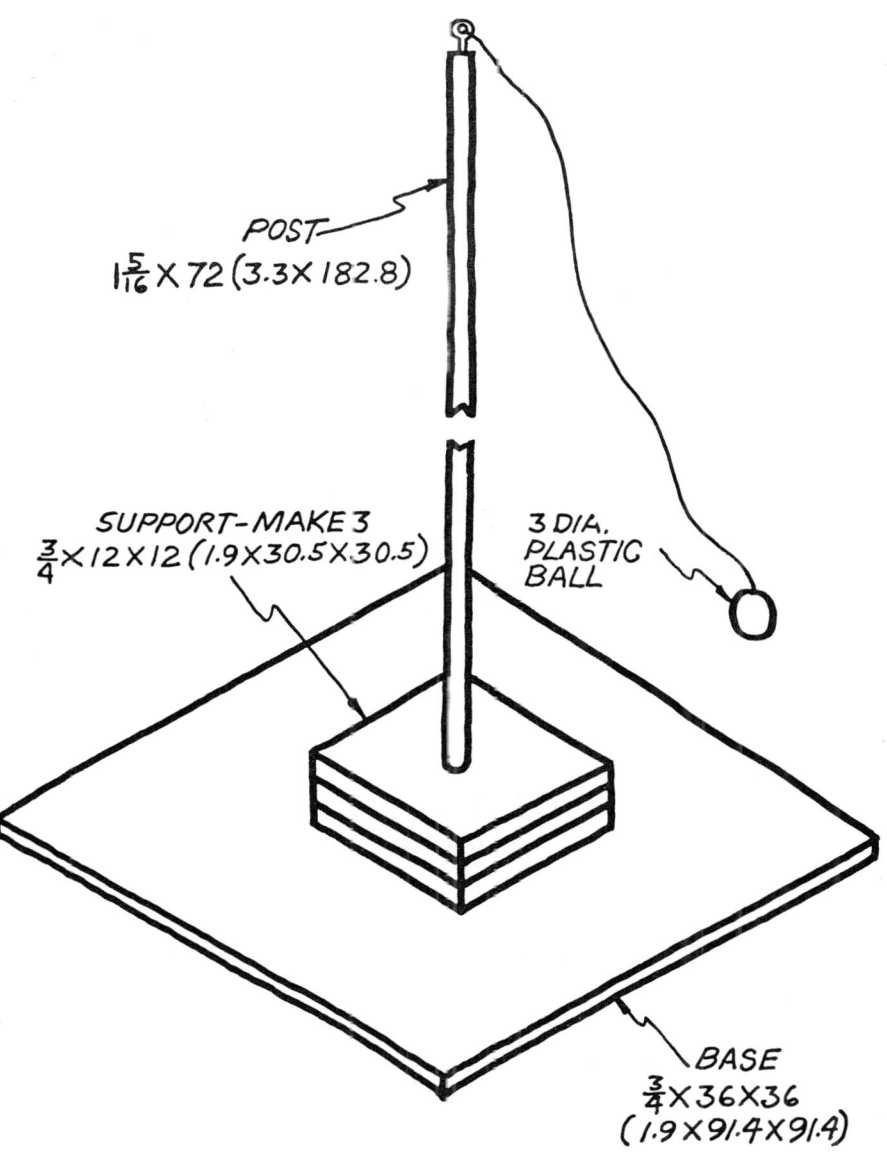

Figure 7-4. Indoor Tether Ball.

Here's How to Make It:

Cut all the pieces to size. Next, locate the centers in each of the support pieces, and drill holes for the pole. Most hole drills this size are seldom able to penetrate more than 1¼", so it will be best to drill each support piece individually. Be absolutely sure that the drill is positioned vertically, or the pole will tilt. Find the center of the baseboard, but do not drill a hole; make a mark that will be used to guide the positioning of the pole support.

Fasten the three sections of the support block together by using glue and nails. It's a good idea to insert the pole while you are making this assembly to insure that the pieces line up and the pole will be perfectly vertical. Don't let the glue squeeze into the hole that the pole goes in.

When the glue has dried in the support assembly, mount it to the center of the baseboard. Use the mark as your guide, and secure the block with glue and screws driven in from the back of the base.

Drive in the screw-eye at the top of the pole and fasten the tether line. To attach the ball, drill a hole through the center, and pull the line through. Knot the line at the bottom and add a dab of glue.

You can paint, stain and varnish or do nothing at all with this fun inside game.

To make storage easier, do *not* glue the pole into position, but merely insert it into the hole in the support and remove when the sun shines again.

BOWL-A-BALL

This is a great game for the kids to play inside on a rainy day—or on the lawn on a bright day. Even we adults have had a lot of fun with it. It's easy to make, fun to use, yet encourages the development of a bowling skill.

Here's What You'll Need:

- Sides—2 pcs ⅜ × 5½ × 12" plywood (1 × 14 × 30.5)
- Supports—2 pcs ½" dia. dowel × 16 (1.3 × 40.6)
- "Pins"—9 pcs ½ × 1¼ × 4½ (1.3 × 3.2 × 11.5)
- Separators—10 pcs ⅜ × ½ × 2 (1 × 1.3 × 5.1)
- Pivot bar and stop:
  1 pc—1.4 dia. × 17½ dowel (.6 dia. × 44.5)
  2 pcs—½ × ¾ × 4½ (1.3 × 1.9 × 11.5)
  2 pcs—¼ × 2 dia. dowel (.6 dia. × 5.1)
  2 pcs—¼ dia. × 1 dowel (.6 dia. × 2.5)
- Axle—1 pc. ¼ rod × 16½, threaded ¼-20 with washers and nuts for each end. (.6 × 41)
- Glue, paint, and/or shellac-stain

Here's How to Make It:

Cut out all the pieces; keep the small pieces in separate containers to prevent loss. When you cut the pieces, you can make several at one time. To do this, make a layout on one

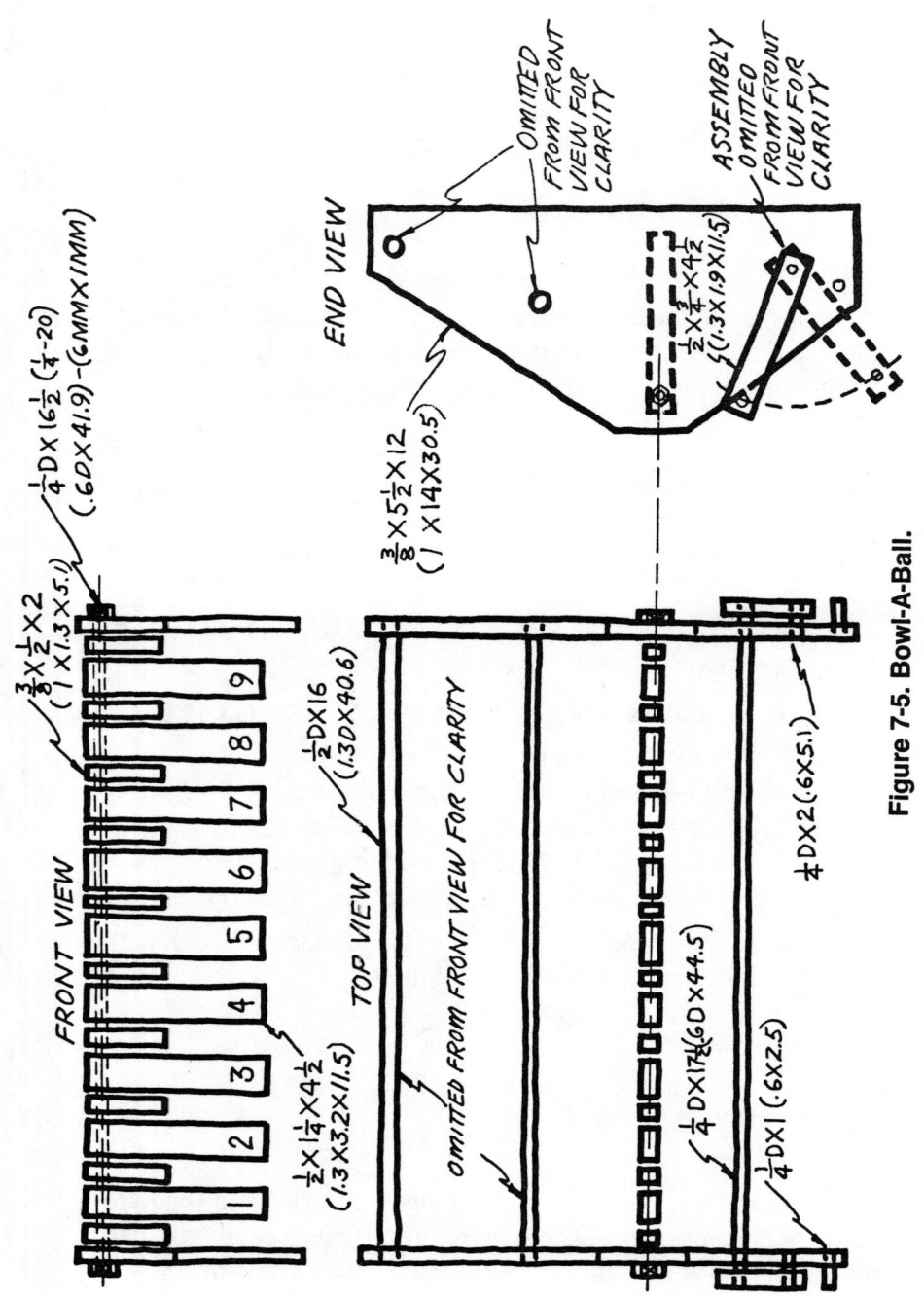

Figure 7-5. Bowl-A-Ball.

Ten Sports Projects

piece and temporarily nail it together with another. Then you can cut the two pieces at the same time. Before you separate the two pieces, be sure to lay out and drill all of the holes through both pieces.

If you'd like to make a jig for drilling the 19 pieces that slide on the axle, set up an open box and clamp it to a drill press table. This will hold the work as well as position it for drilling.

Sand all pieces before you begin assembly. To assemble, slide the dowels into the prepared holes. Be sure that the project is square and sitting firmly on the workbench. Clamp and glue the dowels in place.

When the assembly is dry, you can assemble the "pins" and separators. The separators allow the pins to swing without interfering with each other. It's best to do the painting or staining and varnishing before going on to the next operations.

After you have stained or painted the pins, apply the numbers. You can use decals, or paint them on yourself. Now, slide the whole business together—axle, pins, separators and all. Be sure that the pins swing freely. If there is any binding, trim a few of the separators until there is no friction. A little wax will help, even if there is no binding.

The pivot bar is made of piece of dowel which is glued between two pieces of wood. The other ends of the wood pieces pivot on two pieces of dowel which spin freely in the sides of the project. To keep the bar from falling too far, two short dowels are set into the sides and glued in place after the pivot bar has been moved back out of the way.

The pivot bar is the scorekeeper. When the pins are hit by a bowled handball, they are held in place by the bar. After a player has taken a turn and recorded the score, move the bar forward and let the pins drop back in place for the next round.

BASKETBALL BACKBOARD

Basketball backboards are usually mounted on heavy posts which have been set in concrete. However, you can save yourself a lot of bother by mounting the backboard on a sloping roof with this simple system. Wherever you mount it, be sure that the rim is exactly 10′ (3.05 meters) from the ground. If it's off even a fraction of an inch, your game will be off when you play on a court where the rim is at the right height.

Here's What You'll Need:

- Backboard—1 pc ¾ × 36 × 48 exterior plywood (1.9 × 91.4 × 121.9)
- Braces—2 pcs 2 × 4 × 31 (5.1 × 10.2 × 78.7)
- Stretchers—2 pcs 2 × 4 × 30 (5.1 × 10.2 × 76.2)
- Supports—6 pcs 2 × 4 × 44 (5.1 × 10.2 × 111.7)
- Lag bolts—10 pcs ½ × 6 galvanized with 2 washers each (1.3 × 15.2)
- Lag screws—4 pcs ½ × 6 (at least) galvanized with 1 washer each
- Wood screws flat head galvanized 2″-12
- Commercial basketball hoop and net
- Paint and nails

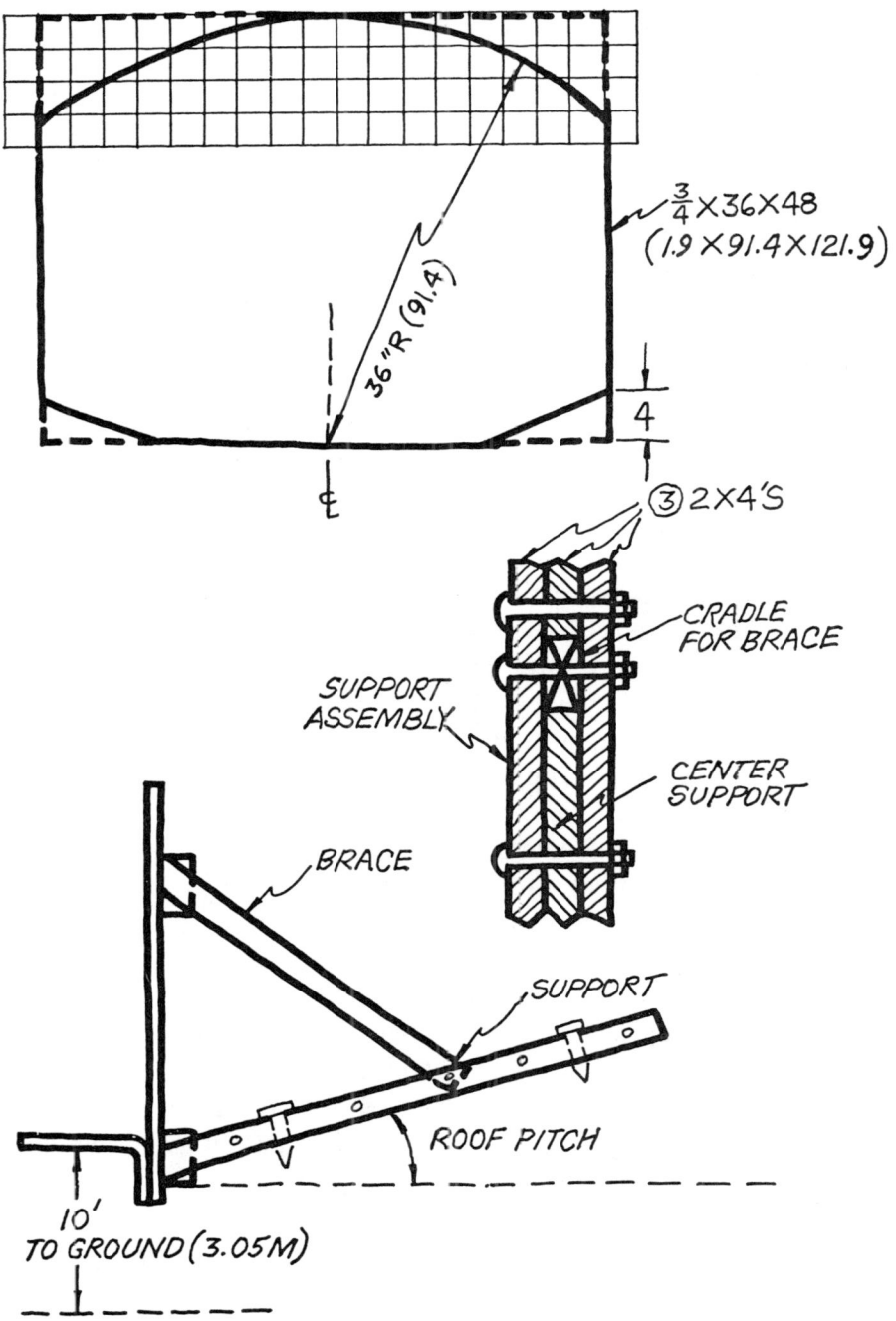

Figure 7-6. Basketball Backboard.

Here's How to Make It:

Cut the backboard to shape, but do not lay out any holes yet. The position of the holes will depend on the spacing and location of the support units.

Locate the rafters on the roof or in the building to which the support units will be attached. Rafters are usually 16" (40.6) apart, although it isn't uncommon to find them spaced 24" (61). Assuming the common 16" distance, you can expect to place the supports about 32" apart (81.3) and 8" (20.3) in from the ends of the backboard. If you can see the rafters from under the roof, you can assure proper mounting by driving a small nail up through the roof next to the two rafters on which the unit will be mounted. The protruding nail will give the perfect location, and the nail hole can be sealed with roofing cement after marks have been made.

There are three pieces to each support. Note that the brace is held in place on the roof by being cradled in a cutout on the center support, and pinned in place by a lag bolt which goes through all supports. It would be best to arrange the supports so that the center section is lined up with the rafter.

Cut the supports to size. Lay out the pieces on a floor as you cut them to insure the proper cutting angles. Follow the diagram in Figure 7-6. Cut the angles where the backboard attaches to the support so that the backboard is vertical. Be sure of the roof pitch. The pitch is the number of inches the roof goes up per foot. A 4" pitch is a rise of 4" per foot run.

Transfer the needed cutting angle for the brace by using a sliding T bevel. If you don't have a T bevel, you can make your own angle-recording instrument by using two thin pieces of wood nailed together to reproduce the angle correctly.

At the support end of the brace centered from the ends and sides, drill a hole for the lag bolts. Following the diagram

Ten Sports Projects

in Figure 7-6, locate the hole on the supports and drill the sides of the supports.

Drill through the support sets and fasten with lag bolts. Position the angle brace, but don't fasten the bolt yet.

Cut the stretchers to size and fasten them in place on the background and to the angle braces and the bottom of the supports.

You can assemble the entire unit on the ground or on the roof. Do it whichever way would be most comfortable and practical for you. At this point it's very important to make sure that the backboard is perfectly vertical and that the rim is exactly 10' from the ground. The hoop height adjustment is made just before you fasten the board to the supports.

Drill holes through the center supports for two lag screws which will go through the 2 × 4, the roof shingles, the sheathing, or "roofers" into the rafter. The screws should be at least 6" long to do the job well. Use washers under the heads and fasten securely with a wrench. It's best to lay a bed of roofing cement where the supports will contact the roof. When the support is laid on the bed and tightened up with the lag screws, it will be just about impossible for any rain to get under the roof through the screw holes.

If the backboard is not absolutely vertical after mounting, you can loosen the assembly and place some shims at either of the lag screws to solve the problem.

Use a good exterior primer before you apply a final coat of paint. Porch and deck paints are best for the finish coat.

CHECKER SHUFFLEBOARD

This scaled-down shuffleboard can be used inside or out. But we thought it up mainly for those who either have checkers they don't use, or have sore arms from playing the real thing. Whatever—you play and score this game just as you do a full-size shuffleboard game.

Here's What You'll Need:

- Board—1 pc ¼ × 12 × 48 plywood (.6 × 30.5 × 121.9)
- Underframe—2 pcs 1 × 1 × 48 (2.5 × 2.5 × 121.9)—2 pcs 1 × 1 × 12 (2.5 × 2.5 × 30.5)
- Glue, nails and paint

Here's How to Make It:

Cut the plywood to size. Be sure that the wood is flat. If you can't find a piece of flat plywood, you can use hardboard or particle board instead.

Fasten the frame to the underside of the board. Use glue and nails for this job. Be sure to sink the nail heads and fill the holes with wood putty. Smooth the putty when it sets.

Follow the pattern in Figure 7-7 for your painting. Paint the board flat black first, and then do the striping with glossy white. If you don't have a striping tool, use masking tape to assure straight lines of even width throughout.

To maintain the scale with a real shuffleboard, be sure

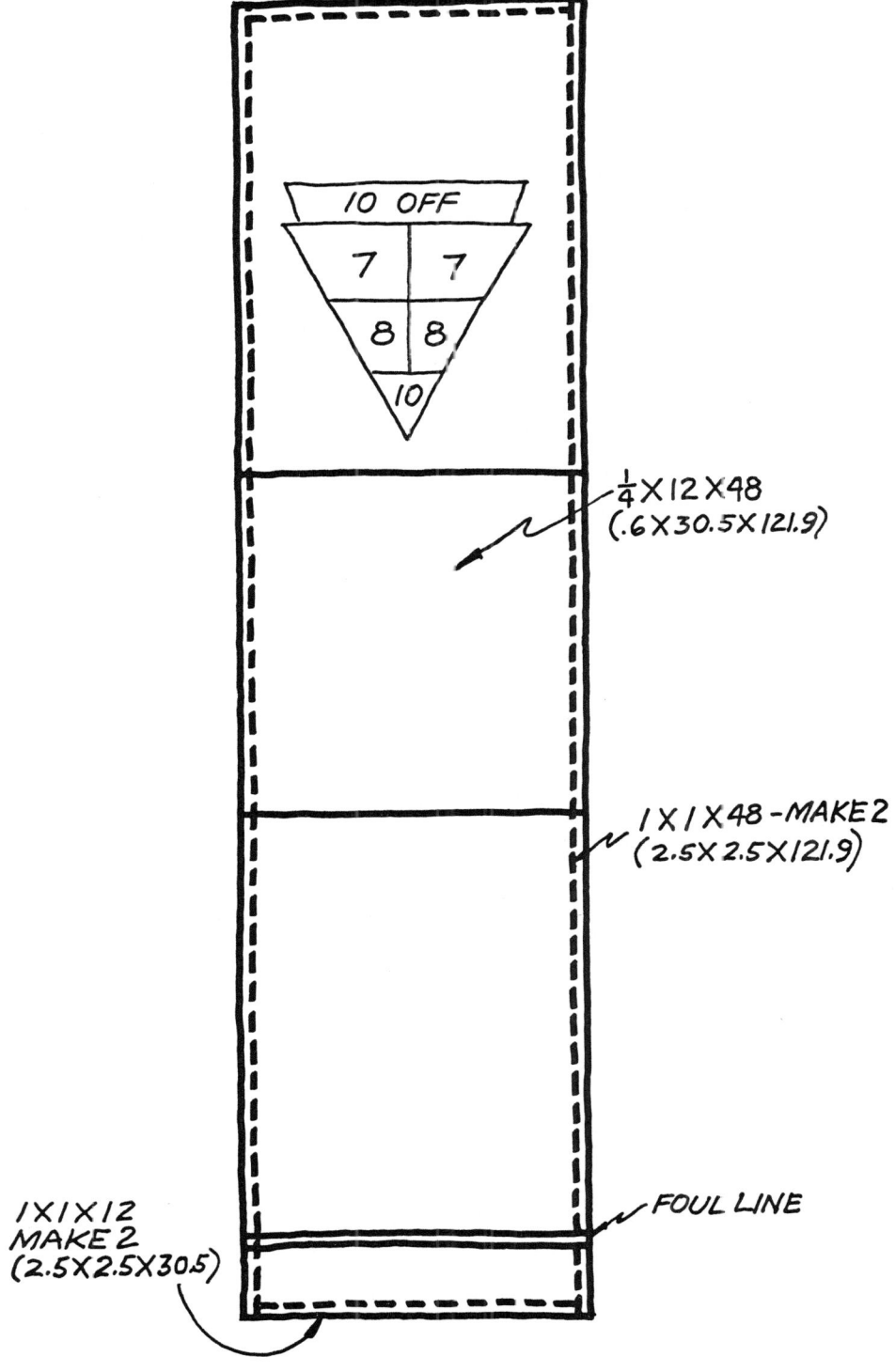

Figure 7-7. Checker Shuffleboard.

to shoot and release your checkers from behind the foul line on the end of the board.

NOTES: If you'd like to make the game easier, place the underframe as an overframe to keep all checkers in the board area.

Just in case you don't have a set of checkers, you can make a set quite easily. Slice a 1" dowel carefully to produce 8 discs that are ⅜" thick. Be sure to sand them thoroughly and apply a coat of paste wax to make them slide easily. You can wax the real checkers too.

LIVE FISH BOX

Nobody catches one fish and heads home right away, unless, of course, it's a big, big fish. For those of you who feel that it takes at least a few fish to make a good meal, this box is the answer to freshness. You can store your catch right in the water it came from until you are ready to take it home. This box, tied to the boat and left in the water, is open on one side and the bottom. The open sides are covered with screening to allow a steady flow of fresh water to reach your fish.

Here's What You'll Need:

- Back—1 pc ½ × 10 × 17 (1.3 × 25.4 × 43.2)
- Top—1 pc ½ × 10 × 18 (1.3 × 25.4 × 45.7)
- Ends—2 pcs ½ × 10 × 10 (1.3 × 25.4 × 25.4)
- Flap—1 pc ½ × 6 × 14 (1.3 × 15.2 × 35.5)
- Flap retainer—1 pc ½ × 2 × 14 (1.3 × 5.1 × 35.5)
- Screen—1 pc ¼" mesh galvanized 18 × 22 (.6 × 45.7 × 55.9)
- Brass or copper nails or screws
- Molding (optional) ½ round × 48 (1.3 × 121.9)
- Hook and eye, 1 pair of brass hinges, 2 handles, knob, rope to tie box to boat or shore paint

NOTE: The wood you use should resist rot. If you can get it, use cedar, cypress, redwood. If you cannot get any of these woods, use pine, but soak it well in pentachlorophenol after you cut the shapes, but before you begin any assembly.

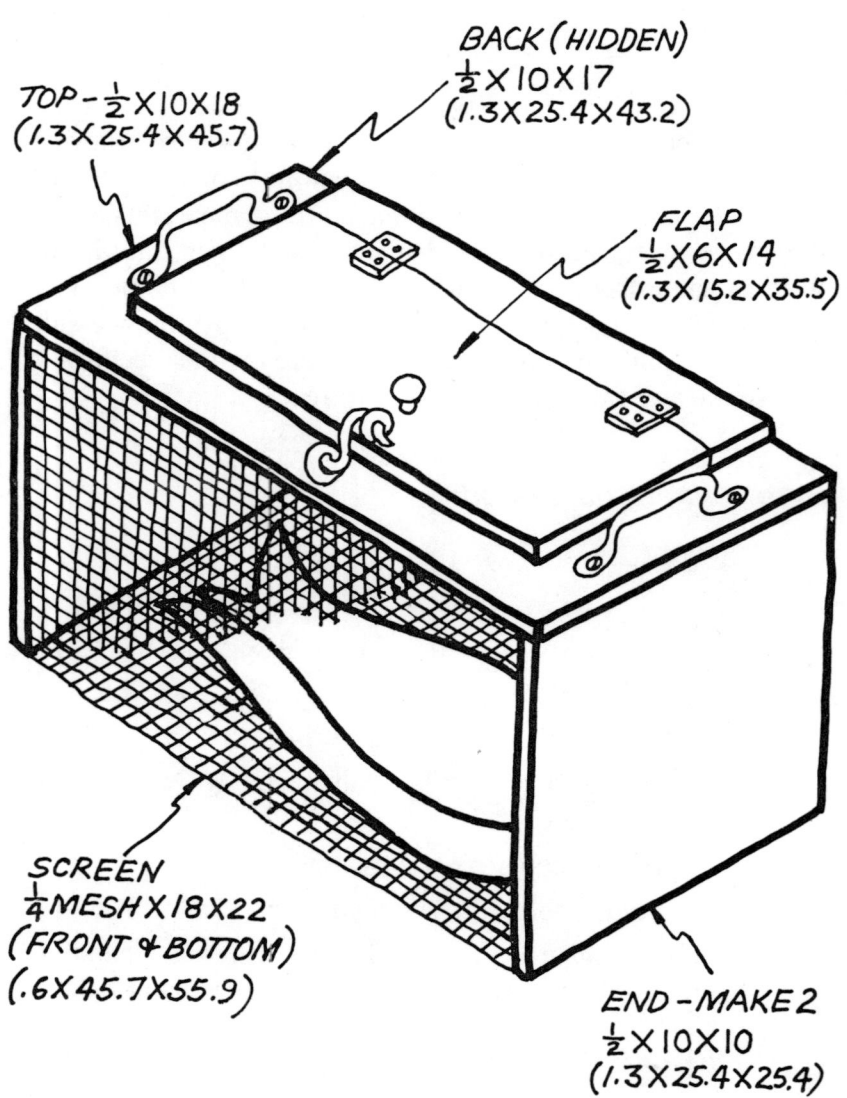

Figure 7-8. Live Fish Box.

Ten Sports Projects 219

Here's How to Make It:

Cut all pieces to size. Assemble the box as shown in Figure 7-8, but be sure to use only copper or brass nails or screws.

Bend and fit the mesh in place. Secure the mesh with small nails or tacks. You can turn the edges of the mesh under before nailing to protect yourself from the ends of the wire, or you can use the ½" round molding to cover the edges. We like the molding—it looks better and is more protective. Miter the corners.

Assemble the cover flap and its retainer with the hinges. Fasten the retainer to the box. Mount the knob in the center of the cover flap. Mount the hook and eye on the flap edge and the top of the box near the knob.

Mount the handles as shown in Figure 7-8. You can bend a sheet (nautical talk), or tie a rope to each of the handles to attach the box to your boat. The box will float, but water will fill it for the fish.

SANDBOX PLAY CENTER

Back when we were kids, a sandbox was a sandbox. It was simply a place to dump some sand for kids to play with. It was a lot of fun, too. Sandboxes are still a lot of fun, but (caught up as we are with words that sound important but mean the same as smaller words) we have seen the phrase "play center" used for the old-fashioned sandbox. Well, ours is no different than the new item or the old sandbox, so we think it's up to you to call it whatever you want. One thing we do know, the kids will call it a lot of fun.

Here's What You'll Need:

- Sides—2 pcs 1 × 8 × 34 (2.5 × 20.3 × 86.3)
  —2 pcs 1 × 8 × 36 (2.5 × 20.3 × 91.4)
- Base—1 pc ½ × 36 × 36 exterior plywood (1.3 × 91.4 × 91.4)
- Legs—4 pcs 1 × 8 × 12 (2.5 × 20.3 × 30.5)
- Seats—2 pcs 1 × 6 × 40 (2.5 × 15.2 × 101.6)
- Nails, paint and waterproof glue, four 2" flat head wood screws

If you can get it, use a rot-resistant wood such as cedar, cypress or redwood. You can also use pine, but be sure that it has been pressure treated for exterior use.

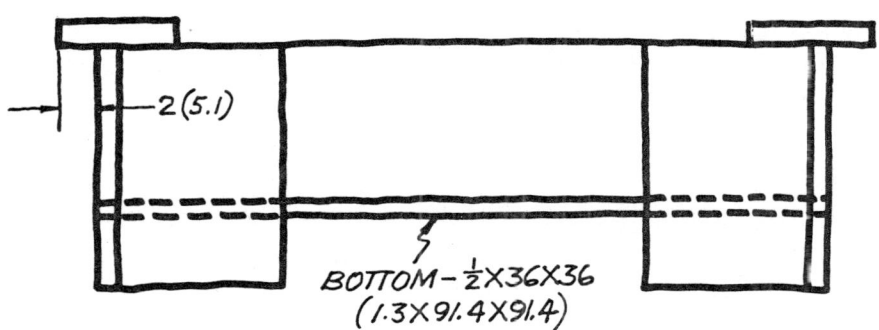

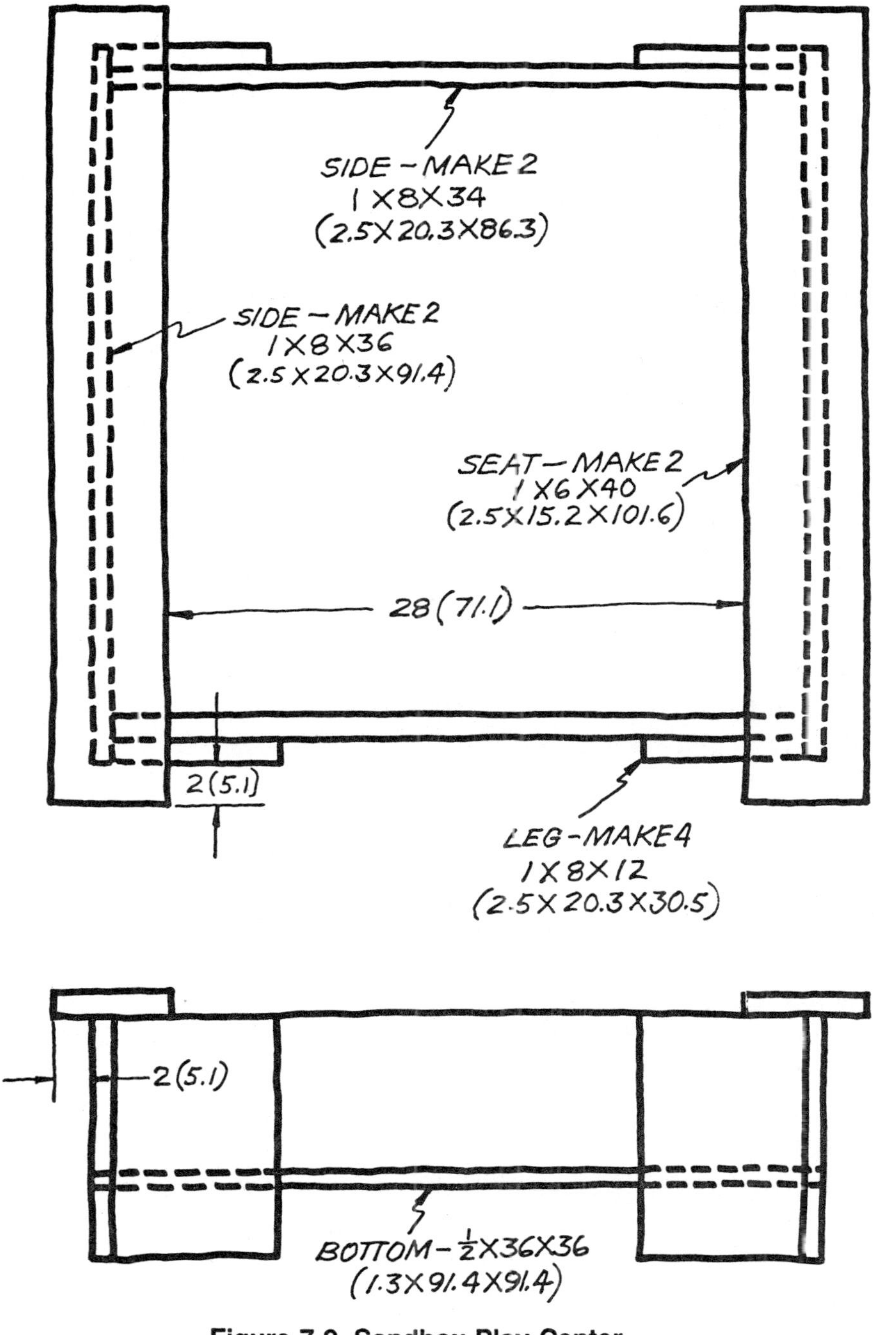

Figure 7-9. Sandbox Play Center.

Here's How to Make It:

Cut all pieces to size and shape.

Assemble the legs to the ends of the shorter side pieces. Be sure to use aluminum or galvanized nails. Wood glue at these and other nailed joints will add considerable strength to the sandbox.

Assemble the long sides to the shorter sides. There are two nailing edges for you to use; one into the other side, and one next to it into the leg. A sandbox needs all the strength you can build into it—use both.

Turn over the box and check it for squareness. Fit the bottom in place and nail securely. Again, use glue along with the nails.

We have made the seats overhang the box for two reasons: to give the kids more room to play, and to give you something to hold onto when you lift the box. You can lift it this way empty, but don't try it when the box is full of sand. Rather than nail the seats in place, use a couple of wood screws in each seat. Countersink the screws and fill the holes with wood putty.

Now you are ready to sand all the edges and surfaces. Do a good job of this; a splinter can ruin a lot of fun in any sandbox.

Give the finished "play center" a coat of natural polyurethane varnish, or use several coats of porch or deck paint.

It's a good idea to make some kind of cover for the sandbox. When it rains, the sand will not only get wet, the water will accumulate and leave you and the kids with a swamp on your hands. Just a sheet of the plastic tarp material painters use will do the job. It's sold by the yard in most hardware stores.

BOUNCE-BALL GAME

There are two ways that you can play this game. If you're a little kid, or have a few you have to entertain once in a while, you can throw the ball directly at the box. But, if you're a big kid (all adults are big kids) you have to play by our rules. Prop the box up against a wall at a 45° angle, get back about 10', and try to get the balls in the highest scoring compartments by giving them one bounce from the floor in front of the box. Still think it sounds easy? Try it. Each player throws three balls.

Here's What You'll Need:

- Base—1 pc ¼ × 19½ × 19½ plywood (.6 × 49.5 × 49.5)
- Sides—2 pcs 1 × 6 × 19½ (2.5 × 15.2 × 49.5)—2 pcs 1 × 6 × 18 (2.5 × 15.2 × 45.7)
- Separators—4 pcs ¼ × 5½ × 18½ (.6 × 14 × 47)
- Glue and finishing nails and paint
- Decals, numbers 1, 3, 6, 10

Here's How to Make It:

Lay out the separators according to Figure 7-10, and make the cuts as indicated. The separators will fit together much like the partitions in an egg crate. Make the grooves in the side walls, as shown in Figure 7-10. Sand all surfaces and edges.

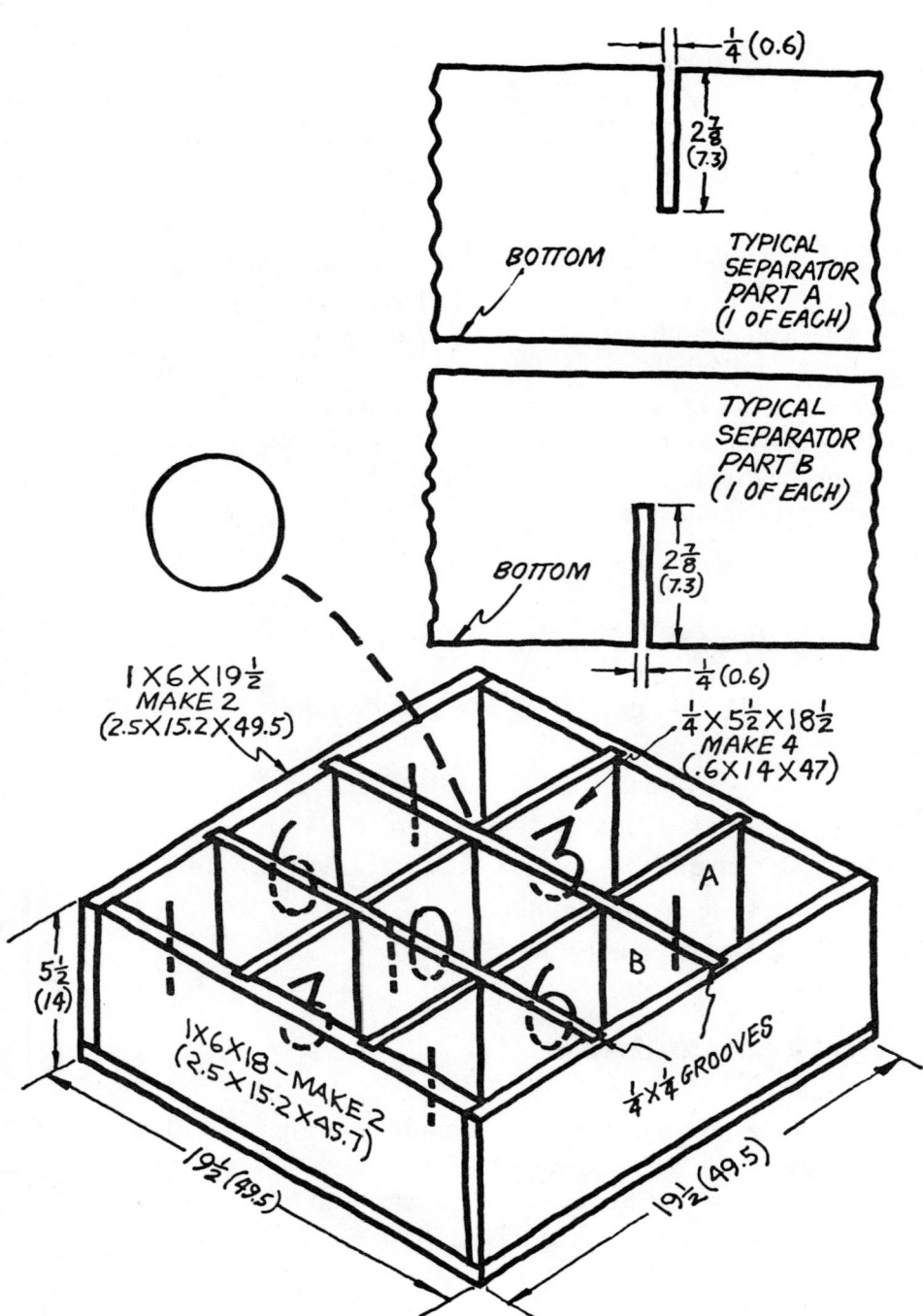

Figure 7-10. Bounce-Ball Game.

Ten Sports Projects

Now you can assemble the box. Begin by gluing and nailing the sides to the base so you have a box with inside dimensions of 18 × 18. Be sure that the walls are straight and square. Apply glue to the grooves you have cut in the sides; slide the separators in place. It isn't necessary to apply any glue where the separators form cross lap joints.

After the glue has set, sand the box and the separators; apply a coat of bright paint. Choose the paint to form a strong contrast with the color of the decal numbers you have selected.

Apply the decals as shown in Figure 7-10. They can either be positioned on the sides of the cells to make them visible when the box is placed at an angle, or you can apply them to the bottoms of each cell.

The game is usually played with three balls. The sum of the scores made by the balls that enter the cells is your score per throw. You can set any limit to the game—10 throws—100 throws—whatever you want.

INDEX

A

Adhesive, contact 93
Axel 180-181, 187, 209

B

Ball, plastic 204
Basketball backboard 210-213
Basket, sewing 76-79
Basswood 148
Benares, Tower of 145-147
Birdbath 111-113
Birdhouse 99-101
Boardfoot 17-18
Boat, jet 163-165
Bolts
      carriage 84
      lay 212
Bottle, plastic 163-165
Bounce-ball game 223-225

Bowl-a-ball game 207-209
Box, kit 72-75
Braces, angle 75, 105
Brooch 62

C

Cable, underground 184
Cage, small animal 89-93
Canvas 97
Carpet 39
Carving, wood 174, 176
Casters 31, 75
Catcher, note 117
Castle, rabbit 102-106
Caulking 42, 53
Chain 132, 144
Chain, lawn 170-173
Chalkboard, easel 57-60
Checker shuffleboard 214-216
Cheese block 47-50
Chisel 174
Clenching, nail 105-106
Clogs, beach 191-193
Clothing, safety 22
Collector, compost 159-162
Concrete 184
Cotton 194
Cooking oil finish 50
Corners, mitering 83, 111-113, 151
Creosote 161
Cuff links 62
Cutting, wood,
    Basketball backboard 212, 213
    Beach clogs 191-193
    Bicycle rack 84
    Birdbath 111-113
    Bird feeding box 109
    Birdhouse 101
    Bounce-ball game 223-225

Index

Cutting, wood *(cont.)*
    Bowl-a-ball 207-209
    Cage 91
    Chalkboard easel 59
    Checker shuffleboard 214
    Cheese block 49
    Child's step stool 36
    Compost collector 161
    Darkroom paper safe 70
    Doghouse 96
    Farmer's hat rack 136
    Folk toys 126-128
    Garden caddy 187
    House number signboard 182-184
    Jet boat 163
    Jewelry 64
    Key rack 139
    Kit box 14
    Kitchen slate 151
    Kites 196-197
    Lawn chair 172
    Light box 82
    Live fish box 219
    Memo pad/pencil holder 133-135
    Newspaper gatherer 31
    Pathway lamp 168
    Photo blind 67
    Picnic box 157
    Picnic salad set 176
    Ping-pong table 202
    Portable planter 53
    Rabbit castle 105
    Sandbox 34
    Sandwich tray 34
    Serving boards 121
    Sewing basket 78
    Spoon racks 44-46
    Sugar scoop 119
    Tether ball 206
    Tower of Benares 147
    Tugboat 42

Index

Cutting, wood *(cont.)*
    Wagon racer 180
    Wall-mounted desk 131-132
    William Tell puzzle 148

D

Darkroom paper safe 68-71
Decals 52, 225
Desk, wall-mounted 129-132
Doghouse 94-98
Dog sizes 94
Dowels 78, 84, 199

E

Eyes, screw 42

F

Fabric 194
Fasteners, hook and eye 92
Fastening wood
    Basketball backboard 212-213
    Bicycle rack 86
    Birdbath 111-113
    Bird feeding box 109
    Birdhouse 101
    Bounce-ball game 225
    Bowl-a-ball 209
    Cage 92-93
    Chalkboard easel 60
    Checker shuffleboard 214-216
    Cheese block 49
    Child's step stool 38
    Compost collector 161-162
    Doghouse 97
    Farmer's hat rack 138
    Garden caddy 187
    House number signboard 184

Index

Fastening wood *(cont.)*
    Jet boat 163-164
    Kit box 74
    Kitchen slate 151-152
    Kites 196-199
    Lawn chair 172
    Light box 82-83
    Live fish box 219
    Memo pad/pencil holder 135
    Newspaper gatherer 31
    Pathway lamp 168-169
    Photopaper safe 70
    Picnic box 157-158
    Ping-pong table 202
    Portable planter 53
    Rabbit castle 105-106
    Sandbox 222
    Sandwich tray 34
    Sewing basket 78
    Spoon rack 46
    Sugar scoop 119-120
    Tether ball 206
    Tugboat 42
    Wagon racer 180-181
    Wall-mounted desk 131-132
Feeding box, bird 107-110
Felt 35
Files 22
Findings, jewelry 64
Finishing wood
    Basketball backboard 213
    Beach clogs 193
    Birdbath 113
    Bird feeding box 110
    Birdhouse 101
    Bounce-ball game 225
    Bowl-a-ball 209
    Cage 93
    Chalkboard easel 60
    Checker shuffleboard 214-216
    Cheese block 50

Finishing wood *(cont.)*
    Child's step stool 38-39
    Compost collector 161
    Doghouse 98
    Farmer's hat rack 138
    Garden caddy 187
    House number signboard 184
    Jet boat 165
    Jewelry 64
    Key rack 141
    Kitchen slate 151-152
    Lawn chair 173
    Light box 83
    Newspaper gatherer 31
    Pathway lamp 169
    Photo blind 67
    Photo paper safe 71
    Picnic box 158
    Picnic salad set 176
    Ping-pong table 202
    Portable planter 53
    Rabbit castle 106
    Sandbox 222
    Sandwich tray 34-35
    Serving boards 123
    Sewing baskets 79
    Spoon rack 46
    Sugar scoop 120
    Tether ball 206
    Tower of Benares 147
    Tugboat 42
    Wagon racer 181
    Wall-mounted desk 132
    Wine glass rack 144
Fishbox 217-219
Flange, pipe 113

G

Garden caddy 185-187
Gather, newspaper 29-31
Gauge, drill 135

Index

Gliders 75
Glass 110
Glue
    epoxy 63-64
    thermo-setting 49
    waterproof 53, 84, 91, 92, 96, 101,
                          106, 109, 111-113
Goggles, safety 22
Gouges 174
Grease 113

H

Hammer, handle 22
Hardwood 19
Hat rack 136-138
Hinges
    continuous 156
    piano 74
    strap 59
Holder
    key 117
    pencil 117
Hooks, cup 141
Hoop, basketball 213
How this book will help you 5

I

Idea starters 6
Instructions, reading 15

J

Jewelry, laminated 61-64

K

Kites 194-199
Knife safety 22

L

Lamp, pathway 166-169
Lamination 61-64
Laminations, butcher block 47
Latch, magnetic 70
Lathe 136
Level, spirit 132
Lifting 22
Light box, photographer's 80-83
Light, diffused 80
Lights, florescent 82
Lock, valise 158
Lumber
        common 20
        factory and shop 20
        pressure treated 177

M

Mass production 6
Mass produced tugboat 42-43
Measuring lumber 16-17
Memo pad pencil holder 133-135
Mesh, galvanized steel 105
Metric equivalents 17
Molding, half-round 111
Money-saving tips 13-26
Muslin, sewing 79

N

Nailing, hemstitch 131
Nails
        aluminum 91
        galvanized 91
Nature projects 89-113
Netting, mosquito 67
Numbers, three dimensional 184

Index

Nuts, speed 82
Nylon 194

O

Oil
    boiled linseed 193
    finish 64
    vegetable 123, 177
O-ring 135

P

Paint 39, 53, 60, 71, 83, 93, 98,
                    101, 106, 113, 120, 132, 141,
                    144, 147, 151, 158, 161, 165,
                    169, 173, 181, 184, 187, 202,
                    206, 209, 213, 216, 222, 225
Paint, blackboard 151
Pan, foil 113
Paper, photographic 68
Pegboard 187
Pendant 62
Photo blind 65-67
Picnic box 155-158
Picnic salad set 174-177
Pincushion 79
Picture-framing tool 151
Pilot holes 34
Pipe 109, 113
Pipe, trick 126-127
Planter 117
Planter, portable 51-53
Plastic 168-169
Plates, mending 75
Plexiglas 110
Polyester 194
Polyethylene 97
Polyfoam 157-158

Practice steps 16
Preservatives, wood 86, 161
Puzzles 145-148

R

Rack
    bicycle 84-86
    key 139-141
    wine glass 142-144
Rags, oily 23
Reel, kite 198-199
Right project, the 6
Reminder, kitchen slate 149-152
Rollers 75
Roofing, roll 106

S

Safety 16, 21-23
Sandbox 220-222
Sawdust 23
Sawhorse 200
Scoop, sugar 117-120
Screening 217
Screen, mesh 91
Screws, brass 86
Sealing compound 71
Serving boards 121-123
Shellac 34, 39, 42, 64, 79, 152, 187
Shellac, application 34
Shingles 93, 97, 106
Signboard, house number 182-184
Sizes, nominal 16
Slate, tempered hardboard 149
Socket, lamp 169, 184
Softwood 19
Splitting, wood 51
Spoon rack 44-46

Index

Stain 53, 60, 67, 79, 83, 98,
                         106, 110, 132, 138, 141,
                         142, 158, 169, 206, 209
Standards 16
Staples 91
Steps, following 16
Step stool 36-39
String, kite 199
Switch, toggle 82

T

Table, ping-pong 200-203
Tape, colored 204
Tape, electricians 71
Tell, William 147-148
Tether ball game 204-206
Tie bar 62
Tie tack 62
Time-saving tips 13-36
Tools,
    dampness 23
    limited number 6
    most useful 24
    sharpening 23
    testing sharpness 22
Toys, folk 124-128
Tray, sandwich 32-35
Tubing, plastic 165
Tugboat 40-43

U

Upholstery nails, decorative 50

V

Varnish 34, 39, 46, 53, 60, 64, 79,
                        83, 93, 98, 106, 110, 138,

Varnish *(cont.)*
                                141, 144, 152, 158, 165,
                                169, 187, 206, 209, 222
Vise 24

W

Wagon racer 178-181
Warping, wood 51
Wax 34, 46, 64, 120, 216
Webbing, canvas 193
Wheels 180-181, 187
Whimmy Diddle 127-128
Whizzer bull roarer 124-126
Wiring, underground 184
Wood,
    colors 32, 61
    combinations 32
    comparison shopping 17
    cost 17
    economical use 16
    firsts 19
    grading 19-21
    hardness 21
    how to buy 17
    nailing 21
    preservative 217
    seconds 19
    selecting 19-21
Workbench, how to build 24-24
Workshop, location 6, 23-24

Y

Yard lumber 20